BELIEVING IS SEEING

The Principle and Patterns Vision in the Scriptures

William J. Bohn

Copyright © 2019 by William J. Bohn

All rights reserved
No part of this book may be reproduced in any form or by any means including electronic reproduction and photocopying without written permission of the author.

ISBN-Print: 9780692127360

Interior design by booknook.biz

Acknowledge

My wife Linda whose reading of the manuscript and encouragement of my writing has been ongoing and invaluable.

Dr. Lowell L. Bennion who introduced me to The Church of Jesus Christ of Latter-day Saints and the gospel of Jesus Christ.

Dr. Friedrich Beißner. His lectures on poetics continue to influence my interest in words and the vision they express in so many ways.

Thomas said, "To see is to believe,"

But Christ answered: "To believe is to see."

–Elder Howard W. Hunter

Embedded within the structure of language is an entire narrative of experience. The relations between things; a consciousness of self, other, and community; an anatomy of action; a sense of time, memory, and potentiality; a method for seeing, shaping, and interpreting reality—all are encoded in the grammar of case and number, tense and conjugation, metaphor and figures of speech. Acquaintance with such structural intricacies reveals just how powerful a tool of apprehension language is, just how strongly the skeleton of words supports the flesh of experience. *–Anonymous*

TABLE OF CONTENTS

Preface	xi
Abbreviations	xiii
Introduction	1
Chapter 1: Faith in the Lord Jesus Christ	9
CHAPTER 2: Believing is Seeing	32
CHAPTER 3: *Poietics* and Aesthetics of Vision in the Scriptures	44
CHAPTER 4: Capturing the Vision	90
Chapter 5: Light and the Three Degrees of Glory	106
Chapter 6: Parables	136
Chapter 7: David and Goliath	157

Chapter 8: Parable of the Good Samaritan   178

Chapter 9: The Lord's Vision of Beauty in the Scriptures   215

Appendix: The Ancient Hebrew Marriage   266

Bibliography   287

Subject Index   299

Image Index   306

Foreword

There is an old adage that goes like this, "happiness was born a twin." I've always liked these simple, yet meaningful words. Simply said, when something "praiseworthy or of good report," (something that has made us happy) happens to us, it is human nature to want to share it with another. Happiness kept only within isn't as fulfilling as sharing it. My friend, Bill Bohn, avid student of the scriptures, serious researcher, author, and humble, knowledgeable teacher, lives this inspired adage; for it is his hope and goal to now share that which he has fervently and enjoyably studied, with others—even happiness.

It has been my pleasure to set at the feet of this man and be taught and edified. His approach to teaching is like his writing. Sincere and genuinely concerned. When a student asks a question, all stops with the presentation, and total, sincere and locked in attention is rendered. Every student matters. Every question is carefully listened to, and patiently, sincerely discussed, with appropriate answers. Brother Bohn encompasses that wonderful quality of sincerely wanting others to understand nurtured Holy Writ. In my opinion, he qualifies for the Savior's revelation wherein he said, "Behold thou hast a gift, and blessed art thou because of thy gift. Remember, it is sacred and cometh from above."

He wishes for the student and now the reader, that same experience the two disciples experienced on the road to Damascus, when the Savior walked with them a distance. When He left, the disciples said one to another, "Did not our heart burn within us, while he talked with us by the way, and while he opened to us the scripture."

I once had a friend who was suffering much in his life. Rebellious children. Unhappy wife. House in disrepair. Loss of employment. It seemed all that could be bad he was experiencing. Being a close friend, we talked about those things that help in daily life—for daily happiness. On that list the subject was mentioned, "Are you reading your scriptures?" His answer totally surprised me when he said, "I've read them!"

In this inspiring text, Brother Bohn opens the door to the importance of ongoing study of the scriptures, for deeper understanding and pleasure. "To see things as they really are." Not just informative---but with testimony building quality—for all; men, women, and children. The information captured between the covers of this remarkable edition is assisted with ongoing guidance from endnotes.

Brother Bohn's approach to the study of the scripture is likened to that which was taught in the SMTC (SENIOR MTC). My wife Ann and I learned this great secret just prior to departing for our recent CES Mission. We learned that when reading the scriptures, we need to apply the "Black and White" method of study. The black referring to the printed word; the white being the spirit which surrounds it. To read for quality and learning---not for quantity only. This is precisely Brother Bohn's underlying message. To receive deeply, clearly, through understanding of the writte4n word, together with the confirmation of the Spirit, the words of the Lord, as recorded in His Holy Writ. We are promised that if it is right, He will "cause that your bosom shall burn within you.

The Savior also admonished, "... seek ye diligently and teach one another words of wisdom; yea, seek ye out of the best books ... even by study and also by faith." Then He personally testified, "Behold, I am Jesus Christ, the Savior of the world. Treasure these things up on your hearts, and let the solemnities of eternity rest upon your minds."

Believing is Seeing: Principle and Patterns of Vision in the Scriptrues is seeking out from a best book; allowing us privilege to see more clearly, the deeper, inspiring and cherished meanings of the words of our Savior. Thank you dear friend, Bill Bohn. And to your sweetheart Linda for her ongoing support and love of this inspiring project.

Most sincerely,
DON J. BLACK

PREFACE

My interest in words and the vision they express began many years ago when I had the good fortune to attend a series of lectures on poetics, which is the study of the forms of literature, at the University of Tübingen (Germany) given by Professor Doctor Friedrich Beissner. His insights changed the way I viewed the printed word: no longer were they simply static spots of organized ink on a page; rather I came to see them, especially words used figuratively, as dynamic lenses into an author's vision of reality. It was a short step to studying the words of scripture as windows into the Lord's vision of reality, i.e., things as they really are, more clearly. This book grew out of those lectures and my subsequent study of poetics as well as years of teaching the scriptures in Church venues, mainly Gospel Doctrine and Institute classes.

Believing is Seeing offers to search the scriptures through the images and parables, both historical and *poietic*, through which the Lord has chosen to reveal some of the deeper truths, or mysteries, of His gospel. While technical terms are occasionally noted, the emphasis is on the organic unity of these words and stories, whereby, with a little research and imagination, line upon line of vision reveals a deeper understanding of the text.

The book first establishes that vision is based on one's faith in Jesus Christ whereupon a discussion of how poetics, or *poietics* as I explain in Chapter 2, functions in a literary context, followed by discussing the mechanics of capturing the vision embedded in the words of scripture. To demonstrate how these mechanics translate into understanding the vibrant language of scripture, three longer studies are included: "Light and the Tree Degrees of Vision," "David and Goliath," and the "Parable of the Good Samaritan." The last chapter, "The Lord's Vision of Beauty," summarizes the supernal vision He has for each of His children.

The main title of this book, *Believing Is Seeing*, is similar to that of a book Wayne W. Dyer wrote a number of years ago, *When You Believe It, You'll See It*. On the surface, the premise of the two books seems to be similar, namely what one believes to be true principles of living conditions how one views the reality around oneself. But the thrust of the two books is quite different: Dyer's was New Age in tenor; *Believing Is Seeing* is scripture-based, examining how by searching the word of God, we can acquire a more exact and deeper perception of God's eternal reality.

Believing is Seeing is the third of three books I've published, the others being *The Beatitudes: From Poor in Heart to Pure in Heart* and *Matthew 25: Symbolic Vision – Parabolic Living*, but is the first of the three in that it establishes the foundation for the study of vision in the other two. However, each of the three stand on their own.

ABBREVIATIONS

ABD	*The Anchor Bible Dictionary*, David Noel Freedman, et al, 6 vols. (New York, NY: Doubleday, 1992).
DNTC	Bruce R. McConkie, *Doctrinal New Testament Commentary*, 3 vols. (Salt Lake City, UT: Bookcraft, 1974-75.
HC	Joseph Smith, *History of The Church of Jesus Christ of Latter-day Saints*, 7 vols. 2nd ed. rev., ed. B. H. Roberts (Salt Lake City, UT: The Church of Jesus Christ of Latter-day Saints, 1932-51; rep. Deseret Book, 1983).
JD	*Journal of Discourses*. 26 vols. (London: Latter-day Saints' Book Depot, 1854-86).
JST	Joseph Smith's Translation of the Bible
Lectures	Joseph Smith, ed. *Lectures on Faith: 1834-35* (Salt Lake City, UT: Deseret Book, 1985.
ODE	C. T. Onions, G. W. S. Friedrichsen, R. W. Burchfield, eds. *The Oxford Dictionary of English Etymology* (Oxford, ENG: Clarendon, 1991).

SOED	Lesley Brown, ed. *The New Shorter Oxford English Dictionary on Historical Principles*, 2 vols. (Oxford, ENG: Clarendon, 1993).
TPJS	*Teachings of the Prophet Joseph Smith*, ed. Joseph Fielding Smith (Salt Lake City, UT: Deseret Book, 1975).
TDNT	Gerhard Kittel, G. W. Bromiley, and Gerhard Friedrich, eds., *Theological Dictionary of the New Testament*. 10 vols. (Grand Rapids, MI: Eerdmans, 1964-1976; rpt. 1993-1995).
TWOT	R. Laird Harris, Gleason L. Archer, Jr., Bruce K. Waltke, *Theological Dictionary of the Old Testament*, 2 vols. (Chicago, IL: Moody, 1980).

All abbreviated references to scriptures are cited according to those found in the front material of the Bible published by The Church of Jesus Christ of Latter-day Saints.

INTRODUCTION

Vision is not what we see, but *how we interpret what we see* according to the principles we accept as true, those principles being significantly influenced by our predominant culture and our past experiences. Vision is central to the history, heritage, and theology of The Church of Jesus Christ of Latter-day Saints: We use the phrase "the First Vision" for the appearance of the Father and the Son to young Joseph Smith in what is now known as the Sacred Grove near Palmyra, New York; moreover, toward the beginning of the book Joseph translated, the Book of Mormon, Lehi's vision sets the tone for what follows in the ancient books comprising that volume of scripture.

Rather than the great visions of the prophets, however, this book focuses on the private revelatory experiences we can have as we engage the dynamic depth of images in the scriptures; we will look at how the Lord reveals the culture of eternal life in the vision of things as they *really* are and how we can access the attendant truths of that vision as we study the scriptures, seeing the principles of the gospel of Jesus Christ in greater depth, identifying the nuances of those principles that can ennoble our daily acts to become more Christlike.

The Divine vision is often apprehended through the visionary words, phrases, and narratives that unfold, line upon line, precept upon precept, subtext upon subtext, as much of the vision as an individual is spiritually prepared to receive, which explains why, after years of studying the scriptures, one day a word, a phrase, or a verse suddenly stands out to us, becoming meaningful for our understanding of the Lord's gospel. This is how the Lord educates His people in the spirit and practices of eternal life.

The visionary pictures He offers us additionally create patterns. "A pattern is a plan, model, or standard," taught Elder David A. Bednar, "that can be used as a guide for repetitive doing or making of something."[3] Applied to the scriptures, the episodes from peoples' lives, the Savior's parables, and images, wherein the patterns of righteousness are revealed, show us how to walk the path leading to reunion with our Heavenly Father. For example, the second great commandment is to love our neighbors as ourselves (Matt. 22:39). The Savior revealed the pattern for living this commandment in the parable of the Good Samaritan. (See Chapter 8.) By intensively studying this narrative, we may feel the spirit of this or that principle and how to enact it more perfectly in our own lives. We can, in the sense of Elder Wilford W. Andersen evocative analogy, go beyond practicing the dance steps of the principle to hear its music, "the joyful spiritual feeling that comes from the Holy Ghost."[4]

The scriptural patterns are *prophetic* in that they testify, in one way or another, that Jesus is the Christ, the Son of the Living God (see Rev. 19:10). Our ability to see the patterns of eternal life is commensurate with our testimony of and faith in Jesus Christ, a testimony borne to us by the Holy Ghost. And only with this divine inspiration do we see "things as they really are" (Jacob 4:13). The word *really* is not an interjection for emphasis; rather it is the adverbial form of "real," indicating the essence of what is truly real eternally which the Holy Ghost helps us perceive without the illusions and delusions of worldliness.

The practice of experiencing and capturing the scriptural vision is discussed at greater length below, but can be concisely stated as follows: the vision in words occurs in four interrelated phases. 1. Imagination: experience the vision of a story or in a word with imagination. 2. Search in depth: search into the object of the vision as deeply as possible. 3. Principles: understand the meaning of the vision by determining the analogous principles involved. 4. Liken: liken the vision and newfound understanding to one's own life.

The scriptures are both codices for doctrinal exposition and handbooks of examples. In studying these ancient texts, including the modern text of revelations, the Doctrine and Covenants, imagination has an important role to play, not in the sense of fanciful, made-up illusions, rather as we use it to reach into the scriptural language and becoming aware of the pictures accompanying our reading. Imagination is a vital cognitive capacity, sometimes rejected as being childish, especially when we become "educated" adults, whereas, in fact, imagination is a childlike, creative power with which the Lord has endowed us to successfully carry out our mortal responsibilities. The act of envisioning includes not only "seeing" but also feeling into the pictures, even motion pictures, running through the imagination and raising that awareness into the conscious mind so as to study them further because in those mental pictures and their attendant emotions are resonant memories of personal experiences by which we relate to whatever it is we are reading. In the awareness of what transpires in the imagination as we read lays the ability to liken the narratives and images of scripture to our individual lives.

Proceeding with the examination of vision, we will be somewhat like archeologists excavating and researching the scriptures and our own imagination. An archeologist carefully digs for artifacts from past cultures, collects the artifacts he finds, and assembles and organizes them to create a picture of the people who lived at a certain time. Our quest is to assemble a picture of the Lord's culture in order to conform our mortal life more and more to the patterns of eternal life "as a guide for repetitively doing" the works of righteousness.

Three Axioms for Searching the Scriptures

Three axioms establish the doctrinal parameters of and frame the discussion in this book. The first asserts that the words of scripture are the Lord's eternal words as recorded in the style of individual prophets. On the face of it, this seems self-evident, but the various books of the Bible are often discussed as if the writer were the author rather than the Lord. For example, the words we read in Isaiah are the Lord's words written in Isaiah's unique style, a style the Lord chose for the particular vision He wanted His followers to see, feel, and understand. Sometimes, under our breath, we seem to blame Isaiah for being unnecessarily obscure, when, in fact, the Lord intended the words in that seminal book to be exactly as they were recorded, though, inevitably, we lose many of the nuances of ancient Hebrew.

A corollary to this first axiom considers all words of scripture to be relevant to people in this last dispensation. When we research Isaiah, we can be assured that the Lord intended it for our day, just as the Book of Mormon was assembled for today and ever after (see 3 Ne. 23:1-3). The same holds true for the Old and New Testament, the Doctrine and Covenants, and the Pearl of Great Price. By assuming the relevance of scripture to us, we can study the words of God without, initially at least, being overly concerned with the socio-historical and cultural background of the time in which they were written down. That can come later, if desired.

The second axiom holds that the Lord's language is thoroughly animated with the extensive use of figurative language. The Savior, as the prime example, often taught principles through analogy, knowing that man on this side of the veil could only comprehend things eternal to any degree with familiar earthly filters. We find, therefore, objects from our common mortal experiences, such as rocks, buildings, streams, light, darkness, et al., used to help us comprehend degrees of eternal principles. However, this is not a book about recognizing particular types of images, though terms such as metaphor and simile appear from time to time; rather it is about experiencing the inner dynamic of the vision embedded in the Lord's words. Appreciation precedes understanding.

The third axiom comes from our eighth Article of Faith: "We believe the Bible to be the word of God as far as it is translated correctly; we also believe the Book of Mormon to be the word of God." In his inspired translation of the Bible, the Prophet Joseph Smith restored and repaired many of the plain and simple truths removed from it, or that scribes in antiquity rephrased and corrupted. Aware of the Prophet's corrections, many of which appear in the footnotes of the Bible produced by the Church, we can study the Old and New Testaments with greater confidence.[5]

Seeing Through the Glass Clearly?

The Apostle Paul's wrote, "For now we see through a glass, darkly" (1 Cor. 13:12), literally, "For now we see through a mirror obscurely."[6] The mirror to which Paul referred to was made in Corinth of highly polished bronze. (Corinth was known in the ancient Mediterranean world for its high-quality bronze.) In the first place, we don't see *through* a mirror; we see the reflection of ourselves and our worldly reality in it. Secondly, at best, such mirrors reflected indistinct images, thus the undermeaning of Paul's image has to do with spiritual matters opaquely discerned.[7] However, in his epistle to the Romans, he wrote, "For the invisible things of him from the creation of the world are clearly seen, being understood by the things that are made, even his eternal power and Godhead" (Rom. 1:20; emphasis added). If, on the one hand, these things can be seen clearly, why did Paul on write, now we see through a mirror dimly?

One key to understanding his intent is the word *now* (Gk. *árti* [ἄρτι], "at this present moment"). When Paul wrote his letter to the Corinthians, scriptures among the Jews meant the uncodified scrolls predating the ministry of Christ, including perhaps books mentioned therein now lost to us, others excluded.[8] In those scrolls were numerous types foreshadowing Jesus Christ, as Augustine of Hippo noted in a circuitous manner: "The New [Testament] is concealed in the Old [Testament], and the Old is revealed in the New."[9] The scrolls remained uncodified until around 70 A.D.; some scholars think that books the early Christians considered to be scripture were excluded from what we now consider to be the Old Testament.[10] Consequently, thanks to incorrect translations, outright deletions, and the early Christian councils, such as at Nicaea,[11] Paul's "mirror" remained obscured until the nineteenth century when the Book of Mormon was introduced to the world, followed by the Doctrine and Covenants and Pearl of Great Price, in which the Lord reveals the fullness of His gospel. Think of what the absence of those scriptures would mean! Our understanding of the gospel of Jesus Christ would be as confused as the plethora of Christian faiths and our vision of eternal life would be blurred. Added to these new scriptures is the tremendous expansion of knowledge in all areas of life in the 2,000 plus years since Paul's statement, especially since the Restoration in 1830, and we now have a much more transparent glass to look through.

Ultimately, the aim of any book such as this should be building testimonies that God the Father and His Son, Jesus Christ, live and are actively involved in the lives of men, women, and children through the power and influence of the Holy Ghost. It should also testify that the scriptures—the Old Testament, New Testament, Book of Mormon, Doctrine and Covenants, and Pearl of Great Price—do, in fact, constitute the library of God's words to man, a library continually added to in this last dispensation by the words of the living prophets of The Church of Jesus Christ of Latter-day Saints. It should testify of Joseph Smith's prophetic, restorative calling; that the Church resulting from his First and subsequent visions is the true and living Church of Jesus Christ of earth today, "living" referring to the continual growth of a body of believers and the infusion of their talents.

Notes to Introduction

1. As used in this study, "eternal life" means the life God lives; "live eternally" denotes living the principles of eternal life during mortality.
2. In the *Phædo*, Plato has Socrates discussing learning (knowledge) as remembering (trans. Benjamin Jowett, in *Great Books of the Western World*, 52 vols., ed. Mortimer Adler [Chicago: Encyclopædia Britannica, 1952], 7:228-231 (= sections 72-76).
3. David A. Bednar, "A Reservoir of Living Water," Church Education System Fireside for Young Adults, Feb. 4, 2007 (https://speeches.byu.edu/talks/david-a-bednar_reservoir-living-water/)
4. Wilford W. Andersen, "The Music of the Gospel," *Ensign* (Nov. 2015), 54.
5. The reader needs to be aware that a great deal of research is being done currently on the influence the so-called Deuteronomists on changing the narratives of the Old Testament and, therefore, the doctrinal thrust of that book. One of the leading proponents of the changes the group may have made is Margaret Barker, a frequent visiting lecturer at Brigham Young University. (In volume 56, no. 1 (2017) of *BYU Studies* a lengthy lecture she gave at Brigham Young University on November 9, 2016 appears, entitled "The Lord is One," with two responses by professors Andrew C. Skinner and David J. Larsen.) Here is a sampling of her thought: "In the world of the Deuteronomists, the Law of Moses replaced the older wisdom teachings (Deut. 4:5-6). Covenant was transformed from the older creation covenant based on loving-kindness into the Moses/Sinai covenant, a very different idea. . . . The fundamental

concept of righteousness, *ṣedheq/ṣedhāqâ*, almost disappeared, and where it did survive it had a new meaning. . . . The expression 'seeing the face of God' disappeared, because this implied a human form" (pp. 85-86). Barker is not alone in the quest to discover what she calls "the older testament"; the bibliographies at the end of her books supply the names of a number of others who are conducting similar research. *However*, and this is a big "however," the Bible published by the Church remains the standard we use in all our Gospel Doctrine, Institute, and Seminary classes. We aren't at liberty to insert the research of Barker or any other researcher as superseding the text in the Bible.

6. Young's Literal Translation; https://www.biblegateway.com/versions/Youngs-Literal-Translation-YLT-Bible/.

7. Paul, as a Hellenized Jew, conversant with Greek thought, was perhaps familiar with the following words found in Plato's *Phædrus* and their attendant undermeaning: "There is no light of . . . any of the higher ideas which are precious to souls in the earthly copies of them: they are *seen through the glass dimly*; and there are few who, going to the images, behold in them the realities, and these only with difficulty" (*Great Books*, trans. Benjamin Jowett, 7:126). Jowett's translation shows Plato's words to be remarkably close to Paul's. Harold North Fowler rendered the same passage quite differently: ". . . only a few approaching the images through the darkling organs of sense, behold in them the nature of that which they imitate, and these few do this with difficulty" (Loeb Classic Library [Cambridge, MA: Harvard University Press, 1960], 485).

Plato gave his own poetic rendering of this statement in his "Allegory of the Cave," in *The Republic*, Bk. VII.

8. See, for example, *The Other Bible*, ed. Willis Barnstone (San Francisco, CA: Harper & Row, n.d.); *The Forgotten Books of Eden: The Lost Books of the Old Testament*, ed. Rutherford H. Platt (New York, NY: Bell Publishing, 2015).

9. Augustine, *Questionum in Heptateuchum* [*Questions on the Heptateuch*], Bk. 2, sect. 73. He also described the Old Testament as the New Testament with a veil pulled over it.

10. A few Christian faiths still include some of those books: Catholicism, Orthodox and Ethiopian Christianity.

11. On the Hellenization of Christian theology, see Richard R. Hopkins, *How Greek Philosophy Corrupted the Christian Concept of God* (Bountiful, UT: Horizon Publishers, 1999).

CHAPTER 1

FAITH IN THE LORD JESUS CHRIST

The first principle of the gospel is "Faith in the Lord Jesus Christ" (A of F, 1:4). Indeed, the Apostle Paul wrote that we walk through mortality by faith (see 2 Cor. 5:7), which is often interpreted to mean learn to obey the commandments of God ever more exactly and follow the counsel of the Lord's living prophets, which are certainly part and parcel of our mortal experience as members of The Church of Jesus Christ of Latter-day Saints.[1] However, this is the point where all too often our discussions of faith end without probing into the essence of faith and deepening our understanding of this fulcrum-principle of our discipleship and exercise it more on an expanded level of ministering.

The Apostle Paul, however, revealed the indispensable core of faith when he wrote that "faith . . . worketh by love" (Gal. 5:6). The Greek verb translated as "worketh" is *energeo*, meaning "to be at work, to effect, to produce."[2] Put in the active voice, Paul's statement might read, "Love *enpowers* faith." Or, in line with the discussion of faith as power, it seem plausible to me that it might read, "Love *empowers* faith, even though the Greek verb of empowers is a different word, but love is perhaps the ultimate source of God's power for "God is love" (1 John 4:8), a power disseminated through light because "God is light" (1 John 1:5; D&C 50:24). Each time we exercise faith in Jesus Christ, in both action and power, we are essentially saying to Him, "I love you." "I love you so much so that I want to become like you and will exercise faith in this or that principle of righteousness to do so." No small wonder, then, that the Savior said, "If ye love me, keep my commandments" (John 14:15). In the fifth chapter of his first epistle, John added further understanding Jesus' statement:

> Whosoever believeth that Jesus is the Christ is born of God: and every one that loveth him that begat loveth him also that is begotten of him.
> By this we know that we love the children of God, when we love God, and keep his commandments.
> For this is the love of God, that we keep his commandments: and his commandments are not grievous.
> For whatsoever is born of God overcometh the world: and this is the victory that overcometh the world, *even* our faith.
> Who is he that overcometh the world, but he that believeth that Jesus is the Son of God? (1 John 5:1-5)

In the book of Revelation Jesus revealed to John the depth of love for all who overcome the world with their faith: "eat of the tree of life" (Rev. 2:7); "not be hurt of the second death" (Rev. 2:11); "eat of the hidden manna" and be given "a white stone" in which "a new name [is] written" (Rev. 2:17); "power over the nations" (Rev. 2:26); "clothed in white raiment," name blotted "out of the book of life," and the Savior "will confess his name before [His] Father, and before his angels" (Rev. 3:5); and so on.[3]

Our faith in Jesus Christ is the major factor in overcoming the world, not only because He represents the opposite of the worldly spirit, but also because "faith gives . . . reality to what we do not see"[4] with our physical eyes; that is, faith allows us to see "things as they really are" (Jacob 4:13). In this sense, it objectifies our vision of reality in a world that attempts to obfuscate eternal truths. Paul wrote:

> But we speak the wisdom of God in a mystery, even the hidden wisdom, which God ordained before the world unto our glory. . . .
> For what man knoweth the things of a man, save the spirit of man which is in him? even so the things of God knoweth no man, but the Spirit of God.
> Now we have received, not the spirit of the world, but the spirit which is of God; that we might know the things that are freely given to us of God. . . .
> But the natural man receiveth not the things of the Spirit of God: for they are foolishness unto him: neither can he know them, because they are spiritually discerned (1 Cor. 2:7, 11-12, 14).

As we continue to progressively come unto Christ at successively higher degrees of faith throughout our lives, refining our discipleship each step along the way under the mentoring of the Holy Spirit, we become the light of faith-filled love Christ asked us to be, when He said:

> Verily, verily, I say unto you, *I give unto you to be* the light of the world; a city that is set on a hill cannot be hid. Behold, do men light a candle [lamp] and put it under a bushel? Nay, but on a candlestick [lampstand]; and it giveth light to all that are in the house.

Therefore, let your light so shine before this world, that they may see your good works, and glorify your Father who is in heaven (JST Matt. 5:16-18; emphasis added).

Moreover, it is His light that we are to let shine: "Therefore, hold up your light that it may shine unto the world. Behold I am the light which ye shall hold up—that which ye have seen me do (3 Ne. 18:24).

There is, in my opinion, a wonderful pictorial representation for faith and light in a work painted by Elder Richard G. Scott entitled *Campfire at Sunset* below that Elder Gerrit W. Gong introduced in the October 2018 General Conference of the Church. For his address, Elder Gong rephrased the title to be "Campfire of Faith."[5] Applying the title of his address to Elder Scott's watercolor, the painting becomes a powerful metaphor for the relationship of an individual's faith in Jesus Christ and the light and faith of heaven, revealing multiple layers of meaning.

Elder's Scott's painting has an Oriental feel to it: the man and his campfire on the left of the work are dwarfed by nature. The atmosphere of the painting is created by the rich, reddish orange radiance of the setting sun, surrounding and infusing all objects, the color matching the faint glow of the small campfire.

As images, fire and light are often companion images of the Godhead and Their influence: "God Almighty himself dwells in eternal fire" and "Immortality dwells in everlasting burnings," the Prophet Joseph tells us[6]; the eyes of Jesus Christ are "as a flame of fire," "his feet like unto fine brass as if they burned in a furnace" (Rev. 1:14, 15); He is, consequently, "the light of the world" (John 8:12; 88:13). Moreover, each person comes into this world with the light of Christ as his or her spiritual essence (see D&C 84:45-46), his or her "intelligence, or light and truth" (D&C 93:29). Thus, Christ is "the true light that lighteth every man that cometh into the world" (D&C 93:2).

Richard G. Scott, Campfire at Sunset. I urge the reader to find the color image of the painting on the internet to fully appreciate it.

As discussed above, light gives definition to objects within its compass, providing at the same time a comforting warmth in the chilly night air, relating spiritually to "the burning in the bosom" man can receive from the Holy Spirit through whom Christ manifests Himself (D&C 9:8; see 1 Ne. 9:11). The spiritual objectivity one gains through the Holy Spirit facilitates spiritually orienting one's self in the ambient world. Darkness on the other hand obscures our ability to become oriented in the world. The image of darkness has long represented evil in its many forms along with the spiritual obfuscation, distortion, and confusion of eternal truths.

Darkness conveys the spirit of worldliness, created by a cacophony of competing voices and images that, if we buy into their snake-oil pitches, can lead us when we let down our guard and drift off the path set out by the Lord. They can also lead us into modern forms of idolatry—such as the need to appear affluent with all sorts of toys, apparel, etc.—putting our focus to things, activities, and the like that divert our singular focus on the glory of the Lord.

The brilliant red-orange glow of the setting sun in Elder Scott's painting I envision as the heavenly fire emanating from the presence of God (and just because the sun is setting, the painting doesn't intimate the demise of the Lord in any sense), a light that always envelops us as the light of Christ, a burning by which the Holy Spirit warms the bosom with the love of God (see Rom. 5:5). If by exercising our faith in Jesus Christ we essentially say to Him, "I love you," then the impressions of the Spirit convey the Savior's love for us, telling us that He has faith in us. There is no feeling remotely close to it.

The metaphoric meaning I draw from my admittedly subjective reading of Elder Scott's painting is as follows. Our small campfire of faith fortified by the divine faith flowing from the Lord, that same love-filled faith by which God created and governs worlds without end, the faith that lights our way along the strait path leading to eternal, cutting a brilliant swathe through the darkness of the philosophies of men—our faith when magnified through the Lord's faith can become a great power for good in the world, especially in the "small and simple things" whereby the Lord bring "great things to pass" (Alma 37:6).

Some Rungs of Faith on the Ladder of Exaltation

The Prophet Joseph declared,

> *When you climb up a ladder, you must begin at the bottom, and ascend step by step, until you arrive at the top; and so it is with the principles of the Gospel—you must begin with the first, and go on until you learn all the principles of exaltation. But it will be a great while*

after you have passed through the veil before you will have learned them. It is not all to be comprehended in this world; it will be a great work to learn our salvation and exaltation even beyond the grave.[7]

There are at least five important rungs on this ladder that disciples climb as they learn to walk by faith (see 2 Cor. 5:7), each representing greater clarity of vision: 1. desire to believe; 2. trust the Lord; 3. hope; 4. faith unto action; 5. the power of faith. (You will likely identify some that I've left out.)

Faith as desire to believe

Alma taught that our faith begins with the simple "desire to believe" in the Atonement of Jesus Christ (see Alma 32:27; 33:22-23), and a willingness to "experiment upon [God's] words, and exercise a particle of faith, yea, even if ye can no more than desire to believe, let this desire work in you, even until ye believe in a manner that ye can give place for a portion of [God's] words" (Alma 32:27).

Developing our faith is analogous to learning a skill set. To begin with, we have to have a modicum of belief in ourselves that, with sufficient training, we will be able to do the skill. At first we may read about it and observe someone proficient in the desired skill to create a mental picture of oneself doing the skill. Or we may seek out a mentor-teacher to help us learn the skill. The old adage, practice makes perfect, is key: we practice the skill, over and over, at first, perhaps, awkwardly, but each attempt brings us closer to the vision of ourselves being competent in the skill. We had a young man in our ward, Levi Crockett, who, at an early age, began playing piano accompaniment for priesthood opening exercises, sometimes missing notes, but still keeping tempo. By the time he left on his mission, he not only played beautifully for a number of different programs in and out of the Church, he had also become a creative arranger of music, enriching and expanding the musical language of compositions, not only for piano, but also for choral presentation. He developed the skillset for playing the piano beyond proficiency to mastery.

We can follow a similar path in our Church callings and responsibilities, *meaning*, in the first instance, nurturing within our family—spouses nurturing one another, and parents their children; *meaning* seeking out one's ancestors to accomplish their temple work; *meaning* ministering to each family we are assigned and others as well, members of the Church or not. It *means* taking ownership of the principles and doing the works of righteousness to the best of one's ability, each such action based on faith. Even on the best of days, few of us can look in the mirror and say to ourselves, "I have exercised my faith one hundred percent of the time today," but we can seek to do better. In addition to praying for direction at the beginning of each day, we might try putting our imagination to work, envisioning comporting ourselves that day in accord with one of the principles of righteousness, having that image in our minds as we interact with others throughout the day. Faithful practice leads to a greater measure of perfection in that one principle. President Harold B. Lee counseled:

> In the kingdom of God there are laws which teach us the way to perfection, and any member of the Church who is learning to live perfectly each of the laws that are in the kingdom is learning the way to become perfect. All of us can learn to live the Word of Wisdom perfectly. All of us can learn to keep the Sabbath day holy perfectly. All of you can learn how to keep the law of fasting perfectly. We know how to keep the law of chastity

perfectly. Now, as we learn to keep one of these laws perfectly we ourselves are on the road to perfection.[8]

Such perfection starts when we experiment upon the words of Christ, trust Him to accompany us with each step of faith.

Trusting Jesus Christ

Trusting in the divinity of Jesus Christ, trusting in His every word, trusting that His pure loving kindness extends to each man, woman, and child personally, constitutes a quantum leap of faith beyond desire. Such trust forms the bedrock of enduring faith: "every word of God is pure; he is a shield [of faith] unto them that put their trust in him" (Prov. 30:5; also Eph. 6:16). This is the kind of trust children have in their parents. King Benjamin described the fundamental qualities for all who trust in and desire to come unto Christ: "the natural man is an enemy to God, and has been from the fall of Adam, and will be, forever and ever, unless he yields to the enticings of the Holy Spirit, and putteth off the natural man and becometh a saint through the atonement of Christ the Lord, and becometh as a child, submissive, meek, humble, patient, full of love, willing to submit to all things which the Lord seeth fit to inflict upon him, even as a child doth submit to his father" (Mosiah 3:19).

In his book, *Believing Christ*, Stephen E. Robinson wrote that "genuine faith in Christ—active acceptance of his power and not just passive belief in his identity—is and must be the very first principle of the gospel. No matter how much of the gospel one learns or even believes as a theory, until we accept the reality of our own salvation, we have not yet turned on the power [of his atonement]."[9] Indeed, "blessed is the man [woman or child] that trusteth in the Lord, and whose hope the Lord is" (Jer. 17:7).

Faith as Hope

When we anchor our faith in Christ (see Ether 12:4), we step on to a further rung on the ladder of faith, the rung of hope. This hope is more than wishful thinking; it expresses confidence that "with God all things are possible" (Matt. 19:26), including fulfilling the measure of one's creation. Through hope our eye of faith sees more clearly as we perceive a vision of positive possibilities. With hope we have confidence that the Lord's Atonement and His "great plan of happiness" (Alma 42:8) include us personally, filling us "with all joy and peace in believing that [we] may abound in hope, through the power of the Holy Ghost" (Rom. 15:13). This represents an important moment in our spiritual journey because once we have hope-filling, trusting faith that the plan of salvation includes us, we are far more likely to become deeply involved in the Lord's work.

With godly hope, we see the "more excellent way" of the Lord (1 Cor. 12:31; Ether 12:11) before us, becoming more resolute in picking ourselves up every time we fall along the way (see Prov. 24:16), "press[ing] forward with a steadfastness in Christ, having a perfect brightness of hope, and a love of God and of all men. Wherefore, if [we] shall press forward, feasting upon the word of Christ, and endure to the end, behold, thus saith the Father: Ye shall have eternal life" (2 Ne. 31:20).

Discussing the gifts of the Spirit, Moroni declared that "there must be faith; and if there must be faith there must also be hope; and if there must be hope there must also be charity" (Moro. 10:20). Someone who possesses a firm hope in Christ does not worry about finishing his race of life first; rather he is focused on helping others finish their races.[10] He understands that mortality is a Special Olympics for everyone and they help others where needed.

Summarizing godly hope, Elder Neal A. Maxwell said:

> Real hope is much more than wishful musing. It stiffens, not slackens, the spiritual spine. . . . Hope is realistic anticipation taking the form of determination—a determination not merely to survive but to "endure. . . well" to the end (D&C 121:8).
>
> While weak hope leaves us at the mercy of our moods and events, 'brightness of hope' produces illuminated individuals. Their luminosity is seen, and things are also seen by it! Such hope permits us to "press forward" even when dark clouds oppress (see 2 Ne. 31:16, 20; see also Heb. 6:19; Ether 12:4; Col. 1:23). Sometimes in the deepest darkness there is no external light—only an inner light to guide and to reassure.
>
> Hope keeps us "anxiously engaged" in good causes even when these appear to be losing causes (see D&C 58:27).[11]

Accordingly, a yet higher rung on the ladder is active faith.

Faith unto Action

In the School of the Prophets, Joseph Smith posited that "faith, and faith only . . . is the moving action in [man]."[12] Moreover, "as faith is the moving cause of all action in temporal concerns, so it is in spiritual."[13] Thus, the Prophet Alma taught, "exercise a particle of faith . . . in a manner that ye can give place for a portion of my words" (Alma 32:27). "Exercise" is an action word; faith leads to action.

Centuries earlier, the Apostle James wrote that "faith, if it hath not works, is dead, being alone" (James 2:17). The converse is also true: works without love-inspired faith are, in Paul's words, "as sounding brass, or a tinkling cymbal" (1 Cor. 13:1): absent the compassionate kindness that empowers faith, such works ring hollow. (In Chapter 8, loving faith is profiled in the discussion of the parable of the Good Samaritan.) Works without faith may satisfy the letter of Christ's law, but they lack the spirit. The syndicated columnist, Sydney Harris, wrote: "Most people wrongly imagine that 'faith' means 'believing in God,' when it really means acting out all the personal and social consequences of such belief; nothing is easier or more conducive to apathy, smugness and self-righteousness than 'believing in God' as an abstraction."[14]

With active faith we can move from the abstraction of a principle to living in and through it; with active faith we can see the next mile marker in our walk of discipleship. If we choose to follow the path outlined by our divinely inspired vision, our first steps may be halting because most of us have to practice a skillset for a time before our actions mirror the vision drawing us on, but with each progressive step of faith, acts and vision will, over time, become one. If we have been reborn in Jesus Christ, the choice can be quite simple because at baptism we commit that we will "serve him to the end" (D&C 20:37).

Faith as Power

Quoting Hebrews 11:3, the Prophet Joseph taught, "By this we understand that the principle of power which existed in the bosom of God, by which the worlds were framed, is faith and that it is by reason of this principle of power existing in the Deity, that all created things exist; so that all things in heaven, on earth, or under the earth, exist by reason of faith as it existed in Him." Therefore, "It is the principle by which Jehovah works [faith worketh by love], and through which he exercises power over all temporal as well as eternal things."[15] Comprehending the magnitude of the power of God's faith is infinitely beyond man's ken, but we can catch a glimpse of faith's power in the many so-called miracles Jesus performed in Palestine. I use the word *so-called* because His miracles were well within the magnitude of His great power of creation, though they transcend man's understanding. Consequently, "Faith . . . is the first great governing principle which has power, dominion, and authority over all things; by it they exist, by it they are upheld, by it they are changed, or by it they remain, agreeable to the will of God."[16]

But, "faith is not only the principle of action, but of power also, in all intelligent beings, whether in heaven or on earth."[17] Thus, when the Savior said, "If ye have faith as a grain of mustard seed, ye shall say unto this mountain, remove hence to yonder place; and it shall remove; and nothing shall be impossible unto you" (Matt. 17:9; see also Luke 17:6), it was more than a mere metaphor. Many of us may read this as a parable to motivate people to have faith, but Moroni recorded that "the brother of Jared said unto the mountain Zerin, Remove! and it was removed. And if he had not had faith it would not have moved" (Ether 12:30). For the faithful brother of Jared, moving a mountain was not a parable.

The great power of faith is often coupled with a sincere prayer of the heart. An oft-told story about Mary Fielding Smith concerns crossing the plains with her little family after her husband, Hyrum, had been martyred with his brother, Joseph, in Carthage Jail. Returning from a journey to obtain supplies in St. Joseph, Missouri, Mary, her son Joseph F. (later to become the sixth President of the Church), and her brother, Joseph Fielding, camped one evening and turned their oxen out to pasture. Across the river was a trail herd. When she arose the next morning, the oxen were missing. After looking for them without success, Joseph F. returned to camp and saw his mother kneeling in prayer, asking the Lord to help them find the animals which were vital to them in their journey. When she stood up, she told her son and her brother to eat breakfast while she looked for the oxen. She crossed over to the other side of the stream by which they were camped and the trail boss pointed in the direction he said he had seen the animals.

Mary, however, proceeded in the opposite direction, straight to where the oxen were tied up, out of sight.[18] The power of her faith in that situation gave her a vision of where to find the animals.

Desire, trust, hope, action, empowerment are only a few of the words that describe the rungs on the ladder as each disciple progresses from faith to faith. And at each higher rung, the vision of eternal life becomes clearer. But, as with climbing a ladder, the opposing force of gravity tries to pull us down; as we climb the ladder of faith, we have to contend with spiritual opposition and opposites, many of which could pull us down from our upward climb toward eternal life.

Some Nuts and Bolts of Building Our Faith in Jesus Christ

Intellectually-Informed Faith

Besides the qualities discussed above, there are several other rungs that are absolutely essential to the development of our faith. One of the first, perhaps accompanying desire, is intellectual that I am terming intellectually-informed faith. "Intellectual," as I'm using the word, refers to the practice of studying and pondering the scriptures—not just once, but many times. We'll never plumb the depths of the scriptures: they are vast and deep as the ocean, but we can and should study them as broadly and deeply as we can.

In the third lecture on faith, the Prophet Joseph taught the following about informed faith:

> 2. Let us here observe, that three things are necessary in order that any rational and intelligent being may exercise faith in God unto life and salvation.
> 3. First, the idea that he actually exists.

4. Secondly, a correct idea of his character, perfections, and attributes.

5. Thirdly, an actual knowledge that the course of life which he is pursuing is according to his will. For without an acquaintance with these three important facts, the faith of every rational being must be imperfect and unproductive; but with this understanding it can become perfect and fruitful, abounding in righteousness, unto the praise and glory of God the Father, and the Lord Jesus Christ.[19]

Accordingly, Elder John A. Widtsoe wrote that "The extent of a person's faith depends in part on the amount of his knowledge. The more knowledge he gathers, the more extensive becomes his field of faith"[20]; likewise, Elder Bruce R. McConkie: "Faith is the child of knowledge. . . . No one can have faith in a God of whom he knows nothing."[21]

Knowledge of God exists in infinite gradations from mere information to the surety of revelation to the kind of personal visitation Joseph Smith was privy to in the Sacred Grove. On the most basic level, we inform ourselves by searching the scriptures. His words act as windows of heaven through which we can discern elements of eternity. The inherent metaphor of "inform" is, first, of a form, meaning an idea or principle that serves as a pattern. Mormon used the word in this sense when he wrote: "For behold, they [the angels] are subject unto him [Jesus Christ], to minister according to the word of his command, showing themselves unto them [the children of men] of strong faith and a firm mind in every form of godliness" (Moro. 7:30). Second, "in" indicates motion into the mind. It is the forms, or patterns, of godliness that we try to envision as we search the scriptures, informing ourselves with those vital truths.[22]

In both the parable of the soils (Matt. 13:3-8, 18-23; Mark 4:4-8, 14-21; Luke 8:5-8, 11-15) and Alma's discourse on faith (Alma 32:27-43; 33:23), the informing process is compared to the planting of a seed, representing the word of God (see Luke 8:11), planted into the heart-soil of a person. Inherent in the seed is its power to grow into "a tree springing up unto everlasting life," a tree whose fruit is "most precious, which is sweet above all that is sweet, and which is white above all that is white, yea, and pure above all that is pure," like unto the fruit on the tree of life in Lehi's vision (Alma 32:41, 42; see 1 Ne. 8:11).

Daily we face a clear and present danger as we are bombarded with desultory seeds of carnality, sensuality, and devilishness (see Mosiah 16:3; Moses 5:13) that would change our vision of reality with form-ideas contrary to the vision of God—such are the bad actors, trained in the artifice of worldliness, that try to sneak into our minds and vie for our attention,[24] often counterfeiting eternal principles to confuse us further. Discussing Satan's lies and deceptions, Elder Larry R. Lawrence wrote the following insightful description of counterfeiting: "The devil has been called 'the great deceiver.' He attempts to counterfeit every true principle the Lord presents. Remember, counterfeits are not the same as opposites [discussed below]. The opposite of white is black, but a counterfeit for white might be off-white or gray. Counterfeits bear a resemblance to the real thing in order to deceive unsuspecting people. They are a twisted version of something good, and just like counterfeit money, they are worthless."[25] However, when we fill our minds with the Lord's words containing the principles of everlasting life, we drive the devil's counterfeit actors from the stage of our imagination. How we interpret the reality around us depends largely on our evaluation of the actors we admit.

When we mentally organize bytes of divine information into coherent patterns, we become intelligent in our faith. Only the inspired confirmation of the Holy Spirit, however, transforms intelligent faith into revealed "knowledge [that] is perfect in [a] thing and [our] faith is dormant" (Alma 32:34). It is through the Holy Spirit that we perceive the reality of what we cannot see with our physical eyes.

By informing ourselves about the righteousness of God, searching and pondering the scriptures, we can grow our faith to the point that we "hunger and thirst after [deeper knowledge of] righteousness" (Matt. 5:6), the blessing of which is to be "filled with the Holy Ghost" (3 Ne. 12:6), leading to a second important rung in growing our faith: Spirit-born testimony of truth.

Spirit-Informed Faith

As we seek after an understanding of righteousness, we soon realize that "the righteousness of God [is] revealed from [one degree of] faith to [the next higher degree of] faith" (Rom. 1:17), then realizing that faith is a gift of God (see Moro. 10:11), given us by "God the third, the witness or Testator"[26] even the Holy Spirit.

This Spirit-informed rung represents the assurance we can receive of the truths we've identified on the informing rung. While we have to continue to exercise faith in most gospel principles, through the revelation we receive from the Holy Spirit, we can *know*[27] the truth of some of the gospel's fundamental principles such as those enunciated in the Articles of Faith, foremost that Jesus is the Christ by virtue of His Atonement and Resurrection; He is the Son of the Living God; moreover, a sure knowledge of the Restoration of the gospel of Jesus Christ through the young farm boy, Joseph Smith, who became the Prophet of the Restoration; a testimony that the Book of Mormon is the word of God and Another Testament of Jesus Christ; a testimony that The Church of Jesus Christ of Latter-day Saints is the one fully true Church of Jesus Christ on the earth today, built as it was at the meridian of time "upon the foundation of the apostles and prophets, Jesus Christ himself being the chief corner stone" (Eph. 2:20), being lead today by living prophets, seers, and revelators, presently *the* Prophet and President of the Church being Russell M. Nelson with Dallin H. Oaks, First Counselor, and Henry B. Eyring, Second Counselor, forming a First Presidency, like Peter, James, and John at the meridian of time. Such revealed truths as these form the foundation of our discipleship under Jesus Christ.

Experience-Born Faith

The third rung I'll mention is faithfully experimenting upon some principle of the Lord's gospel in the spirit of Jesus' declaration, "If any man will do his will, he shall know of the doctrine, whether it be of God, or whether I speak of myself" (John 7:17). To use an overused popular phrase, this is where the rubber hits the road. If we have faith that a principle is true and don't try to comport ourselves in the spirit of that principle, we don't really have faith in its veracity. Or, to use a phrase from the self-development circuit: "To know and not to do is not to know." By doing the truth we know and that we have faith in, we let the light of our testimony shine, in essence telling others, We love Jesus Christ and know He is the Savior of the world.

Opposition

Climbing the figurative ladder toward exaltation can be as exhausting as climbing the ladder up to a very high tower because of the pull of gravity drawing us downward. As we climb this ladder, we learn that opposition is a fact of life; it either helps or hinders our progression, depending on how we view and use it. If we want to condition our bodies, we exercise our muscles using various types of aerobic and anaerobic resistance; if we want to become educated, we exercise our minds with a wide spectrum of intellectual experiences, like solving math problem, writing essays, or performing experiments; if we want to become an accomplished in the playing of a musical instrument, we practice the instrument over and over, mastering the resistance of different muscles to the discipline we exact from them.

So it is with our spirits. Father Lehi taught his children, "For it must needs be, that there is an opposition in all things. If not so . . . righteousness could not be brought to pass, neither wickedness, neither holiness nor misery, neither good nor bad. Wherefore, all things must needs be a compound in one; wherefore, if it should be one body it must needs remain as dead, having no life neither death, nor corruption nor incorruption, happiness nor misery, neither sense nor insensibility" (2 Ne. 2:11).

Every day we face opposition in one form or another; many times we might privately wish it were otherwise, but opposition is one of the fundamental principles of the gospel we joyously sustained in the pre-mortal council of heaven before we came into mortality (see Job 38:7; D&C 128:23). We call moments of spiritual opposition trials of faith: they are the isometrics of faith that can help us build spiritual strength and grow into godliness, or they can neutralize and/or regress our progress if we take the tact of thinking, "This trial is too heavy to bear." Peter valued trials of faith as being "more precious than of gold that perisheth, though it be tried with fire" (1 Peter 1:7). He is counseling us that we may not *see* nor understand the significance of a trial when we are in the midst of it. We must be on guard, not allowing trials to confuse our minds with darkness so that we feel we have lost our spiritual orientation. But, in His infinite wisdom, the Lord gives us trials to hone our faith in Jesus Christ that we may learn to see our ultimate objective even when befogged by proximate circumstances. Isn't this what happened in the life of the teenage Joseph Smith? When he knelt to pray to the Lord, a darkness enveloped him and depressed his spirit, but he continued to pray even more fervently because he had faith in James' promise, "If any of you lack wisdom, let him ask of God, that giveth to all *men* liberally, and upbraideth not; and it shall be given him. But let him ask in faith, nothing wavering. For he that wavereth is like a wave of the sea driven with the wind and tossed" (James 1:5-6). In the Sacred Grove, Joseph was determined not to be a vacillating wave; with childlike faith he prayed until the satanic darkness was driven away by the glory of Heavenly Father and Jesus Christ. And Joseph saw as few others mortals have! In small measure, something similar can happen with our trials if we faithfully endure them, for we "receive no witness until after the trial of [our] faith" (Ether 12:6).

During the Sesquicentennial year of the Church, the Saints were reminded that it takes "faith in every footstep" to reach any goal. Any given step along the way may present a trial of trust— in the Savior, in the process, in ourselves—but if we have a vision of who we are and of our next step, if we keep our eye of faith single to the glory of God, eventually we will come out of the darkness into the light of salvation and exaltation once again. So long as we persevere in learning to walk by faith, we will develop the vision that allows us to see the path ahead. Steadily we can move toward the subject of our faith, even Jesus Christ, and toward the life that He lives, even eternal life. That is why the principle of faithful vision plays a central role in the lives of disciples.

Believing is seeing!

Notes to Chapter 1

1. Anyone who has achieved some degree of skill in a profession, avocation, or some endeavor has experienced obedience to the principles of the skill from the most elementary to the higher principles thereof. I'm reminded of an episode in the career of Artur Rubenstein, one of the premier pianists of the

twentieth century. After one of his performances, an audience member said to him, "I'd give anything to be able to play as you do." To which Rubenstein replied: "No you wouldn't!" He went on to explain the number of hours he had spent learning to be an accomplished pianist and the number of hours he continued to practice to maintain his high level of performance.

2. Georg Bertram, "ἐνεργέω," *TDNT*, 2:652.
3. I discuss all of the promises enunciated in Revelation to those who overcome in my book *The Beatitudes: From Poor in Heart to Pure in Heart* (np: Amazon, 2016), 107-191.
4. This translation of Hebrews 11:1 was rendered by G. B. Caird in his and L. D. Hurst's *New Testament Theology* (Oxford: Clarendon Press, 1995), 39.
5. Gerrit W. Gong, "Campfire of Faith," *Ensign* (Nov. 2018), 40.
6. *TPJS*, 368.
7. *TPJS*, 348; *HC* 6:306-07.
8. *The Teachings of Harold B. Lee*, ed. Clyde J. Williams (Salt Lake City, UT: Bookcraft, 1996), 165-66.
9. Stephen E. Robinson, *Believing Christ* (Salt Lake City: Deseret Book, 1992), 12.
10. At the end of Disney-Pixar's animated movie, *Cars*, the rookie race car, Lightning McQueen comes to a screeching stop just before crossing the finish line of the biggest race of his short career that would have made him the number one race car. His whole vision had been to win the "Piston Cup" and gain the sponsorship of the number one racing team. But having learned a powerful lesson helping others in "Radiator Springs," he sees that the long-time, ready-to-retire champion has crashed. Remembering what a crash had done to his unofficial mentor, Doc, McQueen goes back and pushes the champ across the finish line, even though he (McQueen) comes in third in a three-car race. The paradox is that in finishing last, he wins, while the winner loses. "Many that are first shall be last; and the last shall be first" (Matt. 19:30; et al).
11. Neal A. Maxwell, "'Brightness of Hope,'" *Ensign* (Nov. 1994), 35, 36.
12. *Lectures*, 1:10.
13. *Lectures*, 1:12.
14. Sydney Harris, "Love Your Enemies," *Detroit Free Press* (June 1973).
15. *Lectures*, 1:15-16.
16. *Lectures*, 1:24.

17. *Lectures*, 1:13.
18. See Don Cecil Corbett, *Mary Fielding Smith: Daughter of Britain* (Salt Lake City: Deseret Book, 1974), 210-13.
19. *LF*, 3:2-5.
20. John A. Widtsoe, *Joseph Smith – Seeker after Truth, Prophet of God* (Salt Lake City: Bookcraft, 1951), 163.
21. Bruce R. McConkie, *A New Witness for the Articles of Faith* (Salt Lake City: Deseret Book, 1987), 166; hereafter *New Witness*.
22. The most famous discussion of form as principle or idea is Plato's realm of pure Forms which he discusses throughout his writings. Plato's view of reality held anything real had to be unchanging, immutable. Consequently, he postulated a world of being in which Forms, or Ideas, exist forever and serve as universal patterns for all things. In that world (somewhere in the ether) everything was perfect because the Forms were eternal. Earth life is a world of becoming, a world of things that are temporary, a world of constant change and dying. Thus, each thing on the earth is a pale shadow of the eternal Forms. For example, all chairs on earth are shadowy imitations of the eternal pattern of the Chair. He gave poetic form to his philosophy of Forms in the "Allegory of the Cave" found in *The Republic*, Book VII. In the "Allegory" men are imprisoned in a cave facing one of its walls. On the wall, they can only see shadows passing in front of them, transitory shadows cast on the wall by puppets passing in front of a fire placed behind them. Because they do not know better, the prisoners are deceived and the shadows become their vision of reality. One prisoner, however, is freed to see the fire creating the shadows and changes his vision as he comes to see the fire as reality. It is not until he is brought into open sunlight that he has a true vision of what is real, the sunlight representing the realm of the Forms. It is a fascinating vision that Plato devised, but, in his ignorance of God, he omitted that God the Eternal Father is the sun and source of all forms of godliness.

    Echoes of Plato's vision are found in the Apostle Paul who wrote that those who were "lovers of their own selves . . . more than lovers of God / [Had] a form of godliness, but [denied] the power thereof" (2 Tim. 3:2, 4-5). That the world we live in every day is not the real world is expressed in verses cited several times in the text of the discussion: "the Holy Spirit speaketh of things as they really are, and of things as they really will be; wherefore, these things are manifested unto us plainly, for the salvation of our souls" (Jacob 4:13). *Real* reality is the Lord's.

23. See Elder Boyd K. Packer, "Inspiring Music—Worthy Thoughts," *Ensign* (Jan. 1974), 27-28.
24. Larry R. Lawrence, "The War Goes On," *Ensign* (Apr. 2017), 36. [33-39]
25. *TPJS*, 190.
26. *DNTC*, 2:36.
27. The prophet Alma taught:

> And now, behold, because ye have tried the experiment, and planted the seed, and it swelleth and sprouteth, and beginneth to grow, ye must needs know that the seed is good.
>
> And now, behold, is your knowledge perfect? Yea, your knowledge is perfect in that thing, and your faith is dormant; and this because you know, for ye know that the word hath swelled your souls, and ye also know that it hath sprouted up, that your understanding doth begin to be enlightened, and your mind doth begin to expand.
>
> O then, is not this real? I say unto you, Yea, because it is light; and whatsoever is light, is good, because it is discernible, therefore ye must know that it is good; and now behold, after ye have tasted this light is your knowledge perfect?
>
> Behold I say unto you, Nay; neither must ye lay aside your faith, for ye have only exercised your faith to plant the seed that ye might try the experiment to know if the seed was good. (Alma 32:33-36)

CHAPTER 2

BELIEVING IS SEEING

The key to seeing the vision of the scriptures is found in the Apostle Paul's definition of faith: "faith is the substance of things hoped for, the evidence of things not seen," or as George B. Caird translated the verse, "faith gives substance to our hopes and *reality to what we do not see*" (Heb. 11:1; emphasis added).[1] Alma expressed the same thought: "faith is not to have a perfect knowledge of things; therefore if ye have faith ye hope for things which are not seen, which are true" (Alma 32:21). There are multitudes of important things we may not see with our physical eyesight but which we can perceive with an eye of faith, e.g., the questions Alma posed to his brethren:

> Do ye exercise *faith* in the redemption of him who created you? Do you *look forward with an eye of faith*, and *view* this mortal body raised in immortality, and this corruption raised in incorruption, to stand before God to be judged according to the deeds which have been done in the mortal body?

I say unto you, can you *imagine to yourselves* that ye hear the voice of the Lord, saying unto you, in that day: Come unto me ye blessed, for behold, your works have been the works of righteousness upon the face of the earth?

Or do ye *imagine to yourselves* that ye can lie unto the Lord in that day, and say—Lord, our works have been righteous works upon the face of the earth—and that he will save you?

Or otherwise, can ye *imagine yourselves* brought before the tribunal of God with your souls filled with guilt and remorse, having a remembrance of all your guilt, yea, a perfect remembrance of all your wickedness, yea, a remembrance that ye have set at defiance the commandments of God?

I say unto you, can ye *look up to God* at that day with a pure heart and clean hands? I say unto you, can you *look up*, having the image of God engraven upon your countenances? (Alma 5:15-19; emphasis added).

Notice the verb "look" appears three times in these verses. In verse 15 Alma tells us to look forward *with an eye of faith*. He used the same phrase in his discourse on faith (see Alma 32:40, 41).

Those who require tangible evidence, or signs, before they will accept anything as verifiably true will likely consider the statement "evidence of things not seen" in Paul's definition of faith an oxymoron, yet, no progress takes place, few discoveries are made, without the underlying factor of faith and vision, albeit secular faith and vision: e.g., Columbus' discovery of the Americas; Sir Isaac Newton's laws of mechanics, or Einstein's theory of relativity.[2] With the development of increasingly powerful microscopes and telescopes, we are now able to observe things that have remained completely hidden to the naked eye, yet many of these phenomena scientists had hypothesized with the vision of faith years, even centuries ago, like worlds of microbes, atoms, and subatomic particles as well galaxies in space, with many now accepting that there are worlds without number and even multiverses, ideas that were deemed to be science fiction not all that long ago.[3]

Every day man exercises faith in the unseen: we cannot see electricity but we have faith that when we want light in our houses, all we have to do is press a switch. (I understand that millions in the world do not live with electricity to near the degree people in the developed world do.) We have this assurance because Thomas Edison and Nikola Tesla envisioned that the invisible power of electricity could be harnessed to provide light and other uses, and they went to work to realize their vision. When asked about the thousands of failed experiments he had conducted, Edison is reputed to have said that each failure brought him one step closer to ultimate success. That is, he had confidence in his vision; it was only a matter of getting it right. Not a bad way to think of experimenting with faith upon the words of God!

Notice too in the Alma quote above that he used the verb "imagine" three times. Many adults undervalue the positive power of imagination, but no less a genius than Albert Einstein valued it highly: "Imagination is more important than knowledge. Knowledge is limited. Imagination encircles the world."[4] When we read, images are constantly flashing though the imagination, but in our visual— and auditory-saturated world, those images we read and silently pronounce hardly register in our consciousness, resulting in the diminution of the likening process that Nephi considered so important (see 1 Ne. 19:23). The next time you study the scriptures, try to capture an image or two in your imagination, seeing them as clearly as possible, and raise them into your conscious awareness, study them out in your mind, and evaluate their relevance to you.

Alma challenges us to take our faith to the level of vision, envisioning the reality of immortality and eternal life. Why? Elder L. Tom Perry answered that question:

> When we think of eternal life, what is the picture that comes to mind? I believe that if we could create in our minds a clear and true picture of eternal life, we would start behaving differently. We would not need to be prodded to do the many things involved with enduring to the end, like doing our home teaching or visiting teaching, attending our meetings, going to the temple, living moral lives, saying our prayers, or reading the scriptures. We would want to do all these things and more because we realize they will prepare us to go somewhere we yearn to go.[5]

The challenge to individual members is to see the Lord's vision themselves. Elder Russell M. Nelson gave an insightful, incisive analogy for seeing as the Lord sees:

> Imagine, if you will, a pair of powerful binoculars. Two separate optical systems are joined together with a gear to focus two independent images into one three-dimensional view. To apply this analogy, let the scene on the left side of your binoculars represent your perception of your task. Let the picture on the right side represent the Lord's perspective of your task—the portion of His plan He has entrusted to you. Now, connect your system to His. By mental adjustment, fuse your focus. Something wonderful happens. Your vision and His are now the same. You have developed an "eye single to the glory

of God" (D&C 4:5; see also Morm. 8:15). With that perspective, look upward—above and beyond mundane things about you. The Lord said, "Look unto me in every thought" (D&C 6:36). That special vision will also help clarify your wishes when they may be a bit fuzzy and out of focus with God's hopes for your divine destiny. Indeed, the precise challenge you regard now as "impossible" may be the very refinement you need, in His eye.[6]

Aligning our vision with the Lord's results from internalizing His words as we search the scriptures, prayerfully seeking the guidance of the Holy Ghost, and toning our spiritual muscle-memory through obedience to the Lord's principles of eternal living.

Vision Words in the Scriptures

Chapter 14 of 1 Nephi records that an angel of the Lord revealed a vision of the latter days to Nephi: "And it shall come to pass, that if the Gentiles shall hearken unto the Lamb of God in that day that *he shall manifest himself unto them in word*, and also in power, in very deed, unto the taking away of their stumbling blocks" (1 Ne. 14:1; emphasis added). The word *manifest* implies that such a manifestation will not be in His personal appearance to the world as will be the case with His Second Coming. How, then, will He manifest Himself? The immediate answer would be that He will do so though the scriptures, especially the Book of Mormon. In the usage of the early nineteenth century, "manifest" was defined as "plain; open; clearly visible to the eye or obvious to the understanding; apparent; not obscure or difficult to be seen or understood."[7] In this sense, "manifest" takes us beyond simply reading the scriptures; it suggests that we can somehow envision the Savior's immanence and *feel* His spirit in His word of scripture as we seek and receive the inspiration of the Holy Spirit (see 1 Ne. 10:11).[8] Elder Robert D. Hales taught, "When we want to speak to God, we pray. And when we want Him to speak to us, we search the scriptures; for His words are spoken through His prophets. He will then teach us as we listen to the promptings of the Holy Spirit."[9] "And thus, we acquire faith."[10] President Howard W. Hunter pointed out that "the Master used few words in his teachings, but each one is so concise in meaning that together they *portray a clear image* to the reader."[11]

The image to which President Hunter referred may be found in the many words and phrases expressing vision found in the scriptures. For example, king Benjamin encouraged his people to "open your . . . minds that the mysteries of God may be *unfolded* [revealed] *to your view* (Mosiah 2:9; emphasis added). We might, of course, consider the word *view* as king Benjamin used it to simply be a common figure of speech, as in "I view the matter as settled," but the Lord, through His servants, the prophets, used and continues to use words with precise meaning, so each has to be considered with care. King Benjamin expounded one view, or vision, after another to the people. We know they caught the vision in his words, for "they . . . *viewed* themselves in their own carnal state, even less than the dust of the earth" (Mosiah 4:2; emphasis added). He helped them *see* and *feel* their condition from an eternal perspective, and they were ashamed of what they observed; however, they also recognized that "through the infinite goodness of God, and the manifestations of his Spirit, [we] now have great *views* of that which is to come" (Mosiah 5:3; emphasis added).

Over and over the Savior emphasized the importance of inner-eye sight. When on the Western continent, encouraging His disciples to follow His example, Christ said: "the works which ye have seen me do that shall ye also do; for that which ye have seen me do even that shall ye do; Therefore, if ye do these things blessed are ye, for ye shall be lifted up at the last day" (3 Ne. 27:21-22). Since the Book of Mormon is intended for our day, we can read His counsel as being directed to us also. He expects us to "see" the works He did, through His words; that is, He wants us to view, to envision, and to experience His reality through intensive study of His words. Moreover, the intent of a great deal of His teaching is to be found in the subtext, below the surface of His words. When asked in Palestine why He taught in parables, Jesus answered:

> He answered and said unto them, Because it is given unto you to know the mysteries of the kingdom of heaven, but to them it is not given....
> Therefore speak I to them in parables: because they seeing see not; and hearing they hear not, neither do they understand.
> And in them is fulfilled the prophecy of Esaias, which saith, By hearing ye shall hear, and shall not understand; and seeing ye shall see, and shall not *perceive*:
> For this people's heart is waxed gross, and their ears are dull of hearing, and their eyes they have closed; lest at any time they should see with their eyes, and hear with their ears, and should understand with their heart, and should be converted, and I should heal them.
> But blessed are your eyes, for they *see*: and your ears, for they *hear* (Matt. 13:13-16; emphasis added).

To perceive is to be percipient, meaning "to perceive something outside the range of the senses."[12] With their physical eyes people may have 20x20 eyesight, yet be far, or nearsighted with their spiritual eyes, not perceiving "things as they really are" (Jacob 2:13) surrounding them because they choose to see the worldly illusion of reality (Jacob 4:13). When such spiritual blindness is removed, one realizes, as did Joseph Smith and Sydney Rigdon, that "by *the power of the Spirit our eyes were opened* and *our understandings were enlightened,* so as to *see and understand the things of God"* (D&C 76:12; emphasis added), and opened they were to what Joseph called "the Vision."

Many Latter-day Saints have known a person whose vision of the Church, when they began their investigation of the gospel, included misleading, deceptive ideas of practices in the Church. In the process of taking the missionary discussions and attending Church meetings, their false ideas about the Church melted away and their vision of reality began to conform with the Lord's. And, because "the light of the body is the eye" (Matt. 6:22; Luke 11:34; 3 Ne. 13:22), their eyes more clearly manifest the Light of Christ in them. This process of correcting one's vision is not restricted to new converts; it will continue through all time and eternity; if we keep the faith, we will see more and more of the eternal truths underscoring the appearance of things.

Vision in The Church of Jesus Christ of Latter-day Saints

Proverbs 29:18 establishes the seminal significance of vision for all disciples: "Where *there is* no vision, the people perish: but he that keepeth the law, happy *is* he." Whenever Latter-day Saints "talk of Christ, . . . rejoice of Christ, . . . preach of Christ, . . . prophesy of Christ" (2 Ne. 25:26), which is most of the time, the subtext of their testimony is Joseph's Smith experience in the Sacred Grove, eloquently and powerfully expressed by Elder Hugh B. Brown observed:

When Joseph came out of the woods, he had learned at least four fundamental truths, and he announced them to the world: first, that the Father and the Son are separate and distinct individuals; secondly, that the canon of scripture is not complete; third, that man was created in the bodily image of God; and fourth, the channel between earth and heaven is open, and revelation is continuous.[13]

Thus, a Latter-day Saint's testimony of the Savior is intimately intertwined with the Prophet Joseph Smith's face-to-face meeting with the Father and the Son.

Joseph was privileged to receive many more visions, as have those men who have succeeded him in the office of Living Prophet and President of the Church. Brigham Young, for instance, had a clear vision of the Saints home in the Great Salt Lake Valley and what it could become. The Lord brought the principle of tithing to the fore through President Lorenzo Snow's windows-of-heaven vision; likewise missionary work when President Spencer W. Kimball stood beside a globe, on which arrows pointed into every corner of the world, explaining his vision of how the missionary work would and should proceed, and asking members to catch the vision and become involved in the work also. President Ezra Taft Benson expounded a vision of how regular study of the Book of Mormon would contribute to members' spiritual growth and also that it should "flood the earth." Said he:

> I have a vision of homes alerted, of classes alive, and of pulpits aflame with the spirit of Book of Mormon messages.
> I have a vision of home teachers and visiting teachers, ward and branch officers, and stake and mission leaders counseling our people out of the most correct of any book on earth—the Book of Mormon.

I have a vision of artists putting into film, drama, literature, music, and paintings great themes and great characters from the Book of Mormon.

I have a vision of thousands of missionaries going into the mission field with hundreds of passages memorized from the Book of Mormon so that they might feed the needs of a spiritually famished world.

I have a vision of the whole Church getting nearer to God by abiding by the precepts of the Book of Mormon. Indeed, I have a vision of flooding the earth with the Book of Mormon. . . .

I do not know fully why God has preserved my life to this age, but I do know this: That for the present hour He has revealed to me the absolute need for us to move the Book of Mormon forward now in a marvelous manner. You must help with this burden and with this blessing which He has placed on the whole Church, even all the children of Zion."[14]

The leadership of President Gordon B. Hinckley was called visionary.[15] Like king Benjamin, he gave the Church one vision after another of where the Lord is guiding His earthly kingdom. At the conclusion of the Sesquicentennial Celebration of the year when the pioneers entered the Salt Lake Valley, he unfolded a sweeping vision of the great work ahead:

I *see* a wonderful future in a very uncertain world. If we will cling to our values, if we will build on our inheritance, if we will walk in obedience before the Lord, if we will simply live the gospel we will be blessed in a magnificent way. We will be looked upon as a peculiar people who have found the key to a peculiar happiness . . . .

We have *glimpsed the future*, we know the way, we have the truth. God help us to move forward to become a great and mighty people spread over the earth, counted in the millions, but all of one faith and of one testimony and of one conviction. . . ."[16]

Latter-day Saints need only reflect on what has transpired in the years since these prophets of God declared His visions to see for themselves the fulfillment of each vision the Lord gave to His servants.

Notes to Chapter 2

1. G. B. Caird, *New Testament Theology* (Oxford: Clarendon Press, 1995), 39.
2. While not mentioning the principle of faith, reading between the lines of Daniel Boorstin's *The Discoverers* (New York: Random House, 1983), one can discern just how indispensable faith unto vision has been to man.
3. See Brian Greene, *The Hidden Reality – Parallel Universes and the Deep Laws of the Cosmos* (New York: Alfred A. Knopf, 2011); Mark Tegmark, *Our Mathematical Universe – My Quest for the Ultimate Nature of Reality* (New York: Alfred A. Knopf, 2014).
4. "What Life Means to Einstein: An Interview by George Sylvester Viereck," *The Saturday Evening Post* (October 26, 1929), 117.
5. L. Tom Perry, "The Gospel of Jesus Christ," *Ensign* (May 2008), 44.
6. Russell M. Nelson, "With God Nothing is Impossible," *Ensign* (May 1988), 34.
7. *Noah Webster's First Edition of an American Dictionary of the English Language* (San Francisco: Foundation for American Christian Education, 2000), s.v. "manifest."
8. President Ezra Taft Benson said, "We hear the words of the Lord most often by a feeling. If we are humble and sensitive, the Lord will prompt us through our feelings" (*Teachings of the President of the Church: Ezra Taft Benson* [Salt Lake City: The Church of Jesus Christ of Latter-day Saints, 2014], 160; hereafter Ezra Taft Benson.

9. Robert D. Hales, "Holy Scriptures: The Power of God unto Salvation," *Ensign* (Nov. 2006), 26-27.
10. Dean M. Davies, "The Blessings of Worship," *Ensign* (Nov. 2016), 95.
11. Howard W. Hunter, *Teachings of the Presidents of the Church: Howard W. Hunter* (Salt Lake City, UT: The Church of Jesus Christ of Latter-day Saints, 2015), 149.
12. *SOED*, s.v., percipience.
13. Hugh B. Brown, *Eternal Quest* (Salt Lake City: Bookcraft, 1956), 134.
14. Ezra Taft Benson, "Flooding the Earth with the Book of Mormon," *Ensign* (Nov. 1988), 6; also Ezra Taft Benson, 144.
15. Elder Jeffrey R. Holland, "'Abide in Me,'" *Ensign* (May 2004), 31.
16. Gordon B. Hinckley, "Look to the Future," *Ensign* (Nov. 1997), 69; emphasis added.

CHAPTER 3

POIETICS AND AESTHETICS OF VISION IN THE SCRIPTURES

Language in General – Scriptures in Particular

Two quotes set the stage for a discussion of the *poietics* and aesthetics of the scriptures. The first, also appearing in the front of the book, concerns language in general.

> Embedded within the structure of language is an entire narrative of experience. The relations between things; a consciousness of self, other, and community; an anatomy of action; a sense of time, memory, and potentiality; a method for seeing, shaping, and interpreting reality—all are encoded in the grammar of case and

number, tense and conjugation, metaphor and figures of speech. Acquaintance with such structural intricacies reveals just how powerful a tool of apprehension language is, just how strongly the skeleton of words supports the flesh of experience.[1]

In other words, language profiles the intricate details of a culture—its morality, sociality, dynamics, political philosophy, and so forth. The culture of the United States is revealed in the language its citizens speak and write, likewise language in Mexico, Germany, France, Japan, or any other culture; each expresses a vision of reality. And there are, of course, subcultures in each. Two ancient cultures inform the original recording of the scriptures: ancient Hebrew and Koine Greek, the nuances of which the translators of the King James Bible sometimes missed, and are often corrected in the Bible produced by the Church. Comprehending the culture of our Heavenly Father, Jesus Christ, and the Holy Spirit is what we are seeking in the words in the scriptures, for it is in the divinely inspired words of the scriptures, conditioned by the culture of each prophet that God's voice may be heard and His description of things as they really are seen and felt.

The second quote appears in the front of the Gideon Bibles; while referring specifically to the Bible, I've expanded it to include all scripture, meaning additionally the Book of Mormon, Doctrine and Covenants, and Pearl of Great Price:

> The [scriptures] contain the mind of God, the state of man, the way of salvation, the doom of sinners, and the happiness of believers. [Their] doctrines are holy, [their] precepts are binding, [their] histories are true, and [their] decisions are immutable.

Read [them] to be wise, believe [them] to be safe, and practice [them] to be holy. [They] contain light to direct you, food to support you, and comfort to cheer you.

[They are] the traveler's map, the pilgrim's staff, the pilot's compass, the soldier's sword and the Christian's charter. Here too, Heaven is opened and the gates of Hell disclosed.

Christ is [their] grand subject, our good [their] design, and the glory of God [their] end. [They] should fill the memory, rule the heart and guide the feet. Read [them] slowly, frequently and prayerfully. [They are] a mine of wealth, a paradise of glory, and a river of pleasure.

[They are] given you in life, will be opened at the judgment, and be remembered forever. [They] involve the highest responsibility, reward the greatest labor, and will condemn all who trifle with [their] sacred contents.[2]

This quote partially identifies the grandeur of heaven and its relationship to man, but so much more is available to mortal man, as Elder Neal A. Maxwell indicated: "For those who have eyes to see and ears to hear, it is clear that the Father and the Son are giving away the secrets of the universe!"[3] On one level those secrets are revealed in the breadth, or topography, and depth of the scriptures. "Breadth-topography" refers to the surface text of the scriptures from the Old Testament through the Pearl of Great Price; depth is found in the image-symbols replete throughout. In the breadth of the scriptures we can find the topographical unity of the Lord's vision; in the depth thereof is the organic unity of His vision.[4] Elder Dallin H. Oaks added what is the most important aspect of our scripture research:

> For [Latter-day Saints], the scriptures are not the ultimate source of knowledge, but what precedes the ultimate source. The ultimate knowledge comes by revelation. ...
>
> The word of the Lord in the scriptures is like a lamp to guide our feet (see Ps. 119:105), and revelation is like a mighty force that increases the lamp's illumination manyfold. ...
>
> We do not overstate the point when we say that the scriptures can be a Urim and Thummim to assist each of us to receive personal revelation.[5]

The revelation of which he spoke comes from the Holy Spirit.

Each abstract word of a principle, such as righteousness or faith, expresses an inherent dynamic. I will mention three of many ways we can access the significance of that dynamic.

- One, if we separate a compound word into its constituent parts, we can often get a sense for the concealed dynamic.
- Two, the Old Testament Hebrew and New Testament Greek words can identify the original meaning intended by the writer of a book. For example, the Old Testament word translated as righteousness is *sūdēq* which "refers to an ethical, moral standard [that] is the nature and will of God." By extension, for man, righteousness "consisted in obedience to God's law and conformity to God's nature [as set out in the scriptures], having mercy for the needy and helpless."[6] Think here of the good Samaritan! The New Testament Greek word translated as righteousness, *dikaiosúnē* (δικαιοσύνη), has much the same meaning.[7]

- Three, by following the etymology of a word back to its source we can often find an original metaphoric base that further reveals an inner dynamic contributing greater meaning to the word.
- By knowing even just a bit about the concrete object informing a word-principle in its primordial beginning, we may identify nuances of the gospel that enhance and deepen our understanding of the scriptures.

As an example, we'll consider the oft-used word in the scriptures "remember." Without digging very deeply we can see that "remember" is a compound word in two parts: the prefix *re-* and the primary noun *member*. At its most basic level, "member" is "a part or organ of the body."[8] Paul used the word metaphorically to describe the Church of Jesus Christ: "For as the body is one, and hath many members, and all the members of that one body, being many, are one body: so also is Christ" (1 Cor. 12:12). "Re-" signifies "again, anew . . . backward, back."[9] The word *remember* suggests looking back to once again assemble the members or parts of something we can see in our imagination from our past and, as the Greek word for "remember," *anamnesis* (ἀνάμνησις) implies, to experience as we did in the first instance."[10] Undoubtedly we do not think of this when we use the word *remember*, but were we to pause and consider the particular memory, we might find a concrete scene crossing that part of our mind we call imagination with the emotion we originally felt.

The ramification of this for our discipleship is substantial. Think of the sacrament prayer we hear each week as the preface to the central moment of our Sunday worship: ". . . [we] are willing to take upon [us] the name of thy Son, and *always remember him* and keep his commandments which he has given [us]; that [we] may always have his Spirit to be with [us]" (D&C 20:77, 79). When we say "Amen" to that prayer, we are saying to ourselves we will experience in our spirits, during the following few minutes, all that our Savior means to us. That is a very sacred moment we commit to each time, a moment Heavenly Father wants us to revere in contemplation, not doodling absent-mindedly on our electronic devices. I sometimes wonder if we read the scriptures during the sacrament, are we removing ourselves from the profound moments of recollection between ourselves, Heavenly Father, Jesus Christ, and the Holy Spirit, unless we read a scripture to help lead us into sacred remembering His inexpressible love for and graciousness toward us.

There's much to regard in the act of remembering! This can also be true of many other gospel principles. Indeed, the Lord has embedded with His word attributes indicative of the heavenly culture He wishes us to emulate in the mortal journey, even "the hidden wisdom, . . . the deep things of God" (1 Cor. 2:7, 10), that can refine and ennoble men and women in their quest to become more like their Savior, Jesus Christ, a quest that will continue well past this mortal life into eternity.

POIETICS

Poietics is the Anglicization of the Greek word *poiein* (ποιεῖν) from the verb *poieō* (ποιέω), meaning "things . . . produced by an inward act of the mind or will."[11] Thus *poietics* refers to the thing made or created, specifically to an artistic work created by an author, artist, sculptor, etc. I use the word, not to be pretentious, but to avoid misunderstanding with the word *poetics*, which English speakers might confuse with literature in verse form. *Poietics* applies to two important aspects of scriptural literature: first, the means and manner an author employs to create the unity of a literary work of art. In the study of "Gen 2:4b - 3:24: A Synchronic Approach," Jerome T. Walsh states: "The 'meaning' of a work of literature is communicated as much by the structure of the work as by surface 'content.'"[12] Secondly, as used by Walsh, "structure," I think, is equivalent, or closely related, to *poietics*: how an author orders the words of his text to convey the meaning and emotions he intends his readers to perceive, what the Age-of-Enlightenment polymath, Giambattista Vico, called "poetic logic,"[13] a logic derived from the imagery, rhythm, rhyme, and other factors of a literary work, all of which directed toward creating an emotive response in the reader. The ramifications of this for the discussion of any literary work is that we look at not only what is said, but how it is said to gain a deeper appreciation and understanding of the work.

Poietics is not used to put a nice dressing on something that could be said in straight-forward prose; rather it is a way to reveal subtexts of meaning to the inquisitive reader, undermeanings that often expand the scope of the vision an author wishes to create. Given the extensive use of imagery and symbolism in the scriptures, would anyone claim that the Lord used images *just* to dress important doctrines in fancy language? His image-symbols intimate things for which no human words exist—things of the highest order of reality, things which are inherently beautiful and layered into the substrata of symbols. Hence, to grasp the scope of the Lord's vision requires exploring more deeply into words.

Aesthetics

The formal study of beauty is aesthetics. The root of the word *aesthetics* is found in the ancient Greek noun *aisthētikós*, "sense perception," from the verb *aisthánomai*, "to feel,"[14] to empathsize with a work of art, a principle discussed in Chapter 2. The deeper one ponders the *poietics* of a work, the greater one's aesthetic appreciation for the beauty of the work, usually, and the better one can understand its intrinsic meaning. When we manifest our serious desire to increase our understanding though study and prayer (see D&C 9:8), the Holy Spirit, building on our initial enlightenment, can release and inspire us with further light that reveals additional truth or nuances of truth to us, whereby we may discern a further degree of the profound beauty of the Lord and His vision.

Western civilization has produced numerous theories of beauty, most of which are, today, relegated to college classrooms and libraries; in Will Durant's delightfully ironic turn of phrase, they exist in "the twilight realm of the praised unread."[15] Curiously, relatively few theologians and religious writers have ventured into the discussion of beauty enunciated in scriptures. Some, like Augustine and Thomas Aquinas, employed the term "beauty" to describe their perception of God's creation, not to address His universal vision of beauty revealed in the Bible.[16] Other writers focus on the concretion of creed in art, e.g., Michelangelo's magnificent paintings on the ceiling of the Sistine Chapel or Leonardo di Vinci's *Last Supper* in the Santa Maria delle Grazie church and monastery of Milan. Representing this perspective of beauty, F. I. G. Rawlins wrote in *The British Journal of Aesthetics* "that, whether deliberately grasped or not, an awareness of the Beautiful is, and has always been, a major factor in the evolution of religion and its impact on mankind."[17] The Eastern Orthodox theologian, David Bentley Hart, has written a comprehensive, erudite study of theological aesthetics, his focus being what earlier theologians have said about aesthetics and religion. The scriptures he cites, with the one exception from the Apocryphal Wisdom of Solomon, do not include important verses about beauty from the Old Testament,[18]—important because they also inform the vision of the New Testament, as well as the Book of Mormon, evidenced by the number of references to the Old Testament in the latter two compilations. Regarding the scriptures themselves, the consensus among scholars who have written about biblical aesthetics seems to be that "neither the Old Testament nor the New Testament has any theory of the Beautiful,"[19] an assertion the following study will seek to show is not what the scriptures indicate.

In twenty-first century United States, "beauty" and "beautiful" are words spoken so casually (much like "love") that any specific aesthetic meaning they might have had has been greatly diminished, if not lost, among people in general. One would be hard pressed to find a consensus as to what constitutes beauty; we have reduced our conception and perception of beauty to the subjective assessment that it is in the eye of the beholder. As a consequence, when we study the scriptures and come across any mention of beauty, we may read over the word without further consideration.

However, on April 26, 1832, the Lord gave the Prophet Joseph Smith a revelation that refutes the claim that no principle of beauty is set forth in the scriptures, also negating the multitude of subjective perceptions of beauty. Said He: "For Zion must increase in *beauty*, and in *holiness*; her borders must be enlarged; her stakes must be strengthened; yea, verily I say unto you, Zion must arise and put on her *beautiful garments*" (D&C 82:14; emphasis added), a statement echoing Isaiah centuries earlier: "Awake, awake; put on thy strength, O Zion; put on thy beautiful garments, O Jerusalem, the holy city" (Isa. 52:1). From the 1832 revelation we know that the Lord does have a standard of beauty.

Hans Robert Jauss wrote that *poietics* also refers to, "the process whereby the recipient [of aesthetic impressions] becomes a participant creator of the work."[20] This is what will be discussed as insight and empathy below.

We will first look at *poietic* expression in imagery per se before turning to scriptural imagery and then to verse in the scriptures. Chapter 7 is a discussion of the vision of beauty underscoring the scriptures and discipleship to Jesus Christ.

WILLIAM J. BOHN

NATURE OF *POIETIC* EXPRESSION

In his book, *The Poetic Image*, C. Day Lewis gives us a working definition for exploring the inner dynamic of scriptural images: "The poetic image is a more or less [sensory] picture in words, to some degree metaphorical, with an undertone of human emotion in its context."[21] Lewis's definition supplies us with four terms to focus our further study of imagery: "poetic," "sensory," "metaphorical," and "undertone of human emotion."

Poietic Expression

According to Owen Barfield, we encounter poetic diction "when words are selected and arranged in such a way that their meaning either arouses, or is obviously intended to arouse, [the reader or listener's] imagination."[22] To illustrate what Barfield means, following is Robert Frost's familiar poem, "The Road Not Taken":

> Two roads diverged in a yellow wood,
> And sorry I could not travel both
> And be one traveler, long I stood
> And looked down one as far as I could
>
> To where it bent in the undergrowth;
> Then took the other, as just as fair,
> And having perhaps the better claim
> Because it was grassy and wanted wear,
> Though as for that the passing there
> Had worn them really about the same,
>
> And both that morning equally lay
> In leaves no step had trodden black,

Oh, I kept the first for another day!
Yet knowing how way leads on to way
I doubted if I should ever come back.

I shall be telling this with a sigh
Somewhere ages and ages hence:
Two roads diverged in a wood, and I,
I took the one less traveled by,
And that has made all the difference.

The stanzaic form alerts us that this is poetry; its rhyme scheme is *a b a a b*. The inversion of words is also a poetic device: e.g., "And sorry I could not travel" and "long I stood." Both "sorry" and "long" are out of normal word order as they would appear in prose, adding emphasis to both words.[23]

The first line of Frost's poem sets the scene with the central image of a fork in a road. The second line evokes dramatic tension with the words "sorry I could not travel both": a choice will have to be made as to which fork to take—the tension of opposites. From the last two lines of the first stanza we glean that the fork connotes the choices we all make on the figurative road of life—physical, emotional, spiritual forks in our paths. By extension, life is really a series of such forks where we have to decide the direction we will go. We may recall the quandary Alice faced in Wonderland when she asked the Cheshire cat which fork in the road she should take. The cat responded by asking her, "Where do you want to go?" "I don't know," said Alice. "Then," said the cat, "it doesn't matter." Knowing our goals in life is the key to deciding which forks in our road to take.

To access Frost's vision, we have to be aware of what we picture in our own imagination, for instance, the image of "a yellow wood," not green, red, or any other color; it's yellow! Changing the color would change the vision the poem creates. Thus, yellow represents *poietic* diction. Then we have to ask ourselves questions. What is our first impression of "a yellow wood"? Fall colors? the color of a dying forest? or something else? Were we to ask about the psychology of colors in our American culture, we would find that yellow projects optimistic energy. In the end, the appreciation of the word *yellow* in his poem remains an individual interpretation, unless we research Frost's body of work more extensively.

These brief considerations only scratch the surface of the *poietic* expression in "The Road Not Taken," but it will suffice as a transition to a discussion of the metaphoric process.

Metaphor and the Metaphoric Process

The dynamic of a *poietic* image derives from the synergy created in the metaphoric process. What is the metaphoric process? Think of mixing red and yellow paint in equal measure on a palette: both are primary colors; when blended, they produce a third color, orange. The third color represents the synergistic inner dynamic of a poetic image, though this is a somewhat bland example of the metaphoric process at work as it unfolds its brilliance in someone's imagination. A number of different descriptions and definitions have been used to try and capture the metaphoric process. Vico wrote that "metaphor . . . confers sense and emotion on insensate objects. . . . every such metaphor is a miniature myth"[24] that contains its own story. In a similar vein, Monroe C. Beardsley, American philosopher of art, described "a metaphor [as] a miniature poem."[25] Central to both Vico's "myth" and Beardsly's "poem" is that the metaphoric process unfolds a narrative of a life, revealing an organic unity, resulting from the synergy of diverse parts. What is "organic unity"? G. N. G. Orsini, professor of comparative literature at the University of Wisconsin, has written that the "organic unity and . . . its cognates like the idea of organic form or of 'inner form'[:] The designation arises from the assumption that a work of art may be compared to a living organism, so that the relation between the parts of a work is . . . as close and intimate as that between the organs of a living body."[26]

The imagery found in the scriptures often imply an organic unity. Jesus used a number of image-symbols drawn from common objects of everyday life in first-century-A.D. Palestine, objects still found in many areas of the world, most of which referred to animate objects possessing an inherent organic unity. (Even inanimate objects such as pearls and rocks, if traced back into their origins, result from organic processes.) The surface image of these objects created in our imagination is only a part, often a small part, of their internal "narratives." For instance, when we observe a plant, we see its outward appearance, but its root system and photosynthetic receptors remain hidden from our view, yet they are important to understanding the unity of the plant's vitality and its contribution to its ecological neighborhood.[27] The same unseen phenomena inheres in an image based on that same plant and can be important for us to more fully understand what the image contributes in comprehending the principle involved in the metaphoric relationship, as well as its contextual significance.

The mustard seed and plant illustrate the principle of organic unity. For years, like many other Latter-day Saints, I had read the Savior's analogy of the mustard seed symbolizing faith and also of the mustard tree being "the greatest among the herbs, and becometh a tree" (Matt. 13:31-32; see also 17:20) without thinking too much about it, except that the mustard seed is very small indeed. One day, when reading His description of the mustard tree, I finally asked myself, what it really looks like and what it could tell me about the Savior's point. A quick search in *Encyclopædia Britannica* on the internet revealed characteristics I had no idea existed, characteristics that can have profound application for understanding the depth of His teaching.

Mustard plants look more like large weeds than trees; it is not a comely plant, especially when compared to the cedars of Lebanon, recalling that the Lord said He would have no particular beauty when He appeared at the meridian of time (see Isa. 53:2; Mosiah 14:2). The Hebrew leadership considered Him a noxious weed to be uprooted and destroyed. Second, the mustard plant has an extensive root system that spreads out until water is found, even where it would not be expected. Faithful disciples are "rooted up and built up in [Christ]" (Col. 2:7); they draw living water from Him who is "the fountain of all righteousness" (Ether 8:6; 12:25). He is the spiritual rock, representing Jehovah-Jesus Christ, from which the living waters of the pure love of Christ flow (see 1 Cor. 10:4; 2 Ne. 11:25). The root system also supports the mustard plant against strong, often inhospitable winds. Correspondingly, with roots grounded in Christ, our faith will bolster us against the winds of doctrine that seek to toss us to and fro, diverting us from the path leading to eternal life (see Eph. 4:14). Even if the spiritual environment in which we live is less than ideal, the roots of faith in Christ will support us. In Jacob's teaching about the olive tree representing the house of Israel, we learn an important truth: the roots below ground and the tree above need to be of "equal strength," for then "the root of the righteous shall not be moved" and "the tree of the righteous yieldeth her fruit," no matter the spiritual soil or climate (Jacob 5:66; Prov. 12:3, 12).

Mustard seeds are also rich in symbolism: when ground up and mixed with the proper liquids, they can be used for healing. Analogously, when we are baptized, we covenant, with a mustard seed of faith, to be healers by joining with the Savior in His mission "to bind up the brokenhearted, . . . proclaim liberty to the captives, and open . . . the prisons to them that are bound" (Isa. 61:1). Accepting the Lord's mission as ours, we assist Him in bringing to others "beauty for ashes [and] the oil of joy for mourning" (Isa. 61:3). Another use for mustard seeds is as a condiment, flavoring foods such as hamburgers and hot dogs in the United States. Likewise, disciples of Christ are called to be condiments, "the salt of the earth," in their social relations, adding savor to others' lives and making their lives more pleasant (Matt. 5:13; 3 Ne. 12:13). With a little research, and pondering what I learned, I was able to see the organic unity within Savior's image of the mustard tree and seed and how it might apply to the life of a disciple.

Someone might well ask if finding this much in a simple image is too much. Certainly the Savior knew all of what I found and far more; He is, after all, the Creator of the universe in all its details and, therefore, of the mustard seed and plant. Accordingly, insights one finds in the details of the object, in its organic unity,[28] that are germane to an image or story, and that can add understanding to the subject when accompanied by the Spirit, help us discern the Lord's vision more clearly.

Many metaphors have become so commonplace that we may be tempted to read over them, thereby missing the radiant dynamic expressed in the synergistic blending of two words, a blending that can offer significant insights into each word as well as their third level of comparison, in Latin, the *tertium comparationis*. "The light of truth" is just such a metaphor (discussed more fully in Chapter 5); though common enough, there is a profound symbiosis that can transpire in one's imagination in just three words. In the first instance, light lends truth the characteristic of luminescence that can give us the feeling of "a warm light shining in our being."[29] Truth, the second element of the metaphor, enlightens the mind (see Alma 32:28), line upon line, with a "knowledge of things as they are, and things as they were, and things as they will be" (D&C 93:24), the eternal verities. The third point of comparison resulting from the blending of light and truth is greater understanding of Jesus Christ, Who is *the* light (see John 8:12; 9:5; 3 Ne. 9:18; 18:16; et al) and *the* truth (John 14:6; Ether 4:12; D&C 93:26), of eternal life (see John 17:3). Frequently, when a word is used figuratively, i.e., metaphorically, in the scriptures, it generally suggests an established relationship with a particular principle of the gospel or a person and is, therefore, a symbol (see below).

C. S. Lewis employs the image of mirrors to describe another aspect of the metaphoric process: "The images in a poem are like a series of mirrors set at different angles so that, as the theme moves on, it is reflected in a number of different aspects. . . . They do not merely reflect the theme, they give it life and form; it is in their power to make spirit visible."[30] Making the spirit of a gospel principle visible is an important function of an image in the scriptures. For example, in Isaiah 35:6, the Lord conveys the spirit of the Restoration of His gospel in these latter days with images of renewal and refreshment: "for in the wilderness shall waters break out, and streams in the desert." Contrast this picture with Isaiah 21:1 (discussed in Chapter 4): "The burden of the desert of the sea." In the latter verse the images convey gloom and emptiness whereas in Isaiah 35:6, streams of water joyously dance across the desert floor. (Anyone who has lived in a desert environment appreciates the feeling of joy when streams flow through the washes during the spring, especially from the snow melt in the mountains.) In both images, the desert represents the spiritual aridness of the world; the difference between them has to do with the composition of the water: a stream in the desert is fresh water, or living water as it is referred to in the Middle East, symbolically representing the love of God and the inspiration of the Holy Ghost (John 37-39; Rom. 5:5; 1 Ne. 11:25). In Isaiah 29:1, sea water, being saline, stands for spiritual depravation in the overall image patterns of Isaiah. Both uses of the water image are intended to evoke our ability to recall the sensory experiences of tasting both fresh and salt water.

Images in the scriptures, then, are intended to relate on one level to our personal experiences, experiences we remember, usually with some feeling attached to them. If we search more deeply into, rather than reading quickly over them, they can often become power catalysts for spiritual change, helping us to "see" patterns of godly behavior, feelingly, and motivating us to refine and conform our spiritual life "unto the measure of the stature of Christ" (Eph. 4:13).

Paraphrasing words of the eminent French philosopher, Paul Ricoeur, *poietic* expression in language make visible modes of being that ordinary vision obscures or even represses.[31]

Poietic Expression in Imagery

Sensory-rich

Scriptural imagery is sensory-rich,[32] "sensory" referring to everything we perceive with our five senses of sight, sound, touch, smell, and taste. Norman Friedman, professor of English at Queens College, City College of New York, offers a psychological description of imagery that captures the sensory-richness of images and can be helpful in studying scriptural imagery: "In literary usage, *imagery* refers to images produced in the mind by language, whose words and statements may refer either to *experiences which could produce physical perceptions were the reader actually to have those experiences* or to the sense-impressions themselves."[33] Though the imagination responds most effectively to visual images and secondarily to images involving the other senses, we have the capacity to remember smells, sounds, or flavors that impressed us from years past.

Every day we are inundated with a veritable flood of sensory-rich images. Advertisers understand their power to create the desire, even need, in us for a wide variety of products, many of which are superfluous to our lives. I once taught this principle in a Gospel Doctrine class and all the wives pointed to their husbands' trucks as an example of a "need" advertisers created for a certain brand and type of truck. (Wisely, their husbands did not point to the images that the wives had accepted as needs.) Unfortunately, Satan understands all too well the power of sensually-rich images, images that are garish, cacophonous, often pornographic to influence people toward his ways when he can get away with it, which is far too often, as is evident by the seriousness with which Presidents Hinckley, Monson, Nelson, and other General Authorities of the Church have repeatedly warned of the danger to become addicted to pornographic images. Given the power of images, Latter-day Saints need to always be on high alert as to those we entertain on the stage of our imagination. One important reason we study the scriptures daily is to plant the Lord's images deeply and firmly in our minds. If His images are playing on the stage of our imagination, tempting images will find it difficult to step out of the wings to get playing time, or even to audition to become permanent members of the company of our images, for that matter. Salacious imagery will find the stage door locked.

Insight

"Insight," as used in this study, means, first, seeing past the exterior of an image into its interior through self-reflection by pausing to consider the image formed in the imagination. Secondly, insight involves studying the salient features of the object to which the image refers, often found in the subtexts, or undermeanings, of an image (discussed in Chapter 3). Third, insight means determining which, if any, features of the object are relevant to a better understanding of a scriptural image by prayerfully pondering the intersections of features, image, and context. President Henry B. Eyring said: "Reading, studying, and pondering are not the same. We read words and we may get ideas. We study and we may discover patterns and connections in scripture. But when we ponder, we invite revelation by the Spirit. Pondering, to me, is the thinking and the praying I do after reading and studying in the scriptures carefully."[34] Janet Williams wrote: "The religious life is one of growth in insight, whereby the individual's ability to envision the divine natures in accordance with practice, with scriptural, ecclecial, and liturgical instruction, and with the suffering of the cross of divine reality."[35] (Instead of singling out the cross, Latter-day Saints would point to the Atonement in general.)

The process can be illustrated by referring to a demonstration of the four-story high screen that is sometimes presented in an I-Max movie theater. When the houselights dim, the audience sees light glowing faintly behind the screen because the screen is perforated with tiny holes. As eyes adjust to the light's glow, they see the scaffolding supporting the screen and the speakers set in the scaffolding that project the front sound in a vibrant surround sound system. Applying this demonstration to our mortal lives, what we see with our physical eyes is like a movie projected on the I-Max screen, perhaps the movie of our own life. Before we came into mortality we knew part of this laboratory of experience would be learning to walk by faith, to see through the worldly façade by keeping an eye single to the glory of God, vicariously seeing through His eyes so as to remain on the path of righteousness leading to eternal life. The light behind the I-Max screen represents the light that is the glory of Jesus Christ, even the Light of Christ, permeating the universe (see D&C 88:12). Perhaps, when we are very young or when we are taught the first principles of the gospel, we may perceive the light dimly, but as our eye of faith adjusts to the light, we begin to discern more of the scaffolding of eternal life behind our daily reality. It is somewhat like the young servant of Elisha who was afraid, seeing the Syrian army surrounding the city, and said to Elisha, "Alas, my master! how shall we do? And [Elisha] answered, Fear not: for they that be with us are more than they that be with them. And Elisha prayed, and said, LORD, I pray thee, open his eyes, that he may see. And the LORD opened the eyes of the young man; and he saw: and, behold, the mountain was full of horses and chariots of fire round about Elisha" (2 Kgs. 6:15-17). For most of us, our eyes are not opened so dramatically and quickly, but with the help of the Holy Spirit, we are able, over time, sharpening our focus, clarifying our insight, and see the otherwise unseen reality of heaven behind the sham reality of worldliness. The stronger our faith, the more often we may experience enlightening moments, and increasingly realize that the veil between mortality and eternity is not a solid shield, but more like a perforated screen through whose minute openings the Light of Christ, the light of truth, continually flows. And the concrete images of scripture provide small windows through with we're able perceive more details of His translucent reality.

Reading faithfully and prayerfully to see deeper behind the surface text into their interior, words of scripture disclose the contours and vitality of the Lord's vision.[36] The rewards of faith-filled exploration of the scriptures can be great and uplifting: each time we return to the same verses, we bring additional experiences to bear on them, resulting in new insights. What we do not clearly see in a first reading may become more evident with a little additional research. If we become stuck in understanding a verse, setting it aside for a few hours or days or months, then coming back to it, may clarify our understanding of the Lord's message. Most of all, we should not be afraid to ask questions for greater insight. Elder Ronald A. Rasband observed that "questions are an indication of a further desire to learn, to add to those truths already in place in our testimonies, and to be better prepared to 'press forward with a steadfastness in Christ.'"[37]

Trusting our impressions is invaluable when trying to see the Lord's vision through His words. And we need not be shy about applying our own life experiences to insights in order to understand a passage better. The scriptures are intended for just such likening, as Nephi taught (see 1 Ne. 19:23). Likening is a symbolic process whereby we superimpose a story or image we study in the word of God unto our own lives for personal edification, enlightenment, and growth.

But it is not just seeing more deeply; seeing the scriptures *feelingly* is equally revealing.

Empathy: "See it Feelingly"

Vision is more than insight; it is insight with empathy,[38] or empathic insight, "see it feelingly,"[39] feeling the consequential emotions of a person, scene, event, etc. described in the scriptures. As used in this study, empathy means feeling into the Lord's words and "feeling after him" (Acts 17:27; D&C 101:8).

So much of discipleship is predicated on feelings, especially righteous feelings. We understand this in a backdoor way from Nephi's condemnation of his brothers, Laman and Lemuel, being "past feeling, that ye could not feel his words" (1 Ne. 17:45; also Eph. 4:19; Moro. 9:20). A fine line exists between feelings that strengthen and feelings that lead away from testimony. Righteous feelings come from the Holy Ghost and are described as a "burning in the bosom" (D&C 9:8), a heavenly, inspiring, burning feeling distinctly different from normal human emotions, which Elder Orson Hyde described as having a "heart . . . fired with celestial light."[40] Sometimes divine impressions direct a disciple to do something specific, even though he may not understand why. (How many of us have had just such impressions that we have rationalized and not acted upon?) Still other times the feelings we receive are immediately translatable into words we can write down in order to retain them. (How many of us have felt thoughts that were stunning insights, only to not write them down because we wouldn't forget them? then forgot them!) The feelings we receive when moved upon by the Holy Ghost represent such sacred moments that we should revere them because they come from a member of the Godhead. At a General Conference session, President Harold B. Lee said, "I am not concerned about how much you remember in words of what has been said here. I am concerned about how it has made you feel."[41] "Spiritual things, like conversion and testimony, come to us in large part by *feelings—the enlightenment* of the Spirit," said Elder Dallin H. Oaks.[42] Catching the vision in the scriptures opens the door for us to feel the Lord's intent. Heaven-sent feeling will always lead us to do the best at any given moment in life; Satan's counterfeit impressions try to dissuade us from the best, the good, or any other worthy feeling—to get us to even blatantly sin.

In his book *Life Before Life*, Richard Eyre identifies three types of knowledge: physical, emotional, and spiritual. "Physical" denotes the type of knowledge we gain through our five senses. To this entry level of cognition I would add the intellectual knowledge we acquire from the educational process. Both sensory and intellectual learning begin as information. Knowledge follows as we organize bytes of information into cogent patterns. "Emotional knowledge," Eyre writes, "is stronger than physical knowledge, but it is also harder to come by." In terms of the gospel, when intellectual understanding of a principle becomes an emotional conviction, we have taken ownership of it and are far more likely to act upon the principle. The third type he identifies is spiritual knowledge, which lies still deeper than emotional knowledge. "It involves and is built upon faith," he writes; "on accepting and trusting in things that are above and beyond the common, physical, everyday experience of this world."[43] From Doctrine and Covenants 9:8-9 we understand that spiritual knowledge is based on feelings of a very refined, eternal order.

Images in the scriptures vie for a reader's attention—to pause, to ponder, to imagine, to feel what they have to reveal. If we make these actions part of our scripture study, any given image can lay open the spirit of a principle. Dr. Dennis Deaton writes: "The more sensory-rich and emotion-laden the images, the more powerful they are to the subconscious, the more quickly they are absorbed; and the more readily they are acted upon."[44] And that is the key: "the more readily they are acted upon!"

Emotion-laden[45]

In her book *Feeling and Form*, Susanne Langer adds the following to our understanding of an image's inner dynamic: "Art [which is inherently *poietic*] is the creation of forms symbolic of human feelings."[46] While the scriptures may not seem to be art in the sense we customarily use that word, yet, in the same sense that a poem is highly structured, one finds ample evidence of literary structure throughout the scriptures[47] and expressions of empathetic insight in the parables and sensory-rich, emotion-laden imagery interlacing and interconnecting the entire corpus of scripture.

Jesus described Himself metaphorically as "the bread of life."

> I am that bread of life.
>
> Your fathers did eat manna in the wilderness, and are dead.
>
> This is the bread which cometh down from heaven, that a man may eat thereof, and not die.

> I am the living bread which came down from heaven: if any man eat of this bread, he shall live for ever: and the bread that I will give is my flesh, which I will give for the life of the world (John 6:48-51).

When thinking of bread, we may remember the fresh-out-of-the-oven, home-baked loaf from Mom's, Grandma's, or some aunt's, cooled just enough to cut a thick slice, slather it with butter and jam, with mouthwatering, anticipating that first bite, just as mine is writing about it. I think the Lord wants us to associate the positive, comforting, sweet taste of bread with Him and His companionship in our lives, ("companion" from Latin *com-* "with, together" and *panis* "bread," literally "bread fellow,"[48]) sustaining each of us with His pure love conveyed through the Holy Spirit. It is as if He were saying, "I am the bread of *your* life. Remember that, because I love you; if you open your heart to me, I will be your manna from heaven. His "bread," like the manna the Israelites received, can satiate our spiritual hunger in the desert wasteland called the world.

Images draw together the far-flung reaches of the scriptures and linking them into a unified whole whose fundamental message relates in one way or another to the Atonement of Jesus Christ. By pondering and researching the images we encounter as we search the scriptures, we may identify plain and simple truths embedded in the subtext of those images—truths that ancient churchmen may have expunged from the Bible, to them uncomfortable truths that conflicted with the theology they wanted to promulgate; truths the Lord intended to be part of His word; truths that can enhance our sensibility (our aesthetic response) to and reverence for the scriptures and deepen our understanding of the restored gospel of Jesus Christ; truths that can grow our testimonies of God the Father and Jesus Christ. Said Jesus, "Search the scriptures; for in them ye think ye have eternal life: and they are they which testify of me" (John 5:39). Understanding that the Lord's vision of beauty weaves through the entire scriptural corpus may help us, from time to time, see a little of the unfathomable beauty in which Elohim and Jesus reside, and where we may reside by becoming a beautiful soul in Their kingdom.

Inward-Outward Dynamic of Images in the Scriptures

What I mean by inward-outward dynamic of an image is demonstrated in the following diagram with an explanation following:

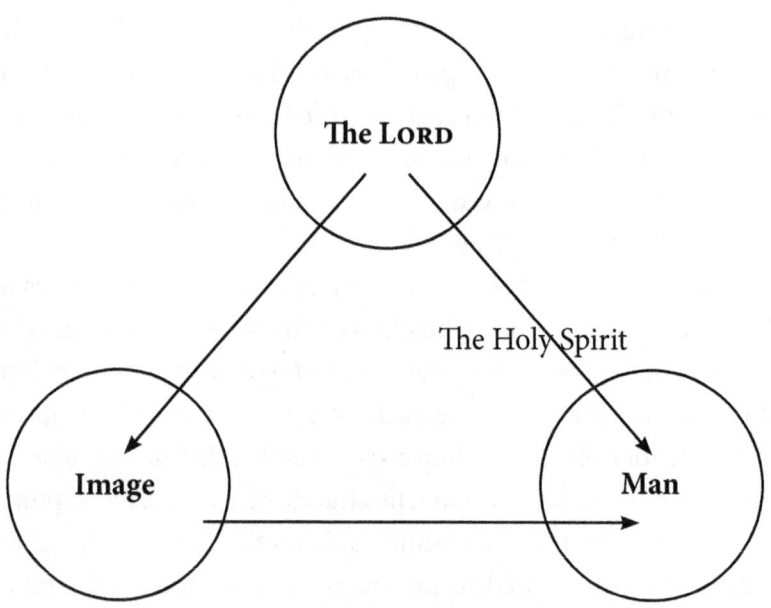

The basic axiom for this phase of the discussion is: The Lord is omniscient and possesses boundless vision, seeing and comprehending all things in their infinitely minute properties, for He created all. In addition, He lives in a timeless state with an all-seeing eye, allowing

Him to view all reality—past, present, and future—simultaneously. Do we have any recorded evidence of such vision? We do! The Lord translated Moses so "that Moses looked, and beheld the world upon which he was created; and Moses beheld the world and the ends thereof, and all the children of men which are, and which were created" (Moses 1:8). Later in the same chapter we read:

> And it came to pass, as the voice was still speaking, Moses cast his eyes and beheld the earth, yea, even all of it; and *there was not a particle of it which he did not behold*, discerning it by the spirit of God.
> And he beheld also the inhabitants thereof, and there was not a soul which he beheld not; and he discerned them by the Spirit of God; and their numbers were great, even numberless as the sand upon the sea shore. And he beheld many lands; and each land was called earth, and there were inhabitants on the face thereof (Moses 1:27-29; emphasis added).

Moses beheld *every* particle of the earth and *all* its inhabitants in the eternal present (see Moses 1). Abraham had a similar experience (see Abr. 3:21-22). In some way, unfathomable to us, the Lord's vison circumscribes "worlds without end" and "the end from the beginning" (Isa. 46:10; Abr. 2:8). And, just as man's creations represent him, all God's creations represent Him.

The dynamic described in the above sketch unfolds as follows:

Phase One: An image obtained its *inward dynamic* at the moment the Lord inspired a prophet to record His revelation, each image *in-formed* with truth-filled, organic vitality, each comprising details of the Lord's omniscient vision. **Phase Two**: The enlightening power of the image lies dormant until the curious reader opens the image's outer shell, releasing its encapsulated *dynamic outward* into the reader's mind, especially the imagination, bearing testimony that Jesus Christ lives and loves the reader for seeking to learn as much of His word as possible, and wants to reveal as much of His vision in the particular word or phrase as the reader is willing to seek after and is spiritually prepared to receive. (This will continue, I would guess, forever.) While every image contains only a particle of the Lord's vision and truth, that particle can be very deep, uncovering layer upon layer of the divine vision, deepening our understanding of gospel principles, while heightening our emotional conviction of it. What on the surface appears to be the verbal representation of an object drawn from this mortal sphere is, upon closer inspection, so much more. **Phase Three:** As the covenant disciple offers a prayer of faith, asking to receive greater understanding of an image, he may be blessed with the inspiration of the Holy Spirit, the intermediary between the Godhead and man, resulting in an enlightening reciprocity between the disciple and the Lord. President Joseph Fielding Smith expounded the deep significance of this reciprocal relationship between God and man, writing: "The man [or woman] who is confirmed receives ... the companionship of the third member of the Godhead. Therefore, *he is back again in the presence of God, through the gift of the Holy Ghost.*"[49]

Thoughts on Searching Images in the Scriptures

Where to start exploring a scriptural image in depth? First, pray to Heavenly Father, indicating desire for enlightenment regarding the image, seeking the guidance of the Holy Spirit during the course of one's research.

Next, part of such research will include simply seeing the object the image represents to us. Many of us want to understand what an image means, for example in Isaiah, before we focus on the image itself to take the measure of it in our experience, remembering some feeling we may have attached to the object as in the example of bread above. If it is an object unknown to us, we can search the internet to find a picture, consult a handbook or encyclopedia to garner more information about it.

Third, the Lord counsels us to "study it out in your mind" (D&C 9:8). Consequently, we do as much research of an image-referent as seems necessary, determining as best we can different connotative levels of meaning. (See below for a more detailed descriptions of ascertaining connotative levels.) Exploring an image may only take a few minutes, and hour, but could extend for a day or more.

Once satisfied we've done as much research as necessary at a particular moment of one's "disciple-scholarship", we submit our findings to the Lord Who has promised, as cited above, "if it is right I will cause that your bosom shall burn within you; therefore, you shall feel that it is right. But if it be not right you shall have no such feelings, but you shall have a stupor of thought that shall cause you to forget the thing which is wrong" (D&C 9:8-9). Oft times that "burning," when indicating the correctness of one's conclusions is very subtle; sometimes the stupor of thought is likewise subtle when we look at our conclusions, and they just don't look right. And we need always remember that a stupor of thought is also revelation.

In searching an image's depth, only a few isolated details may first become apparent, but as our eyes adjust to the spiritual light the image releases, and we continue refocusing our vision, i.e., do more research, more and more details can emerge, forming an expanded panorama in sharp relief. Referring once again to the I-Max screen, we might compare the screen to the veil drawn between mortality and immortality. The dynamic of images reveals itself through the multitude of "windows" in the veil, through which a byte of the Lord's vision can be discerned. Gradually, we might realize that the different panoramas revealed are really the same vision with different details, "a compound in one" (2 Ne. 2:11). Because there are a vast number of image-perforations in the veil, we will only make a small beginning in mortality in capturing the Lord's omniscient vision—but a beginning it is, preparing us for the immensely grander vision we may see in the spirit world, not to mention the magnificent Moses-like vision of reality from the mountain peak of the celestial kingdom, for which vantage point all things will appear in their proper order.

To understand how any of this may become possible, the Lord has stated that the celestialized earth will become a great Urim and Thummim revealing "all things pertaining to an inferior kingdom or all kingdoms of a lower order, will be manifest to those who dwell on it. In addition, each person blessed to dwell on that "sea of glass mingled with fire" (Rev. 15:2) will receive a white stone "whereby things pertaining to a higher order of kingdoms will be made known" (D&C 130:9-10). From our present earthly station it is very difficult to comprehend the grandeur of it all.

Images as Symbols

In the introduction to his wonderful photographic study of Louisiana plantations, Clarence John Laughlin well described the symbolic attribute of the poetic process:

> The method of poetry [*poietics*] is to abstract symbols from *the stuff of living experience*; to embody these symbols not only in *emotive language*, but, by means of the creative use of these symbols, to ... give us *a reality* which is not only complexly sweetened or embittered

by the perceiving mind, but *more extensive in time than that reality which is immediately apprehensive*; since now elements of the past and of the future play equal parts with that of the present. In *the superior reality of poetic vision* we enter *a plane where symbols have a life of their own*; and here perhaps *we transcend*, temporarily and incompletely, *the limitations which time*, or rather, our three-dimensional realization of time places on us.⁵⁰

By "abstract[ing] the stuff of living experience . . . to give us a reality . . . more extensive in time than that reality immediately apprehensive," symbols in the scriptures reveal "things as they really are" (Jacob 4:13), God's eternal reality. Thus the power of any image is the reality it represents. In a remarkable address delivered at the Mutual Improvement Association Conference on the evening of June 12, 1927, Elder Orson F. Whitney gave a cosmic dimension to the principle of *poietic* symbolism:

> I have long held the view that the universe is built upon symbols, whereby one thing bespeaks another; the lesser testifying of the greater, lifting our thoughts from man to God, from earth to heaven, from time to eternity. . . .
>
> God teaches with symbols; it is his favorite method of teaching. The Savior often used them. . . .
>
> The Gospel is replete with symbolism, with poetry— poetry of the highest type. The very essence of poetry [*poietics*] is in symbolism and the power of suggestion. . . .

> The greatest poem in existence is the Gospel of Jesus Christ. . . .
>
> Anything is poetic that stands for something greater than itself. [51]

(Several generations before Elder Whitney, the Scottish philosopher-essayist, Thomas Carlyle, found that "[t]he universe is but one vast Symbol of God,"[52] that is, there is a vast, true reality behind the symbol.)

The Apostle Paul stated that "the invisible things of him from the creation of the world are clearly seen, being understood by the things that are made, even his eternal power and Godhead" (Rom. 1:20), echoing the Lord's declaration to Adam, "behold, all things have their likeness, and all things are created and made to bear record of me, both things which are temporal, and things which are spiritual; things which are in the heavens above, and things which are on the earth, and things which are in the earth, and things which are under the earth, both above and beneath: all things bear record of me" (Moses 6:63). Thus, "While we look not at the things which are seen, but at the things which are not seen: for *the things which are seen are temporal; but the things which are not seen are eternal*" (2 Cor. 4:18; italics added). The invisible things of God are the mysteries of godliness that reveal themselves as we study the scriptures, opening the outer shell of a symbol and searching its meaty kernel for the deeper truths, especially as we do so under the influence of the Holy Spirit who "searches . . . the deeper things of God" (1 Cor. 2:10) where the ancient "hidden wisdom, which God ordained before the world unto our glory" (1 Cor. 2:7) is found. Nor should we shy away from these mysteries; Joseph Smith said: "The Savior has the words of eternal life. . . . I advise all to go on to perfection, and search deeper and deeper into the mysteries of Godliness."[53] Discovering the deeper truths of the mysteries helps us sense the efficacy of Elder Whitney's assessment of Christ as the greatest poet ever, "Not because he wrote verses, for we have no record of his having written any; but because he saw deepest into the mystery of life, into the divine symbolism of the universe—His own creation."[54]

Others have made similar observations. The English Romantic poet-critic, Samuel Coleridge, asserted: "A symbol . . . is characterized . . . above all by the translucence of the eternal through and in the temporal."[55] Or as the English theologian and Bible scholar, G. B. Caird wrote, the Lord "us[es] the human known to throw light on the divine unknown."[56] And since the divine is infinitely vast, no one need worry that they will plumb the depths of the gospel, for it is "inexhaustible."[57]

At the heart of searching the mysteries revealed through image-symbols in the scriptures are perception and percipience. Perception is "1. The state of being or process of becoming aware or conscious of a thing, spec. through any of the senses. The intuitive or direct recognition of a moral, aesthetic, or personal quality, e.g. the truth of a remark, the beauty of an object"; percipience, defined above, refers to "one who perceives something outside the range of the senses."[58] William Blake, English poet and artist, said, "If the doors of perception were cleansed every thing would appear to man as it is, infinite."[59] President James E. Faust personalized Blake's thought, when he said, "The lens can be lightened and become crystal clear through the influence of the Holy Ghost."[60]

An image in the scriptures becomes a symbol in several ways: principally, either when it reappears in similar contexts paired with a specific principle of the gospel, such as the light of truth, or a person, such as the good shepherd, or as it appears in similar scriptural contexts, e.g., "living waters." Once the symbolic relationship is established between an image and a principle, person, or situation, the image can often appear by itself without being followed by the object, yet implying the object, e.g., the image of light. This metaphor is so constant that the figurative use of light by itself inherently suggests the principle of truth, depending, of course, on the context in which it appears. Such images become "trigger words" because they "trigger" specific association in the mind. Another example of a trigger word is the past participle *filled*, in 3 Nephi 12:6: "filled with the Holy Ghost." After we recognize this association, wherever we find "filled" by itself, again depending on the context, we can often mentally add "with the Holy Ghost" for greater insight into the intent of the scriptural verse in which it appears. A symbol, then, retains the dynamic quality of the image, but it is more.

Ancient Hebrew *Poietics*

I would like to add the following observations made about ancient Hebrew *poietics*, which explains the Hebrew mindset informing the writing of the Bible and the Book of Mormon. *The Cambridge History of English and American Literature* (think American literature in the early 1800s, around the time Joseph translated the Book of Mormon) includes a short assessment into the nature of Old Testament Hebrew whose "most noticeable feature is its deficiency in abstract and general terms. . . . Nearly every word presents a concrete meaning, clearly visible even through figurative use. Many of its roots are verbal, and the physical activity underlying each word is felt through all its special applications." Moreover,

> every general truth expressed by the Hebrew is rendered with the utmost directness, and in phraseology as pictorial, . . . as stimulative to imagination and feeling, as could be possible. Such a language is the very language

of poetry. The medium through which poetry works is the world of sensible objects. . . . What is necessary to make poetry out of such materials is intensity of feeling, with elevation and coherence of thought.[61]

Notice this last sentence that resonates with the discussion of insight and empathy in Chapter 2. Expressing a similar thought in her book *Life and Language in the Old Testament,* Mary Ellen Chase described biblical Hebrew as "primarily a language of the senses and the emotions, one which was seemingly made to arouse and startle. Many, if not most, of its words were direct, concise, concrete, vivid and vigorous."[62] And the renowned scholar of Romance literature, Erich Auerbach, added the following regarding biblical narrative, but his thought is equally applicable to the study of imagery: The "aim [of biblical stories] is not to bewitch the senses, and if nevertheless they produce lively sensory effects, it is only because the moral, religious, and psychological phenomena which are their sole concern are made concrete in the sensible matter of life."[63]

POIETIC EXPRESSION IN VERSE

Rather than rhyme and rhythm heightening the imagery, as Westerners know it, Hebrew scriptural *poietics* employed what has been described as "thought rhyme," better known as parallelism. Parallelism is not easily discerned in the King James Bible because of its paragraph formatting, but with a little understanding, parallelisms can add to our appreciation for and understanding of biblical and Book of Mormon scriptures and the meaning the Lord intended for us to appreciate more deeply and fully.

Parallelism

In 1753, Anglican Bishop and Oxford professor of poetry, Robert Lowth, lectured on a feature of the Bible of biblical poetics that had remained in the background of Bible studies, namely the technique known as parallelism. Lowth demonstrated that parallelism was a foundational principle of biblical *poietics*.[64] Ever since, this verse format has been considered the distinctive verse form in the Bible; it is also evident in the Book of Mormon.[65] Rather than correspondence based on rhyme, scriptural parallelism is based on the correspondence of thoughts by which the Lord advances His message.

What is parallelism? Parallelism, from the Greek meaning "side by side," denotes "a state of correspondence between one phrase, line, or verse with another."[66] Viktor Shkloevsky made an important point when he asserted, "The purpose of parallelism, like the general purpose of imagery, is to transfer the usual perception of an object into the sphere of a new perception. . . ."[67] Robert Alter, professor of Hebrew and comparative literature at the University of California, Berkley, has written insightfully of the inner dynamic of parallelism:

> Biblical poetry [meaning parallel verses] is characterized by an intensifying or narrative development within the line; and quite often this "horizontal" movement is then projected downward in a "vertical" focusing movement through a sequence of lines or even through a whole poem [or passage of scripture]. What this means is that the poetry of the Bible is concerned above all with dynamic process moving toward some culmination. The two most common structures, then, of biblical poetry are a movement of intensification of images, concepts, themes through a sequence of lines, and a narrative movement—which most often pertains

to the development of metaphorical acts but can also refer to literal events, as in much prophetic poetry.[68]

The intensification, or heightening of thought, "is in part associated with the movement from cause to effect and from general to specific statement."[69]

Recognizing parallelism in order to use it in understanding the Lord's meaning can be difficult: for one, verses in the King James Translation does not distinguish parallel verse, which appear as prose; for another, anciently, parallelism developed a fair number of variations. We will confine ourselves to the most common and least complicated form, found in Psalm 23:

> The Lord is my shepherd, I shall not want.
> He maketh me to lie down in green pastures:
> he leadeth me beside the still waters.
> He restoreth my soul:
> he leadeth me in the paths of righteousness for his name's sake.
> Yea, though I walk through the valley of the shadow of death,
> I will fear no evil: for thou art with me;
> thy rod and thy staff they comfort me.
> Thou preparest a table before me in the presence of my enemies:
> thou anointest my head with oil, my cup runneth over.
> Surely goodness and mercy shall follow me all the days of my life:
> and I will dwell in the house of the LORD for ever.

The first line is built around an internal parallelism: "I shall not want" heightens, with specificity, what it means to have the Lord as one's shepherd. Lines two and three build on not wanting by describing "green pastures," then, still waters, both of which describe, on one level, a peaceful, idyllic landscape, on another, sources of nourishment for sheep, and on yet another, symbolic level, spiritual nourishment via the Holy Spirit for the sheep of the Lord's fold. Restoration of soul is intensified by being led in the paths of righteousness because of the Lord. The straight-forward parallelism builds to the climatic "I will dwell in the house of the Lord forever," recalling the psalmic verse proclaiming to dwell in the house of the Lord forever "to behold the beauty of the Lord" (Ps. 27:4). From beginning to end, the Lord advances the imagery of the whole to this last line by intensifying each subsequent image through the use of parallelism.

Chiasmus

A variation of parallelism, much discussed among Latter-day Saints' scholars over the past few years, is the form called chiasmus, from the Greek letter X (chi), indicating a crossover of thought through inversion of word order, which Joh T. Walsh asserts, "is the commonest symmetrical pattern in biblical Hebrew narrative."[70] A well-known example of chiasmus is found in Isaiah 5:20 (emphasis added):

> Woe unto them that call *evil good, and good evil*,
> that put *darkness for light, and light for darkness*,
> that put *bitter for sweet, and sweet for bitter*.

In the first line "evil good" is reversed to "good evil," emphasizing that society has become degraded to the point of disparaging the good by calling it evil, something that dominates in United States society today. The subsequent chiasmi have the same effect. But chiasmi structuring longer passages have also been deciphered. 1 Chronicles 11:1–12:41 appears as following[71]:

    A David become king of all Israel at Hebron (11:1-9)
    B   David gains support at Hebron (11:10-47)
    C   David gains support at Ziklag (12:1-7)
    D   David gains support at "the stronghold" (12:8-15)
    D´   David gains support at "the stronghold" (12:16-18)
    C´   David gains support at Ziklag (12:19-22)
    B´   David gains support at Hebron (12:23-37)
    A´ David becomes king of all Israel at Hebron (12:38-40)

D/D´ constitutes the turning point of chiasmus. Professor John W. Welsh, who has conducted ground-breaking research into the appearance chiasmus in the scriptures, particularly the Book of Mormon, explains that the interpretive significance of chiasmus is focusing attention on the center lines "to elevate the importance of a central concept or to dramatize a radical shift of events at the turning point."[72] Following is an example from the Book of Mormon, namely Lehi's vision (1 Ne. 8:10-12)[73]:

    9 And it came to pass that I beheld a tree
    10 A whose fruit was <u>desirable</u>
           B to make one <u>happy</u>
    11   C And it came to pass that I did go forth
               and <u>partake of the fruit thereof</u>;
              D a and I beheld that <u>it was most sweet</u>,
                  b <u>above all</u> that <u>I ever</u> before tasted
              D´ a´ Yea, and <u>I beheld</u> that the <u>fruit
                    thereof was white</u>,

           b´ <u>to exceed all the whiteness</u> that <u>I had ever seen</u>.
12   C´ And as <u>I partook of the fruit thereof</u>
        B´ it filled my soul with exceeding great <u>joy</u>;
   A´ wherefore, I began to be <u>desirous</u> that my family should partake of it also; for I knew that it was desirable above all other fruit.

The turning point D/D´ draws our attention to the exceeding sweetness and whiteness of the fruit, both symbols of beauty, which is what the tree represents in one of the subtext (see 1 Ne.11:8). In another subtext it represents Jesus Christ (see 1 Ne. 15-21), therefore, in a further subtext it is "the love of God," the pure love of Christ, "which sheddeth itself abroad in the hearts of the children of men; wherefore, it is the most desirable above all things" (1 Ne. 11:22; see Rom. 5:5). When we read the above verses in the original chiastic format, it becomes far more apparent where the emphasis of Lehi's vision lies. In prose, that emphasis is only faintly apparent.

In the discussion of beauty in the scriptures, John Welch writes: "The form [chiasmus] can be aesthetically very pleasing, due in part to its vast potential to coordinate rigorous and abrupt juxtapositions with a single unified literary system, all while focusing on a point of central concern."[73]

Notes to Chapter 3

1. A Common Reader Catalog (Oct. 2004), 68.
2. http://blog.gideons.org/2010/12/the-bible-contains-the-mind-of-god/
3. Neal A. Maxwell, "Meek and Lowly," devotional address given at Brigham Young University (Oct. 1986), 9; speeches.byu.edu.
4. For a discussion of the topography and depth of one chapter, see William J. Bohn, *Matthew 25: Symbolic Vision – Parabolic Vision*.

5. Dallin H. Oaks, "Scripture Reading and Revelation," Jan 1995, 7.
6. *TWOT*, 1878-79.
7. *TDNT*, 2:187-95.
8. *SOED*, s.v. "member."
9. *The American Heritage Dictionary of the English Language*, 4th ed. (Boston, MA: Houghton Mifflin, 2000), s.v. "re-" pref; see also *The American heritage Dictionary of Indo-European Roots*, ed. Calvert Watkins (Boston:MA: Houghton Mifflin, 2000), s.v. "re-."
10. The British theologian, G. D. Caird, wrote: "Through the phenomenon known as *anamnesis* those who 'remember' an event actually relive it" (*New Testament Theology*, ed. L. D. Hurst (Oxford, ENG: Clarendon Press, 1995), 151, note 29.
11. Spiro Zodhiates, *The Complete Word Study Dictionary: New Testament* (Chattanooga, TN: AMG Publishers, 1993), 1187; hereafter Zodhiates. (Strong no. 4160). In the first Greek translation of the Old Testament, the Septuagint, "[*poieín*] denotes the activity of Yahweh in the creation of the world." Creativity, specifically artistic creativity, is the sense in which I use the word *poietics*. It also extends to morality: "[*poieín*] is used generally for doing good to one's neighbour. . . . The establishment of joy and peace . . . and the demonstration of friendliness . . . are expressed by [*poieín*]" (*Theological Dictionary of the New Testament*, ed. Gerhard Friedrich, trans. Gerhard Friedrich [Grand Rapids, MI: Wm. B. Eerdmans Publishing, 1995], 6:459, 477.
12. Jerome T. Walsh, "Gen 2:4b-3:24: A Synchonic Approach," *Journal of Biblica Literature* 96 (1977), 172.
13. Giambattista Vico, *New Science* (It. *Scienza Nuova Prima*), trans. David Marsh (New York: Penguin Books, 2001), 157-59; hereafter Vico.
14. *OED*, 23.
15. Will Durant, *The Renaissance: A History of Civilization in Italy from 1304-1576 A.D.* (New York: Simon and Schuster, 1953), 34.
16. See Augustine, *Confessions*, 10, 53; *The City of God*, Bk. 11, Chap. 4. Thomas Aquinas, *Summa Theologica*, Part 1, Q39, Art. 8; Par6, Suppl. Q91. See also Umberto Eco, *The Aesthetics of Thomas Aquinas*, trans. Hugh Bredin (Cambridge: Harvard University Press, 1988). This personal religious aesthetic can be found in writers from Boethius and Jakob Boehme to the present.
17. F. I. G. Rawlins, "Religion and Aesthetics," *The British Journal of Aesthetics* (Oct. 1966), 375-76. Rawlins concentrates on the plastic arts employed by

Nicene Christianity to teach and decorate. In an article entitled "Das Schöne im Alten Testament," Claus Westermann shows that the emphasis before Christ was on the art of words and music (*Beiträge zur alttestamentalischen Theologie. Festschrift für Walter Zimmerli zum 70. Geburtstag*, ed. Herbert Donner [Göttingen: Vandenhoeck und Ruprecht, 1977], 479-97). Latter-day Saint scholars have also concentrated on works of the plastic arts when discussing beauty, e.g., Merrill Bradshaw, "Toward a Mormon Aesthetic," *BYU Studies* 21, no. 1 (winter 1981), 91-99; Michael Hicks, "Notes on Brigham Young's Aesthetics," *Dialogue: A Journal of Mormon Thought* 16 (1983), 127-30. *Theological Aesthetics: A Reader*, ed. Gesa Elsbeth Thiessen (Grand Rapids, MI: William B. Eerdmans Publishing, 2005) offers a beginning anthology for the study of beauty from a religious perspective. It does include brief excerpts from the philosophical writings of Kant and Hegel. By including the aforementioned philosopher, it is interesting that the editor omitted excerpt from Plato and Aristotle.

18. David Bentley Hart, *The Beauty of the Infinite – The Aesthetics of Christian Truth* (Grand Rapids, MI: Wm. B. Eerdmans Publishing, 2003). The Swiss theologian, Hans Urs von Balthasar, has written a multi-volume study of aesthetics entitled *The Glory of the Lord: A Theological Aesthetic*, trans. Erasmo Leiva-Merikakis (San Francisco: Ignatius, 1982) that goes far beyond the scope of the present discussion.

19. C. Henton Davies, "Beauty," in *The Interpreter's Dictionary of the Bible*, 5 vols., ed. George Arthus Buttrick, et al (Nashville, TN: Abingdon Press), 1:371. Two exceptions to this dismissal of any theory of beauty in the Bible are William A. Dyrness, "Aesthetics in the Old Testament: Beauty in Context," *Journal of the Evangelical Theological Society* 28, no. 4 (1985), 421-32 and Timothy Polk, "In the Image: Aesthetics and Ethics through the Glass of Scripture," *Horizons in Biblical Theology: An International Dialogue* 8, no. 1 (1986), 27-59.

20. Hans Robert Jauss, *Aesthetic Experience and Literary Hermeneutics*, trans. Michael Shaw (Minneapolis, MN: University of Minnesota Press, 1982), 56.

21. C. Day Lewis, *The Poetic Image* (London: Cape, 1969), 18, 22.

22. Owen Barfield, *Poetic Diction – A Study in Meaning* (Hanover, NH: Wesleyan University Press, 1984), 41. Barfield, a renowned scholar in his own right, was a close friend of C. S. Lewis, though they frequently disagreed on a variety of issues.

23. The technical term for such poetic inversions is "anastrophe," a word derived from ancient Greek meaning "inversion or unusual order of words or clauses" (*SOED*, s.v. "anastrophe).

24. Vico, 159.
25. Monroe C. Beardsley, *Aesthetics: Problems in the Philosophy of Criticism* (Indianapolis: Hackett Publishing, 1981), 144.
26. Gian Napoleone Giordano Orsini, "Organism," in *Dictionary of the History of Ideas: Discussion of Selected Pivotal Ideas*, ed. Philip P. Wiener (New York: Charles Scribner's Sons, 1973), 3:421.
27. For example, see Peter Wohlleben, trans. Jane Billinghurst, *The Secret Life of Trees: What They Feel, How They Communicate* (Vancouver, CAN, Berkley, CA: Greystone Books, 2016); German: *Das geheime Leben der Bäume: Was sie fühlen, wie sie kommunizieren* (Munich, GER: Random House, 2015).
28. The Apostle Paul described the organic unity of Christ's Church to the Corinthian saints: "For as the body is one, and hath many members, and all the members of that one body, being many, are one body: so also is Christ. For by one Spirit are we all baptized into one body, whether we be Jews or Gentiles, whether we be bond or free; and have been all made to drink into one Spirit. For the body is not one member, but many" (1 Cor. 12:12-14). Every part is vital to the whole corpus of the Church. He filled in the details of the organic unity in his letter to the Ephesian saints: "And he gave some, apostles; and some, prophets; and some, evangelists; and some pastors and teachers; For the perfecting of the saints, for the work of the ministry, for the edifying of the body of Christ: Till we all come in the unity of the faith, and of the knowledge of the Son of God, unto a perfect man, unto the measure of the stature of the fulness of Christ" (Eph. 4:11-13). So Christ's Church today—The Church of Jesus Christ of Latter-day Saints. Jesus Christ is the Head; by revelation, He calls a living prophet, seer, and revelator to represent and receive revelatory guidance from Him, at the moment that Prophet is Russell M. Nelson. Through *the* Prophet, Christ calls counselors in the First Presidency of the Church, members of the Quorum of the Twelve, and other general authorities. This same organizational structure is also found in the stakes of the Church. What is not nearly as visible are the acts of kindness performed by individual members, resulting from their testimonies of Jesus Christ, of Joseph Smith's First Vision, and the resulting true and living Church growing therefrom. President Harold B. Lee said: "Perhaps the most important reason of all for the growth of the Church is the individual testimonies of the divinity of this work, as would be multiplied in the hearts of the individual members of the Church. For the strength of the Church is not in the numbers, nor in the amount of tithes and offerings paid by faithful members, nor in the

magnitude of chapels and temple buildings, but because in the hearts of faithful members of the Church is the conviction that this is indeed the church and kingdom of God on the earth" ("'Strengthen the Stakes of Zion,'" Ensign [July 1973], 6). Implicit in the pithy call to service, serve locally, but think globally, is the vision that what is done on the local level of the Church has ramifications for its global growth.

29. Boyd K. Packer, "Personal Revelation: The Gift, the Test, and the Promise," 11/94, 60.
30. C. Day Lewis, 60.
31. Paul Ricoeur, *Interpretation Theory: Discourse and the Surplus of Meaning* (Fort Worth, TX: Texas Christian University Press, 1976), 60.
32. The terms "sensory-rich" and "emotion-laded" are borrowed with permission from Dr. Dennis Deaton, President and CEO of Quma Learning in Mesa, Arizona. He discusses the phrases in *Mind Management* (Mesa, AZ: MMI Publishing, 1995), 189-93.
33. Norman Friedman, "Imagery," in *Princeton Encyclopedia of Poetry and Poetics*, ed. Alex Preminger (Princeton, NJ: Princeton University Press, 1990), 363; emphasis added.
34. Henry B. Eyring, "Serve with the Spirit," *Ensign* (Nov. 2010), 60.
35. Janet Williams, "Judging Judgment," *Theology Today* (Jan. 2002), 544.
36. See James E. Talmage, *The Vitality of Mormonism* (Salt Lake City, UT: Deseret News Press, 1919).
37. Ronald A. Rasband, "Standing with the Leaders of the Church," *Ensign* (May 2016), 46-47.
38. The German verb *einfühlen*, "feel into," describes well how "empathy" is being used in this study. "Empathy" is a compound noun: the "em-" prefix is the same as "en-" prefacing a word—"into"; "-pathy" derives from "passion," "feeling," thus, "feel into."
39. The phrase "see it feelingly" is spoken by King Lear in Shakespeare's tragedy of the same name. See William Shakespeare, *King Lear*, ed. Kenneth Muir (London: Methuen & Co., 1966), act iv, sc. Vi, line 150.
40. Orson Hyde, "The Man Called to Lead God's People, etc.," *JD*, 26 vols., ed. G. D. Watt (Liverpool, ENG: F. D. & S. W. Richards, 1854), 1:22.
41. Harold B. Lee, "A Blessing for the Saints," *Ensign* (Jan 1973), 134.
42. Dallin H. Oaks, "Nourishing the Spirit," *Ensign* (Dec 1998), 10.

43. Richard Eyre, *Life Before Life: Origins of the soul . . . knowing where you came from and who you really are* (Salt Lake City: Shadow Mountain, 2000), 57-59.
44. See note 14 above.
45. Deaton, *Mind Management*, 189
46. Susanne Langer, *Feeling and Form* (New York: Charles Scribner's Sons, 1955), 40.
47. See, for example, *The Literary Guide to the Bible*, ed. Robert Alter and Frank Kermode (Cambridge, MA: Harvard University Press, 1990); Robert Alter, *The Art of Biblical Narrative* (New York, NY: Basic Books, 2011); Alter, *The Art of Biblical Poetry* (New York, NY: Basic Books, 2011); Donald W. Parry, *Poetic Parallelism in the Book of Mormon: The Complete Text Reformatted* (Provo, UT: The Neal A. Maxwell Institute for Religious Scholarship, 2007).
48. http://www.etymonline.com/index.php?l=c&p=50&allowed_in_frame=0; also *OED*, s.v. "companion."
49. *DS*, 1:41; emphasis added.
50. Clarence John Laughlin, *Ghosts along the Mississippi* (New York: Bonanza, 1961), n.p.; italics added.
51. Orson F. Whitney, "Latter-day Saint Ideals and Institutions," *Improvement Era* (Aug. 1927), 851, 861-62; hereafter Whitney.
52. Thomas Carlyle, *Sartor Restarus*, iii, Chapter 3 (https://books.google.com/books? id=C4EQ AAAA YAAJ& printsec= frontcover&source=gbs_ge_summary_r&cad=0#v=onepage&q&f=false), 223.
53. *TPJS*, 364.
54. Whitney, 851; emphasis added.
55. *The Statesman's Manual* [1816], in *Samuel Taylor Coleridge: A Critical Edition of the Major Works*, ed. H. J. Jackson [Oxford: Oxford University Press, 1985], 661
56. G. B. Caird, *The Language and Imagery of the Bible* (Grand Rapids, MI: William B. Eerdmans Publishing, 1997), 19.
57. See Neal A. Maxwell, "The Inexhaustible Gospel," *Ensign* (Apr. 1993), 68.
58. *SOED*, s.v. "perception" and "percipience."
59. William Blake, "The Marriage of Heaven and Hell, Plate 14," in *The Norton Anthology of English Literature*, ed. M. H. Abrams, et al (New York: Norton & Co., 1968), 2:74.
60. James E. Faust, "It Can't Happen to Me," *Ensign* (May 2002), 47.

61. *The Cambridge History of English and American Literature*, 14 vol.s, ed.s A. W. Ward and A. R. Waller (1907-1921), vol. 4, sect. II (The "Authorized Version" and its Influence), §3 (The Nature of the Hebrew language, poetry and prose.); http:// www. bartleby. com/ 214/0203.html; search "concreteness of biblical Hebrew language."

62. Mary Ellen Chase, *Life and Language in the Old Testament* (New York: W.W. Norton, 1955), 143.

63. Erich Auerbach, *Mimesis: The Representation of Reality in Western Literature*, trans. Willard R. Trask (Princeton, NJ: Princeton University Press, 2003), 14.

64. Lowth published his research under the title of *On the Sacred Poetry of the Hebrews*. *The New Cambridge Paragraph Bible* of the King James translation is arranged to show the poetic verses in both Old and New Testaments (ed. David Norton [Cambridge, ENG: Cambridge University Press, 2005]).

64. See Donald W. Parry, *Poetic Parallelism in the Book of Mormon: The Complete Text Reformatted* (Provo:UT: The Neal A. Maxwell Institute for Religious Studies, 2007), 15; http://publications.mi. byu.edu/publications/ bookchapters/Poetic_Parallelisms_in_the_Book_of_Mormon_The_Complete_Text_/ Poetic%20Parallelisms%20in%20the%20Book%20of%20Mormon.pdf.

65. Robert E. Elliott, "Parallelism," in *Princeton Encyclopedia of Poetry and Poetics*, ed. Alex Preminger (Princeton, NJ: Princeton University Press), s.v. "Parallelism."

66. Viktor Shkloevsky,"Art as Technique," https://warwick.ac.uk/fac/arts/english/currentstudents/undergraduate/ modules/fullist/first/en122/lecturelist-2015-16-2/shkloevsky.pdf, 5

67. Robert Alter, "The Characteristics of Ancient Hebrew Poetry," in *The Literary Guide to the Bible*, ed.s Robert Alter and Frank Kermode (Cambridge, MA: Harvard University Press, 1990), 620.

68. Robert Alter, *The Art of Biblical Poetry* (New York: Basic Books, 2011), 78.

69. Jerome T. Walsh, *Style & Structure in Biblical Hebrew Narrative* (Collegeville, MN: Liturgical Press, 2001), 13.

70. Walsh, 28.

71. In *Chiasmus in Antiquity*, ed. John W. Welch (Provo, UT: Research Press, 1981), 10; see also John Breck, *The Shape of Biblical Language* (Crestwood, NY: St. Vladimir's Seminary Press, 1994, 59-61. Others have observed the chiastic principle outside of the scriptures: e.g., James L. Ferrell sees the history of the earth organized chiastically with the Atonement of Jesus Christ being at the center of the pattern (*The Hidden Christ – Beneath the Surface of the*

Old Testament [Salt Lake City: Deseret Book, 2009], 208-09). One has to be cautious not to ascribe chiasmus to phenomena that do not warrant it. Dr. Welch has cautioned about what constitutes a valid chiasmus in the scriptures (see John W. Welch, "Criteria for Identifying and Evaluating the Presence of Chiasmus," in *Chiasmus Bibliography*, ed. John W. Welch and Daniel B. McKinlay [Provo, UT: Research Press, 1999], 154-74). Boyd F. and W. Ferrell Edwards have established rigorous criteria for determining a chiastic pattern in the Book of Mormon ("Does Chiasmus Appear in the Book of Mormon by Chance," *BYU Studies* 43:2 [2004], 103-30).

72. In Donald W. Parry, *Poetic Parallelism in the Book of Mormon*, 15. The importance of this vision is found not only in the message itself, but also in the method of delivery, namely in a pillar of fire that descended from heaven and "dwelt upon a rock before him [Lehi]" (1 Ne. 1:6). Such experiences are rarely recorded, so when they are, it indicates something very special and very sacred, such as Moses and the burning bush. The Hebrews termed such pillars of fire the Shekinah, meaning "the glory and presence of God."

73. Welch, 12.

CHAPTER 4

CAPTURING THE VISION

Capturing the vision expressed by the words of a narrative or poem begins when we slacken the pace of our reading, even pause, to become aware of what we are envisioning, i.e., seeing it feelingly. When we were children and read a story, we lived with the characters, felt their emotions, anticipated the dramatic twists and turns in the plot, and, afterwards, could go out and play the parts we liked best. Our formal education taught us to become analytical; we lost the wonder of our young imagination. In this chapter, we will seek to revive the wonder of the imagination, combine it with the analytic abilities we've developed, providing a framework for searching deeper into a text to discover the eternal verities layered below its surface.

Concrete Virtual Realities

Technically, a concrete virtual reality refers to "the generation by computer software of an image or environment that appears real to the senses."[1] Artists have been creating such realities since man began to paint and tell stories. When you were young, you may have experienced the virtual reality of a story while sitting around a campfire at night, an adult telling a frightening tale that had you looking into the darkness for something resembling the terror he was describing. You may have smiled nervously as he finished (after all, it wasn't *really* real, was it?), but many a boy and girl did not sleep well after such stories because the virtual reality of the storyteller's words lived so concretely in their imaginations. Bards in antiquity were able to draw people into their protracted stories in such a way that their audiences lived them vicariously. The storyteller's verbal vision created a virtual reality in the imagination of his audience.

With the advent of the printing press, and the resulting increase of literacy, the printed word began replacing the storyteller (though, even today, there is nothing like listening to a good storyteller). Reading became a private experience between the reader and the author. Reading allowed a person to pause and ponder what he or she was reading, allowing the imagination to probe more deeply into the text. With popular fiction especially, people experience the visionary, virtual realities of stories and plays, e.g., the Harry Potter tales. The world of wizards and witches creating the novels virtual reality draws the reader in almost from the first words of the first book. Wizards and witches don't really fly around in England, and there is not a Hogwart's School of Wizardry, but, reading the stories, it is difficult not to live right along with central characters J. K. Rowling created. The same is true of many other works of popular fiction, including fiction written by Church-member authors, such as *The Work and the Glory* series of Gerald N. Lund, who told me that more than a few people, when visiting Nauvoo, asked where the Steed's house was, so captivated were they by the virtual reality Lund created. With works of literature written by authors such as Herman Melville, Dante, Goethe, etc., capturing the vision, living the virtual reality created, is much more difficult because so much of it lies below the surface of the text; it takes several readings before the parts come together in the imagination.

Though not fiction, the scriptures fall into this latter type of literature; they reveal a reality that transcends mortal life and continue to reveal greater and greater depth as we search them over a lifetime. The principle of vision is implicit in Nephi's likening of the scriptures unto himself and his people (see 1 Ne. 19:23). He likened, or superimposed, the narratives of peoples' lives in the Old Testament unto the lives of his people. In the telling, Nephi brought the scriptural narratives to life in peoples' imaginations so that they could *experience* the lives of those Old Testament figures. That is, he helped them capture the vision in the narratives so that they understood deep within their spirits how to build on the righteousness of their ancestors and avoid whatever mistakes they had made. The reality of the past served the reality of the present.

Latter-day Saints today are heirs to the inspired narratives and poetry found in the Old Testament, New Testament, Book of Mormon, and Pearl of Great Price[2] in which the Lord has expressed His pure, unadulterated vision of "things as they are, and as they were, and as they are to come" (D&C 93:24), a vision He hopes we will wholeheartedly adopt, overcoming any lingering elements of the natural man, emulating the principles of eternal life with increasing exactness, and imitating our Savior's example. Fortunately, in General Conference, the prophets, seers, and revelators of our time liken the scriptures unto us for our profit and learning.

Text, Context, Subtext

Read as a literary text, concrete virtual realities in the scriptures have both breadth and depth. One way to understand the level of meaning in a literary text was expressed by the renowned Canadian literary theorist and ordained minister in the United Church of Canada, Northup Frye, who examined literary works by their surface "overthought" and hidden "underthought," terms he borrowed from the English Victorian poet Gerard Hanley Hopkins. For Frye,

> The overthought is the surface meaning of the poem [or any literary passage, really] as presented: it covers most of what the poet's contemporary readers took in and probably, as a rule, most of what the poet himself thought he was producing. This is mainly the syntactic or conscious meaning of the poem. The *underthought* consists of the *progression of imagery and metaphor* that supplies an *emotional counterpoint to the surface meaning*, which it often supplements, but also often contradicts.[3]

For practical reasons we will formulate the over- and underthought into three interrelated layers of meaning: text, context, and subtext, "text" denoting the surface, or literal, meaning of words, their dictionary definition, or overthought. For Latter-day Saints, there is an additional sense of "literal" in that we consider the words of scripture to be inspired and, therefore, literally the words of God (see 2 Tim. 3:7).

"Context" identifies a second layer of overthought in the words surrounding a particular word or phrase, often adding nuances of meaning to a word thereby supplementing its literal meaning. Using a word or phrase out of context can diminish, even distort, what the Lord intends for a reader to understand.

"Subtext" refers to the underthought, the connotative meanings and themes of a word.[4] The connotative meaning of words is most often associated with the figurative language of images and symbols, implying something other than the literal meaning of words, for example, in the phrase, "Blessed are all they who do hunger and thirst after righteousness" (Matt. 5:6; 3 Ne. 12:6). Because of the phrase "after righteousness," we understand that "hunger and thirst" do not imply physical hunger and thirst, rather they represent a craving, i.e., intense desire, to learn about and assimilate into one's being the principles of righteousness. Often when a word is used literally in the surface narrative of the scriptures, subtexts may lay beneath it.

The following schematic illustrates the text, context, and subtext of words in a narrative or poem and the lines of intersection radiating from them:

Surface Text:	Word 1	Word 2	Word 3	Word 4 (etc.)
	(Context)	(Context)	(Context)	
Subtext 1:				
Subtext 2:				
Subtext 3:				
Subtext 4:				

The horizontal line under the four words represents the surface level of the text. Each of the four words also functions as a context for the others words. We might think of the lines descending from each word as an abstraction for the roots that spread throughout the scriptures and intersect, or intertwine, with one another. (The picture of Thorncrown Chapel outside Eureka Springs, Arkansas, (below) shows what the schematic looks like in an architectural format.[5]) Any word or passage of scripture may have one or more subtexts. Capturing the vision in the subtexts below the surface of the text facilitates the reader's ability to discern the organic unity of an image and its deeper meaning.

"The Burden of the Desert of the Sea"

To illustrate the practical application of text, context, and subtext in the scriptures, we will look at the first few words of Isaiah 21:1: "The burden of the desert of the sea," an introduction the biblical scholars have found opaque, but which Restoration scriptures help to explain. Three words are of interest in the verse: burden, desert, and sea in their relationship to one another, particularly desert and sea. Placed on the surface text of the schematic above, they appear below the picture of Thorncrown Chapel.

Thorncrown Chapel, Eureka Springs, Arkansas

Text:	Burden	Desert	Sea

A footnote to Isaiah 21:1 in the Church-published scriptures tells that "burden" means "a message or prophecy of doom to Babylon."[6] At first blush, the pairing of "desert" and "sea" may seem an odd couple, but since these are the Lord's words, we know they offer a vision of the burden He will place upon Babylon. Our challenge is to explore the pairing and bring our personal experiences to bear on it in order to determine their common denominators and see the vision they project.

I live in Arizona, much of which is desert. One of the greatest threats anyone faces in the desert, especially during the summer months, is dehydration; a person loses body moisture rapidly in this arid climate, and without sufficient drinking water they may experience severe sunstroke and, unfortunately, sometimes even death. Lack of fresh water to drink is as great a threat at sea as in the desert. One of the most famous lines of poetry in English literature comes from Samuel Coleridge's *Rime of the Ancient Mariner*: "Water, water, everywhere, . . . Nor any drop to drink."[7] One subtext shared by the desert and the sea, then, is the lack of potable water, illustrated as follows:

Text:	Burden	Desert	Sea
Subtext 1:			Lack of Fresh Drinking Water

In the scriptures, fresh, or running, water is figuratively described as living water, representing the inspiration flowing from the throne of God through the Holy Ghost (see Rev. 22:1; John 7:38-39). From Lehi's vision of the iron rod we learn that living water also represents the love of God, "shed abroad in our hearts by the Holy Ghost" (Rom. 5:5; see 1 Ne. 11:25). Inspiration, in its many forms, conveys not only truth, but also God's love, meaning that each time someone is privileged to receive divine inspiration; the Lord is also saying, "I love you." With regard to the burden to be placed on the Babylonians, who had developed an advanced civilization in which many discoveries important to the advancement of Western civilization were made—the Babylonians would be without the inspiration of Jehovah that had likely helped them with their discoveries. Following is the partial schematic of the desert-sea image into the second, third, and fourth subtexts:

Text:	Burden	Desert	Sea
Subtext 1			Scarce Drinking water (Living Water)
Subtext 2:			Absence of inspiration
Subtext 3:			The Holy Ghost Withdraws
Subtext 4:			Spiritual drought

The depth of this burden is stunning, and we know it was fulfilled.

Another line of subtexts in this verse derives from the topography shared by, for example, the Saharan Desert of the Middle East and the sea. A relatively calm sea appears featureless to the untrained eye; swells provide some definition, but becoming oriented at sea is daunting without navigational instruments or training in navigating by celestial bodies. Picture now the Sahara Desert. Dunes break up the flat surface, but the landscape is otherwise indeterminate. In the novel, *Lonesome Dove*, Larry McMurtry describes a fictional cattle drive across the western territorial plains of the United States. The cowboys were disturbed by the emptiness around them; all they could see were "the mirages [that] shimmered in the endless distances. Even a man with a good sense of direction," they recognized, "could get lost with so few features to guide him. Water was always chancy."[8] We can imagine that the English and Scandinavian pioneers crossing the plains felt much the same way, even though they were on the Lord's errand, with a clear goal in front of them. By analogy, the adversary tries to flatten the spiritual landscape for people so that the mountain revelations of the Lord's gospel are indefinite, and people can easily lose their moral direction. Metaphorically, such loss of spiritual orientation is often described with the images of darkness, or, in the extreme instance of falling inexorably under Satan's influence, the metaphor of chains (see 2 Ne. 28:19; Alma 13:30).

Following is the schematic of Isaiah 21:1 with both legs of subtexts filled in:

Text:	Burden	Desert	Sea
Subtext 1:		Featureless Topography	Dearth of Fresh Water (Living Water)
Subtext 2:		Spiritually Disoriented	The Holy Spirit Withdraws
Subtext 3:		Spiritually Adrift	Absence of Inspiration
Subtext 4:		Darkness/Chains	Spiritual Drought

Admittedly, this schematic is an abstract means for looking at a very imaginative verse of concrete images, but if we can see the symbolic vision represented by the desert-sea image complex, perhaps we can have an overview of what occurs if we become spiritually disoriented.[9] It reminds me of an experience two of my sons and I had during a vacation to San Carlos, Mexico, when a family invited us to go ocean fishing with them. After an hour or so fishing, suddenly a huge cloud of fog rolled in over us so that we could barely see from stem to stern. Most of us had no idea in which direction shore was. Most, but not all of us! Without hesitation, our old guide pointed us to shore—not only to shore, but almost exactly to the boat dock. He was never disoriented. Don't we all feel befogged to one degree or another at some time in our lives? And aren't we grateful when we finally feel the still, small voice of our Divine Guide pointing the way to shore and reorientation?

The Lord, I think, wants us to liken the desert-sea image to ourselves and experience it vicariously so that we avoid future spiritual disorientation by envisioning just how important abiding by His words in the scriptures is and how important the living waters of inspiration are when "the mists of darkness" try to envelop us in their suppressing, depressing vapor (1 Ne. 12:17; 3 Ne. 8:22). A picture in the imagination can sink deeper into the spirit than a verbalized admonition. The vision of Isaiah 21:1 was a warning to Isaiah's contemporaries as well as to people today who are facing a world of moral decay: If we do not heed His words, if we think we know more than His Apostolic Watchmen, we can easily lose our way spiritually in the worldly wilderness. And the Lord goes on to show in Isaiah that the worldly wasteland is devoid of inspiration and revelation to guide man through the shifting sands of moral relativity; it can even foster idolatry.

Feeling the anxiety inherent in Isaiah 21:1, of being enveloped in the mists of darkness that try to block out divine enlightenment, parching one's spirit, making us impervious to God's love—feeling the implicit anxiety in this Isaianic verse is as important, if not more so, than seeing the vision. Such feeling can act as a powerful motivation to remain on the strait and narrow path outlined by the Lord. Donald

B. Calne, director of the Neurodegenerative Disorders Center at Vancouver Hospital and emeritus professor of neurology at the University of British Columbia, wrote: "The essential difference between emotion and reason is that emotion leads to actions while reason leads to conclusions."[10]

In sum, we capture the visions in the scriptures and take ownership of them by pausing in our search of God's word to ponder what He wants us to see and feel. Pausing and pondering does slow the pace of reading, but it immeasurably enriches and enlarges our comprehension because: **IN THE SUBTEXTS WE FIND THE EVIDENCE OF THINGS NOT SEEN, AND THUS THE VISION AND SPIRIT OF THINGS AS THEY REALLY ARE.** To pass over them without pausing for a deeper look is to overlook a great deal of what the Lord has embedded in the scriptures. Letting the various image-pictures and narrative motion pictures take root in us helps us experience a little better what the Lord sees and feels.

Assembling the Vision

The scriptures are like a great disassembled puzzle," wrote M. Catherine Thomas, Assistant Professor Emeritus at Brigham Young University. "If we want to know what one section means, we may have to assemble additional pieces of scriptures [from other sections] for a fuller picture."[11] Imagine looking at the pieces of a puzzle spread out on a table. At first they seem confusing, but as we study the pieces, we begin to see how one piece fits here with another piece there. Fitting the first several pieces together may not seem like much, but each time we are able to fit pieces together, we come a step closer to completing the puzzle.

The first step in assembling the scriptural-gospel puzzle is simply reading the scriptures, all of them, if not from beginning to end of each volume, then every book randomly,[12] searching the scriptures in breadth, acquiring an overview of the scriptural topography. With each subsequent reading, we will remember more of that topography and see better how the pieces fit together, i.e., how revelation in one book clarifies revelation in another. It has to be said that in this life we may only be able to assemble a small part of the puzzle making up the Lord's vision of reality, but in the discipline of searching we gain in the process will carry with us into the spirit world. The great promise is: "Whatever principle of intelligence we attain unto in this life, it will rise with us in the resurrection. And if a person gains more knowledge and intelligence in this life through his diligence and obedience than another, he will have so much the advantage in the world to come" (D&C 130:18-19).

In-depth research is akin to an archeological excavation where we dig into several layers of meaning below the surface, as demonstrated in Isaiah 21:1 above, searching for hidden gems of truth, collecting our findings and sorting them into similar groups, all the while prayerfully asking for the help of the Holy Ghost. Said Elder Neal A. Maxwell: "The scriptures offer us many doctrinal diamonds, and when the light of the Spirit plays upon their several facets, they sparkle celestial sense and illuminate the path we are to follow."[13] The geological process by which coal becomes diamonds is well known and has its own important spiritual application. Rough diamonds are found through arduous excavating, and can be passed over unless one knows what to look for. So it is with doctrinal diamonds: they may lay in the surface text or subtexts, going unnoticed unless the reader is searching for the deeper layers of meaning, the deeper truths called mysteries often found in the image-symbols of the scriptures. Elder John A. Widtsoe noted the eternal significance of scriptural symbols: "As man develops, he learns to be content to know eternal truths only in great symbols. . . . Back of symbols lies the whole Great Plan in its many gradations and divisions. . . . By frequent reference to [the great symbols of the gospel] the realities of eternal life are constantly held before us."[14]

Tools of the Trade

In recent years the Church has provided members with a number of exceptional tools for searching the scriptures, scriptures containing exhaustive footnotes offering a wealth of information such as cross references, notes explaining the original meanings of Old Testament Hebrew and New Testament Greek words, verses from the Joseph Smith translation of the Bible that correct and/or expand the translations of the King James committee, and more. Located at the end of the main body of text are the Topical Guide, the Bible Dictionary, excerpts from the Joseph Smith translations, a Gazetteer, and maps of ancient Palestine and pictures of Palestine today and the same for upstate New York at the time of Joseph Smith in the Book of Mormon.[15]

All the tools mentioned above are also available in a searchable database of www.lds.org/ scriptures which can be downloaded on to mobile devices. Whereas the Topical Guide in the book edition is necessarily limited, the search feature in the computer database looks for every appearance of a particular word or phrase in the standard works. Another tool I have found useful is located at http://scriptures.byu.edu/ where one can select a scripture from any of the standard works and find quotes by the Presidents and Apostles, and other General Authorities of the Church, referring to the selected scripture. Add a good dictionary to these tools and you are ready to seriously research the scriptures.[16]

Notes to Chapter 4

1. *SOED*, s.v., "virtual reality."
2. The Doctrine and Covenants is not included in this list because it contains more statements on doctrine rather than narratives or poetry. However, the principles discussed in this chapter can be applied equally in this compilation wherever the Lord used images to explain doctrine, which was quite often.

3. Northrup Frye, *Words with Power: Being a Second Study of "The Bible and Literature,"* New York: Harcourt Brace, Jovanovich, 1990), 57.
4. *American Heritage Dictionary*, 4th ed. (Boston: Houghton Mifflin, 2000), s.v. "subtext."
5. Faye Jones, the creative architect of Thorncrown Chapel, was perhaps the most famous Arkansas architect. He studied under Frank Lloyd Wright at Wright's Taliesin West studio located in Scottsdale, Arizona.
6. See also *TWOT*, 2:600-01 (# 1421 d-e).
7. *Samuel Taylor Coleridge: A Critical Edition of the Major Works*, ed. H. J. Jackson (Oxford: Oxford University Press, 1985), 52 (vv. 121-22). Coleridge introduced his work with a quote in Latin from T. Burnet, the first sentence of which reads: "*Facile credo, plures esse Naturas invisibiles quam visibiles in rerum universitate*" (I believe that there are more invisible than visible natures [creatures?] in the universe), exactly what the scriptures reveal, though quite a bit different than what Burnet surmised.
8. Larry McMurtry, *Lonesome Dove* (New York: Simon and Schuster, 1985), 462.
9. For the Israelites at the time of Isaiah, the subtext laying closest to the surface of the text was a reminder of the spiritual wasteland they created for themselves by adopting the idolatrous practices of their neighbors and captors. Repeatedly the Lord had described the house of Israel as the adulterous bride who had betrayed her intended, the Lord Himself, by worshipping idols in direct contradiction of the first three of the Ten Commandments. It is from these three commandments that the subtext draws its meaning and power (see Exod. 20:3-6).

    In this implicit reminder was also the burden, i.e., the prophesy of doom, concerning what was to come in the not-so-distant future. Past, present, and future merged for the Jews in this one introduction. It is also a reminder and message for people today that they could fall away by worshipping others gods—gods of wealth, of education, of performing skills, and so forth.
10. Donald B. Calne, *Within Reason – Rationality and Human Behavior* (New York: Vintage Books, 2000), 236.
11. M. Catherine Thomas, "King Benjamin and the Mysteries of God," FARMS Reprint.
12. For most people, this represents a considerable commitment of time; however, if one simply prepares for the Gospel Doctrine class each Sunday, reading entire chapters rather than selections, one can, for the most part, accomplish

reading each work from beginning to end in four years. The exception to this is the Old Testament because a great deal of material is, of necessity, omitted from the Gospel Doctrine course of instruction. I would encourage you, however, to read most of the Old Testament; the more I have studied the scriptures over the years, the more I've come to realize how great an influence the Old Testament has on the New Testament and the Book of Mormon. A British scholar by the name of Margaret Barker has done a great deal of research into the Old Testament's influence in the New Testament, writing about what she terms "temple theology." Basically, Ms. Barker has concluded that the theology and practices of the *first* temple, King Solomon's temple, rather than the second, Herod's temple, forms the core theology of the New Testament. While discussing her ideas here would be a diversion, the reader can read an introduction to her work in Margaret Barker, *Temple Theology: An Introduction* (London: Society for Promoting Christian Knowledge, 2004). This is not an endorsement of Ms. Barker work, nor should this become a substitute for reading and searching the scriptures for oneself. Her ideas are simply thought provoking because when one reads Isaiah, Hebrews, or Revelation, it is evident that the temple experience of an LDS temple ceremony adds significantly deeper understanding of those books. It can be said that she has also found friendly reception among BYU scholars, and has lectured there several times.

When reading the Old Testament, the reader could pass over Leviticus and Numbers which speak to the specifics of the Law of Moses. Moreover, if you find it tedious or difficult to read the standard works from beginning to end, try selecting book at random to read. Random reading is like going to a library shelf and taking a book, reading it as quickly as possible. Whatever works for you, follow the motto on a plaque on President Kimball's desk that read: "Just do it!" The rewards for consistent, persistent scripture study are great.

13. Neal A. Maxwell, "According to the Desires of [Our] Heart," *Ensign* (Nov. 1996), 68.
14. John A. Widtsoe, *A Rational Theology* (Salt Lake City: Deseret Book, 1966), 175-76; see also Boyd K. Packer, *The Holy Temple* (Salt Lake City: Bookcraft, 1980), 40-41.
15. The most authoritative English dictionary is the twenty-volume *Oxford English Dictionary of Historical Principles* (2nd ed. 20 vols. Oxford: Oxford University Press, 1989). I prefer the two-volume version, *The Shorter Oxford English Dictionary* (*SOED*) because it contains most of the essential words of the

language and because it is also available in an inexpensive software edition. For specific American English usage, I turn to *The American Heritage Dictionary of the English Language*. However, any number of good dictionaries is more than adequate to assist in one's research.

16. The Church has announced a new version of the New Testament for 2019, published by the Maxwell Institute at Brigham Young University.

CHAPTER 5

LIGHT AND THE THREE DEGREES OF GLORY

The Spirituality of Light

The Evangelist John wrote, "God is light" (1 John 1:5); Jesus declared, "I am the light and life of the world" (3 Ne. 9:18). Some may consider His declaration as simply rhetorical images, but John's apocalyptic vision reveals that, in His exalted state, Christ is a being of light: "His head and his hairs were white like wool, as white as snow; and his eyes were as a flame of fire; And his feet like unto fine brass, as if they burned in a furnace; and his voice as the sound of many waters" (Rev. 1:14-15; also 2:18), statements confirmed in modern revelation: "His eyes were as a flame of fire; the hair of his head was white like the pure snow; his countenance shone above the brightness of the sun; and his voice was as the sound of the rushing of great waters, even the voice of Jehovah" (D&C 110:3). The light radiating from His and His

Father's glory is the light radiating from the heavenly city of God (see Rev. 22:23).

In Doctrine and Covenants 88:3-13, the Lord identified this light, but also revealed just how powerful and extensive it is:

> Wherefore, I now send upon you another Comforter, even upon you my friends, that it may abide in your hearts, even the Holy Spirit of promise; which other Comforter is the same that I promised unto my disciples, as is recorded in the testimony of John.
> This Comforter is the promise which I give unto you of eternal life, even the glory of the celestial kingdom;
> Which glory is that of the church of the Firstborn, even of God, the holiest of all, through Jesus Christ his Son—
> He that ascended up on high, as also he descended below all things, in that he comprehended all things, that he might be in all and through all things, the light of truth;
> Which truth shineth. This is the light of Christ. As also he is in the sun, and the light of the sun, and the power thereof by which it was made.
> As also he is in the moon, and is the light of the moon, and the power thereof by which it was made;
> As also the light of the stars, and the power thereof by which they were made;
> And the earth also, and the power thereof, even the earth upon which you stand.
> And the light which shineth, which giveth you light, is through him who enlighteneth your eyes, which is the same light that quickeneth your understandings;

> Which light proceedeth forth from the presence of God to fill the immensity of space—
> The light which is in all things, which giveth life to all things, which the law by which all things are governed, even the power of God who sitteth upon his throne, who is in the bosom of eternity, who is in the midst of all things.

That He is the life of the world is expressed in the first-person singular, "I am," which echoes the sacred name by which Moses was to identify Him to the Israelites: "I AM THAT I AM" (Exod. 3:14), meaning that He "is a self-existent being,"[1] having life in Himself. He disclosed as much in Palestine when He declared: "For as the Father hath life in himself; so hath he given to the Son to have life in himself" (John 5:26) These verses enunciate the Lord's astrophysics and metaphysics based on the ubiquity of light in the universe: astrophysics because they address some of the fundamental physical realities of the cosmos; metaphysics because light conveys truth (see D&C 84:45).

Modern science is just beginning to catch up with this 1832-1833 revelation. Columbia University professor of physics, Brian Greene, has written: "In concrete terms, in *every* cubic meter of the universe—including the one you now occupy—there are, on average, about 400 million photons that collectively compose the vast cosmic sea of microwave radiation."[2] The implications of this assessment are great: first, we have to remember, most light is not visible to the naked eye; second, Greene's statement means that even in darkness, we are surrounded by light; third, this light is the Light of Christ; fourth, the Holy Spirit can communicate with us at any time through the Light of Christ, as Elder Bruce R. McConkie explained: "The Light of Christ, the all-pervading, universally present Spirit, is the vehicle used by the Holy Ghost to operate and function in all the world. That is, the Holy

Ghost uses the Light of Christ to manifest his power and make available his gifts to all men everywhere at one and the same time."[3]

To bridge the discussion of the Light of Christ in the preceding paragraphs with the discussion to follow, we need to acknowledge here that our Heavenly Father is "the Father of lights" (James 1:17; D&C 67:9)[4] and men and women are "children of light" (John 12:6; Eph. 5:8; 1 Thess. 5:5; D&C 106:5), possessing the Light of Christ, the vast database of eternal truths (see D&C 84:45-46; D&C 93:29). Pondering these and related scriptures, Truman Madsen concluded: "These revelations suggest that man is more than a receptacle of degrees of light; he is somehow in his primal makeup composed of light."[5] Elder Mark A. Bragg remarked, "We are children of God. Receiving light, continuing in God, and receiving more light are what we are created to do. . . .Seeking the light is in our spiritual DNA."[6]

Notice, in the thirteenth verse of Doctrine and Covenants 88 that the Light of Christ "is in all things [and] giveth life to all things . . . is [also] the law by which all things are governed, even the power of God." *Light is the power of God!* (Webster's 1828 *Dictionary* defined "quicken" as "to make alive in a spiritual sense; to communicate a principle of grace."[7]) The wording in this verse bears a striking similarity to the description of faith as power found in the *Lectures on Faith*:

> . . . faith is not only the principle of action, but of power also, in all intelligent beings, whether in heaven or on earth. Thus says the author of the epistle to the Hebrews (11:3):
>
> Through faith we understand that the worlds were framed by the word of God, so that things which are seen were not made of things which do appear.[8]

> By this we understand that the principle of power which existed in the bosom of God, by which the worlds were framed, was faith; and that it is by reason of this principle of power existing in the Deity, that all created things exist; so that all things in heaven, on earth, or under the earth, exist by reason of faith as it existed in Him.
>
> Had it not been for the principle of faith the worlds would never have been framed, neither would man have been formed of the dust. It is the principle by which Jehovah works, and through which he exercises power over all temporal as well as eternal things. Take this principle or attribute—for it is an attribute—from the Deity, and he would cease to exist.[8]

The similarities of this description of faith to Doctrine and Covenants 88:13 are so striking that they can't be mere coincidence; consequently, we can speak of them as one: faith is light, light is faith. We apprehend from this relationship that our inherited Light of Christ is the generative power of faith in Jesus Christ, serving as the catalyst for advancing His work, usually in the small acts that contribute to "his great and eternal purposes" (Alma 37:7). This spiritual interaction of light and faith may occur as the Holy Spirit inspires us with a heavenly spark from the divine fire.[9]

President Gordon B. Hinckley taught, "Faith lights the way,"[10] not just metaphorically, but also literally, expressed in the following adaptation of his sentence, using the New-Testament verb form of faith, *pisteuo* (πιστεύω), (the noun denoting "faith" being *pístis* [πίστις], as in "Faith [*pístis*] without works is dead" [James 2:20]): "Light *faiths* the way," awkward, to be sure in English, but giving expression to faith as an active agent in man. The long version of light *faiths* the way is: "With our inborn, genetic Light of Christ, we generate the faith in Jesus Christ to light the way of Christ before us." By walking beyond the edge of the light we've generated at any given moment, we step into and activate latent zones of this Light of Christ in us, thereby unsealing greater faith in eternal truths and nuances of truths, opening greater vistas of godly opportunities, and leading further along the path of eternal life for us and for others, all of which circumscribes the adventure of discipleship.

Because mercy, meaning loving/compassionate-kindness, or "the pure love of Christ" (Moro. 7:47), defines who Jesus Christ is, we can assume that His love informs the Light of Christ as the Light of Christ informs our exercise of "faith, which," in turn, "worketh by love" (Gal. 5:6), making man both a receptacle of the godly love shed forth in his heart as a burning in the bosom by the Holy Spirit (see Rom. 5:5; D&C 9:6) and someone who, having been the recipient of godly love, has the responsibility to bestow His comforting love on others: "Blessed be God, even the Father of our Lord Jesus Christ, the Father of mercies, and the God of all comfort; Who comforteth us in all our tribulation, that we may be able to comfort them which are in any trouble, by the comfort wherewith we ourselves are comforted of God" (2 Cor. 1:3-4). Given the relationship between the Light of Christ, the pure love of Christ, or mercy, and our faith, the deeper meaning of the Savior's commission to the Nephites becomes clearer, to "hold up your light that it may shine unto the world. Behold I am the light which ye shall hold up—that which ye have seen me do" (3 Ne. 18:24). What greater testimony can any disciple manifest than the faith-filled emulation of the works of the Lord?

There are other evidences of the Light of Christ shining through doing the Lord's will. An esoteric example is the image of the lamp the virgins carry in the parable of the ten virgins that gives visual form to their inner Light of Christ. Proverbs 20:27 states that "the spirit of man is the [lamp (Hebrew *nîr*)] of the Lord searching all the inward parts of the belly."[11] "The inward parts of the belly" connotes the innermost part of a person's soul, his Light of Christ. The wise virgins light the way for the Second Coming of the Bridegroom with their love- and faith-filled Light of Christ, sharing His gospel with others in their every act.[12] A more transparent example appears in the Sermon on the Mount and before the Temple at Bountiful, when the Savior said: "Behold, do men light a [lamp (Greek *lúchnos*, λύχνος)] and put it under a bushel? Nay, but on a [lampstand (Greek *luchnía*, λυχνία)], and it giveth light to all that are in the house; Therefore, let your light (Greek *phōs*, φῶς) so shine before this people, that they may see your good works and glorify your Father who is in heaven" (Matt. 5:15-16; 3 Ne. 12:15-16).[13] In Isaiah, the Lord refers to his disciples' light, expressing what can happen when they tend to the needs of the poor by living the law of the fast:

> Is it not to deal thy bread to the hungry, and that thou bring the poor that are cast out to thy house? when thou seest the naked, that thou cover him; and that thou hide not thyself from thine own flesh?
>
> Then shall *thy light break forth as the morning*, and thine health shall spring forth speedily: and thy righteousness shall go before thee; the glory of the Lord shall be thy rereward. . . .
>
> And if thou draw out thy soul to the hungry, and satisfy the afflicted soul; then shall *thy light rise in obscurity*, and thy darkness be as the noonday:
>
> And the Lord shall guide thee continually, and satisfy thy soul in drought, and make fat thy bones: and thou

shalt be like a watered garden, and like a spring of water, whose waters fail not.

And they that shall be of thee shall build the old waste places: thou shalt raise up the foundations of many generations; and thou shalt be called, The repairer of the breach, The restorer of paths to dwell in (Isa. 58:7-8, 10-12; emphasis added).

In his discourse on faith, Alma compared the word of God, meaning the Atonement of the Word of God, the Light to the world, Jesus Christ (see Alma 33:21-23), to a seed that, when planted in a person's heart and nourished by their faith, would germinate and take root. As the seed gestates, he said, "it beginneth to enlarge my soul; yea, it beginneth to *enlighten* my understanding" (Alma 32:28; emphasis added). A few verses on in the discourse, he writes: "O then, is not this real? I say unto you, Yea, *because it is light*; and whatsoever is light, is good, because it is discernible" (Alma 32:35; emphasis added). While the great light of the gospel is the Savior's Atonement, and all other principles are "only appendages to it,"[14] Alma seems to imply that each word of God—word of God in many instances meaning the principles of the gospel of Jesus Christ—contains a measure of divine light with its attendant power to communicate absolute truth and a vision of "things as they *really* are." Indeed, when preaching in the land of Mormon, he ascribed the conversion of the people to having "their souls . . . illuminated by the light of the everlasting word" (Alma 5:7). Again these references may simply seem to be basic scriptural metaphors, but I would suggest that they may be understood literally, as evidencing a real entity.

The culmination of Alma's analogy follows logically, and the image is breathtaking. As seeds grow into plants, the light-filled seed in Alma's analogy, diligently nurtured by the light-generated faith of a committed disciple of Christ, grows into "a tree springing up unto everlasting life" (Alma 32:40-41). Eternal ramifications lie behind this image, beginning with its most important subtext: the reality of the Savior's Atonement. His original disciples compared the cross upon which He was crucified to a tree (see Acts 5:30; 13:29; 1 Peter 2:24), the tree of His ultimate, redeeming sacrifice to reconcile man with His Father in heaven. A second, interrelated subtext alludes to trees representing the life of man (see Deut. 20:19). Discipleship, then, means taking up one's cross, one's personal tree, and following the Savior (see Matt. 16:24); "for a man to take up his cross, is to deny himself all ungodliness, and every worldly lust, and keep my commandments" (JST Matt. 16:26),[15] forgoing personal pleasures to bless the lives of others, thus assisting Christ in the great work of "bring[ing] to pass the immortality and eternal life of man" (Moses 1:39). A disciple's acts of compassionate-kindness may seem small, perhaps even insignificant, but Alma assures us that "by small and simple things are great things brought to pass; and small means in many instances doth confound the wise. And the Lord God doth work by means to bring about his great and eternal purposes; and by very small means the Lord doth confound the wise and bringeth about the salvation of many souls (Alma 37:6-7).

By engaging in the salvific work of Christ's Atonement, a disciple becomes an earthly pivot point of what can become a sacred circle of light, love, and faith represented by Alma's tree. A constant stream of the light- and love-filled faith, the Savior's faith in His disciples and others, descends from heaven, sheds forth into the hearts of people by the Holy Spirit (see Rom. 5:5). When a disciple requites the Savior's faith in him or her with faith born of love for the Savior by investing his or her time, talents, and means in lightening others' burdens, empathizing with those that mourn,[16] comforting those in need of comfort, that disciple's proactive faith in Christ ascends to heaven where the Savior receives it as having been done unto Himself (see Matt. 25:40), whereupon more inspiration descends upon the disciple. "The liberal [free in giving,[16] beneficent] soul shall be made fat: and he that watereth shall be watered also himself" (Prov. 11:25). The first mention of water in this verse refers to the inspired acts a disciple does for others; the second mention of water is the "pure river of water of life, clear as crystal, proceeding from the throne of God and of the Lamb" (Rev. 22:1), representing the love of God enfolded in the Savior's faith and in the Light of Christ, through which the Holy Spirit inspires man.

It is in the fruit of Alma's tree that a disciple's acts of faith becomes clearer, fruit "which is most precious, which is sweet above all that is sweet, and which is white above all that is white, yea, and pure above all that is pure" (Alma 32:42), fruit whose qualities mirror the fruit of the tree of life in Lehi's vision (see 1 Ne. 8:11), fruit *whose color is the color of light*. Proverbs 11:30 summarizes the significance for individual disciples of the image of the tree discussed here: "The fruit of the righteous is a tree of life; and he that winneth souls is wise." As the tree of the cross became a tree of immortality and eternal life with the Savior's Resurrection, so a tree springing up unto everlasting life becomes a tree of life as disciples selflessly embark upon the Lord's errand.

The circular flow of light from heaven to earth and back is implicit in Jesus declaration to a Samaritan woman at Jacob's Well: "Whosoever drinketh of this water shall thirst again: But whosoever drinketh of the water that I shall give him shall never thirst; but the water that I shall give him shall be in him a well of water springing up into everlasting life" (John 4:13-14), the Savior's water being the water viz. light flowing from the throne of the Father and the Son. To drink or "taste this light" as Alma taught (Alma 32:35), is to accept the principles of the gospel of Jesus Christ as true and everlasting, first through the baptisms of water and fire, followed by Christlike actions, enduring faithfully to the end, "lay[ing] up . . . treasures in heaven" (Matt. 6:20; 19:21; Mark 10:21;

Luke 12:33; 18:22; Hel. 5:8, 25; 3 Ne. 13:20; D&C 6:27), indicating thereby the return of a disciple's inspired acts to heaven. Essentially, Christ made the same declaration during the last day of the Jewish feast of the Tabernacles: "If any man thirst, let him come unto me, and drink. He that believeth on me, as the scripture hath said, out of his belly shall flow rivers of living water" (John 7:37-38). Parenthetically, John added: "But this spake he of the [Holy] Spirit, which they that believe on him should receive" (John 7:39). As the living waters of inspiration flow from heaven to earth into the heart of His disciples, so living water-light flows from disciples into the lives of others, returning, then, to heaven as inspired works. I term such discipleship "prophetic" because, "the testimony of Jesus is the spirit of prophecy" (Rev. 19:10), and one's testimony is manifest in both word and work.

There is an inclusive meaning of the word *prophet*, expressed in Moses' lament, "Would God that all the Lord's people were prophets, and that the Lord would put his spirit upon them! (Num. 11:29). It would be easy to dismiss this as Moses' wish that each Israelite who complained to him might spend some time in his shoes to appreciate what he had to put up with from them, but President Harold B. Lee acknowledged that

> In a sense, the word *prophet* might apply to all faithful Church members. I do not mean that we have the right to receive revelations as to how this church might be run, or that members may have revelations as to how or who should be named in a stake or ward organization. But I do say that the bishop in his place, the mission president in his place, the stake president in his place, the quorum president, the auxiliary leader, the seminary teacher, the institute teacher, a father and mother in the home, a young person in his or her quest for

a proper companion in marriage—each of us has the right to revelation.

No group of people have a gift so widely diffused as the gift of prophecy. You recall the definition as contained in the book of Revelation. John quoted the angelic messenger who came to him as saying, ". . . I am thy fellow-servant, and of thy brethren that have the testimony of Jesus: . . . for testimony of Jesus is the spirit of prophecy." (Revelation 19:10.) . . .

[A]nyone who enjoys the gift by which he may have God revealed has the spirit of prophecy, the power of revelation, and, in a sense, is a prophet within the sphere of responsibility and authority given to him.[18]

Biblical Hebrew and Greek reveal the inner dynamic of the word *prophet* as it relates to the verb "springing up." In ancient Hebrew the word for prophet was *nābî*, the underlying metaphor of which is to spring up, as water from an artesian well springs up. "Used in the form of a noun," wrote Joseph Fielding McConkie and Robert L. Millet, "it means one in whom the message of God springs forth or one to whom anything is secretly communicated."[19]

Another dimension of the spirit of prophesy is expressed by the Greek New-Testament words for prophet and prophesy, respectively *prophētēs* (προφήτης) and *prophēteía* (προφητεία). When referring to time, the *pro*-prefix of these compound words signifies "before," "earlier than." (While a prophet may foretell events when the Lord delegates seeric ability to him, his "primary role is to be a forthteller, . . . declaring the word of God."[20]) The basic stem of both words is *phēmi* (φημί) from the obsolete verb *pháō* (φάω), denoting "to *shine*," "to *bring forth into the light,"* "*enlighten.*" The noun form of *pháō* is *phōs* (φῶς), signifying "light" or "fire"; it comes into English as "photo" in all its derivatives. *Phōs* also denotes the light emitted by a luminous body, such as a lamp or candle, as in, "Let your light [*phōs*] so shine before men. . ." (Matt. 5:16). It is in this figurative sense that the deep image of the word *prophet* is found. This light is "the spiritual light and knowledge which enlightens the mind, soul, or conscience. . . . Metonymically, a light [is] the author or dispenser of moral and spiritual light."[21] The verb *phaínō* (φαίνω), meaning to give light, to illuminate, derives from *phōs*; both words are found in John 1:5: "And the light [*phōs*] shineth [*phaínō*] in darkness; and the darkness comprehended it not." The Savior's prophets are those who reflect His light to a world enveloped in moral darkness and ignorance. Every disciple, however, can also be a prophetic light within his sphere of influence; that's why the Savior taught us to let our light shine before men: it isn't our light, which is really His light that we reflect (see 3 Ne. 18:24), light which radiates from the Spirit of Christ and the enlightenment of the Holy Ghost within us; it is the light that highlights the potential in others; it projects a better future to those in spiritual darkness if they will exercise just enough faith to see through the eyes of the Christ. The essence of such discipleship has been given anonymously in five short lines:

> Obedience is the price.
> Faith is the power.
> Love is the motive.
> The Spirit is the key.
> Christ is the reason.

For a moment, let's dispense with the formal first-person "we" and "our" and personalize the following paragraph with the second-person "you." Considering all the factors that contribute to a prophetic inclination—the Light of Christ in and surrounding you; the free flow of revelation from the throne of God and the Lamb to you; your companionship with God the Holy Spirit; the faith of the Godhead in you, expressed in each instance of inspiration; your faith, born of love for your Savior, resulting in acts of kindness toward the Lord's other children—these factors and more create a sacred bond of trust between you and Jesus Christ: He trusts that you will be spiritually sensitive to His still, small voice and that you will do whatsoever He prompts you to do; you trust Him implicitly that He is perfectly merciful, loving you with a kindness transcending all the kindness you can ever experienced in mortality, that His only motive is that you become more like Him in thought and deed. So long as you sustain your part of the trust, it is as if you were enveloped in a heavenly, fiery pillar of refreshing love, such as descended from heaven surrounding the Nephite children with angels ministering unto you, "angels [who] speak by the power of the Holy Ghost; wherefore, they speak the words of Christ" (2 Ne. 32:3). Abiding in the pillar, or not, is always your choice. With the pulls of daily living and the constant temptation around you, stepping out of your personal pillar into the moonlight of terrestriality or the starlight of telestiality, is an ongoing challenge, but the pillar remains, ready to descend and surround you at any moment you are spiritually ready, for your Savior is a constant God Who wants nothing more for you than to desire to live with Him eternally in the sunlight of celestiality, and act accordingly, that He might "confess [your] name before [His] Father, and before his angels" (Rev. 3:5).

What we do with our Light of Christ, and that additional enlightenment of revelation we receive during mortality, may, to some degree, determine the degree of glory we will ultimately receive in eternity. By being yoked with Christ through the constant companionship of the Holy Spirit, we can cultivate the Light of Christ in us unto a measure of the life of Christ by, one, obeying, then, two, willingly doing the commandments of the Lord that are the principles of eternal life. Each everlasting kingdom is a realm of glory, or light: the sun represents the celestial glory, the moon the terrestrial glory, and the stars the telestial glory (see D&C 76:70-71, 81; 1 Cor. 15:40-41). Each image suggests the differing degrees of light and truth men and women choose to follow while on earth. The focus in the following discussion is, therefore, *not* on the degree of glory to which spirits will be assigned at the Last Judgment; rather it is on the relationship people establish with light and truth during their mortal probation and the lifestyle that results from their predominant focus.[22] To identify these different relationships, we will examine the subtexts of each image the Lord has given us: starlight, moonlight, and sunlight.

The Starlight of Telestiality

In your mind's eye, recall a moonless night when you were far away from city lights and able to clearly see the Milky Way lighting the heavens with its ethereal, cloud-like luminosity. It is a spectacular, even awe-inspiring sight. With the Hubble telescope we have seen pictures of the Milky Way's magnificent vistas, invisible to the naked eye. But as beautiful and luminous as they may be, they do not provide any real light for man on earth to see. Were we alone in a forest looking at the Milky Way, and brought our eyes down to ground level, we would be surrounded by darkness; without some other means of light, we would only be able to see the outlines of objects very close to us. While not the absolute, light-extinguishing "vapor of darkness" the Nephites and Lamanites experienced immediately before the Savior appeared at the temple in Bountiful (see 3 Ne. 8:20-25), the darkness of starlight could be disorienting and frightening. Were we in the middle of an ocean or a desert, we might find it challenging to orient ourselves unless we were experienced in navigating by the stars. Such is the spiritual life with only the starlight of truth. Even the light of truth is dim in spiritual darkness.

The telestial world in which we live is called nature. It can be peaceful and gentle, allowing a sense of intimacy with our Creator; but, at times, it can rage with volcanos, fires, earthquakes, floods, tsunamis, and much more. On this telestial world, man has created civilizations—predominately Occidental, Oriental, and African, as well as multiple subcultures. While these civilizations have created much good, great works in many fields, discoveries, arts, etc.,[23] they have also fostered wars and prejudice toward other cultures and peoples. Satan hides in the darkness, attempting to control the thoughts and actions of man. Confusion rules through disinformation, double speak, and lying, resulting in spiritual darkness, many "call[ing] evil good, and good evil; . . . put[ting] darkness for light, and light for darkness; . . . bitter for sweet, and sweet for bitter" (Isa. 5:20; 2 Ne. 15:20). Our man-made world is full of cabals and gangs held together by secret combination inspired by Satan; they lurk in the dark, immoral alleys of spiritual, moral, political, and social anarchy in a variety of forms, and such anarchy is happening worldwide today. In order to survive and thrive in the starlight of telestiality, some people choose to become "a law unto themselves" (Rom. 2:14). Their preferred time to create mischief is night time; deception is their *modus operandi*; the Ten Commandments of no concern, much less the higher law of Christ. It is a world of disillusionment, discouragement, and depression for many. To live according to telestial light is to avoid any form of enduring truth. We might compare the starlight of telestiality to a mirror ball whose star-like flecks of light seem brilliant at first, but, if followed, they disappear into darkness. For as Jesus said, "he that walketh in darkness knoweth not whither he goeth" (John 12:35).

Yet, though we live in this telestial world, faintly illuminated by the starlight of truth, we do not have to participate in a telestial lifestyle. The vast majority of people around the world exercise their Light of Christ to live a terrestrial lifestyle, illuminated with certain enduring truths.

The Moonlight of Terrestriality

The moonlight of terrestriality refers to how we perceive reality, not to the terrestrial state in the Garden of Eden, the Millennium, or Paradise. Like the other two modes of perception, the telestial and the celestial, terrestrial vision has both a cognitive and a moral dimension, that is, what we perceive and how we evaluate our perceptions. What "terrestrial" means is more elusive than the other degrees of light, and the moon is an apt image for it.

Once again, imagine being in a forest. This time a bright, full moon lights the night sky, such as the moon described in the famous Christmas poem, "Twas the Night before Christmas": "The moon on the breast of the new-fallen snow, Gave a lustre of midday to objects below." A full moon can be bright, but it creates a deceptive vision, for the moon is not an independent source of light; the light we see shining from its surface is the reflected light of the sun. Lowering our gaze to ground level, we find a very different scene than when we only had the starlight to illuminate the scene around us. In such moonlight we can discern some features of objects close to us, as well as the dim outlines of those farther away. Yet a strange feeling persists about what we observe: everything seems blanketed with a shadowy light. We only have minimal depth perception; color is drained from everything. Our surroundings become a dimly lit world in which we can easily imagine something moving in the periphery of our vision. In C. S. Lewis' *Prince Caspian*, Lucy finds herself in a dense forest with her sister, Susan, and her brothers, Peter and Edmund. Lucy sees "whole patches or pools of moonlight, but the moonlight and the shadows were so mixed that you could hardly be sure anything was or what it was."[24] We may find this terrestrial illumination as being eerie rather than scary, though the difference may be minimal.

In the cognitive sense, the passage from *Prince Caspian* relates to people living a terrestrial life who are "forever learning, and never able to come to a knowledge of the truth" (1 Tim. 3:7). Morally, they can be "tossed to and fro, and carried about with every wind of doctrine, by the sleight of men, and cunning craftiness, whereby they lie in wait to deceive" (Eph. 4:14). In this analogy, those waiting to deceive live a telestial vision, like the unseen robbers in the parable of the Good Samaritan; they try to delude those living terrestrially into seeing things their way. Terrestrial people can all too often think they are being objective and progressive when they accept the latest, most loudly promoted idea, when, in fact, they are often digressing or regressing, morally.

How appropriate the moon image to characterize a terrestrial pattern of life! As a representation of spirituality, the moon allows only a vague hint of "things as they really are," an in-between zone Satan prefers where he can tell a little truth to cover a big lie, trying to confuse our vision of the divine order of things. Most of the philosophies of men lie in a shadowy zone: they come and dissipate quickly because they are as opaque as the vision that spawned many of them. In the end, they are not sustainable; they are bound to time and place rather than transcending both and being anchored in eternity. Those that endure do so as academic surveys in universities, such as Plato's forms or Kant's critiques; because the light of eternal truths glows ever so faintly in them, they do not appeal to the broad spectrum of mankind. Like the moon's light, they are not the true light, at best its indefinite reflection.

Perhaps thinking of the starlight of a telestial mentality or the moonlight of a terrestrial disposition, the Apostle Paul wrote, "now we see through a glass, darkly" (1 Cor. 13:12). The things of God were obscured by a number of factors: Jewish Deuteronomists had yet to codify what we now term the Old Testament, trying to obviate any references in the Hebrew manuscripts that the new Christian sect considered to reference Christ; the New Testament was not yet, bits and pieces being transmitted by word of mouth; the vast majority of people were, in any case, illiterate and wouldn't have been able to read the Bible if available; even after the two Testaments were codified, up until the advent of the printing press that made available the courageous vernacular translations of Martin Luther, John Wycliffe, William Tyndale and others. The priestly class withheld the Bible from their parishioners, deeming it too dangerous in the hands of the uneducated, untrained masses, therefore, people were unable to take the true measure of things eternal for themselves.

Since the advent of the printing press, literacy has grown in quantum leaps in many areas of the world; the Bible is readily available to anyone who wants it in hard copy or digitally, and, with the publication of the Book of Mormon, the knowledge of eternal truth has expanded for those who are sincerely seeking it, also available in hard copy and digitally. Unfortunately, for various reasons, many have turned their backs on spiritual knowledge and, therefore, have not allowed the latent light in the seeds of God's words to germinate them, resulting in a breakdown of civility and morality. Elder Jeffrey R. Holland said: "[S]omeday I hope a great global chorus will harmonize across all racial and ethnic lines, declaring that guns, slurs, and vitriol are *not* the way to deal with human conflict."[25] Because moral values have become hazy and distorted, people find it more difficult to discern the vistas of eternal life; or they discern just enough to deceive themselves into thinking they have seen all the light of truth available, when, in truth, they are still seeing through the glass, darkly. Stephen R. Covey observed that "each person sees the world not as *it is*, but as *he* or *she is*."[26] The couplet, "Two men looking through bars / The one saw mud, the other stars," expresses this well.

The difference in perception between a terrestrial and a celestial vision was well expressed by President Ezra Taft Benson, who, as U. S. Secretary of Agriculture, had a great deal of experience dealing with solving societal problems. He vividly contrasted the world's plan for helping the downtrodden with the Lord's way:

> The world works from the outside in. The world would take people out of the slums. Christ takes the slums out of people, and then they take themselves out of the slums. The world would mold men by changing their environment. Christ changes men, who then change their environment. The world would shape human behavior, but Christ can change human nature.[27]

President Benson's vision expands what is, in eternity, a microcosmic moment of impoverishment into the macrocosmic realization of an individual's divine potential.

Being deceived into believing the shadows of light represent what is real is to settle for a lesser perception of what life can be. People who live by a terrestrial vision are "honorable men of the earth, who were blinded by the craftiness of men" (D&C 76:75). Many do good in their lives, but how many give the glory to God for their good works whereby they could help others come unto Christ? If done in the sunlight of celestiality, the good they do could have greater eternal effect.

The Sunlight of Celestiality

Sunrise, such as the one pictured on the cover of the book, is one of the most beautiful and inspiring sights in nature. Birds sing joyous greeting to the first rays of the sun; Navajo Native Americans likewise greet the new day with song.[28] In those dawning minutes, people experience a refreshing serenity that brings peace to the soul. As an image, daybreak dissipates the misgivings of the night, the mysteries hidden by darkness. Order and objectivity return to our personal world as objects once again become clearly defined in our vision.

As Latter-day Saints, and those investigating the Church, we bask in the sunlight of celestiality when, with "a sincere heart and real intent" (Moro. 10:4), "desir[ing] to believe" (Alma 32:27), we receive the affirming witness of the Holy Spirit that Jesus is, in fact, the Living Christ, the Son of the Living God, that the Father and the Son visited the boy Joseph Smith and restored through him the ancient church, "built upon the foundation of the apostles and prophets, Jesus Christ himself being the chief corner stone" (Eph. 2:20), now known as The Church of Jesus Christ of Latter-day Saints. We bask in the sunlight of celestiality by searching the scriptures, believing them to be the words of Christ written down in the styles of individual prophets, identifying the "forms of godliness" and with "strong faith and a firm mind" (Moro. 7:30), planting those forms in our spirits, "precept upon precept" (Isa. 28:10, 13; D&C 98:12). We bask in the sunlight of celestiality by obeying the commandments of God, doing the truths given in each commandment thereby coming to the light, "manifest[ing] that [our deeds] are wrought in God (John 3:21). We bask in the sunlight of celestiality as we abide in the companionship of the Holy Spirit whereby we are back again in the presence of God.[29]

Taken together, all of these acts help us to "know the truth of all things" (Moro. 10:5; D&C 124:97) and a vision of things as they really are. They are acts representing the process of true objectivity whereby we gain an unadulterated view of correct principles, helping us to envision that all things represent the Lord (see Moses 6:63). In contrast, the world's concept of objectivity is based on believing only what can be determined with our five senses, especially sight, not understanding that this is only the beginning of identifying truth. Centuries ago Jehovah warned about the shortcoming of sight when he told the Prophet Samuel, "the Lord seeth not as man seeth; for man looketh on the outward appearance, but the Lord looketh upon the heart" (1 Sam. 16:7). Ours is an appearance-oriented culture; e.g., men and women constantly work on their appearance as if that tells others who they are, but who they *really* are is found in the spirit.

With celestial vision we look into the eyes of our spouse and see an equal, a companion of infinite worth, someone to cherish, not just till death do us part, but forever; a son or daughter of God who loves us so much that they choose to share mortality and eternity with us; someone whose well-being is of utmost concern to us. We look into the eyes of a child and see a precious newly-arrived offspring of God, perhaps thinking of their potential when we ask, as does Elder M. Russell Ballard, "Who are you, little one? What will you become through the Atonement of Christ?"[30] Each of us has, literally, infinite potential, most importantly, to become as our Savior.

In the sunlight of celestiality we see more clearly those who need help and how to help them. Seeing through the spiritual darkness with an eye of faith, we know when to stop and help the beaten-down stranger off the side of the spiritual road.

In the sunlight of celestiality we notice when a sheep has gone astray and leave the ninety and nine to rescue the one, the central message of President Thomas S. Monson's ministry, a principle he acted upon throughout his life. We will want to greet the new and returning sheep with open arms, like the father in the parable of the prodigal son. Elder Maxwell recognized the tender, precarious moment of return and counseled active members to take note:

> When all these individuals have come from so great a distance, surely we can go a second mile in

friendshipping and fellowshipping them! If with quiet heroism they can make their way across the border into belief, surely we can cross a crowded foyer to extend the hand of fellowship. Has it been so long that we have forgotten our first anxious day at a new school or our timidity in a new neighborhood? In the city of Zion, there are constantly new kids on the block!

Since priesthood leaders have determined that the newcomers' visas are in order, let us greet them genuinely—not with frowns and skepticism. It will be our job to lift them up—not to size them up. They will have known much rejection; now let them know much acceptance.[31]

We are reminded, perhaps, that in the City of Enoch, the City of Holiness, "there was no poor among them (Moses 7:18).

The sunlight of celestiality is a revealing light of faith and love; it is a privilege and responsibility to bask in its divine rays. This light encourages us to "learn and live the celestial law here," as President Harold B. Lee counseled, "so that when the time comes you can go on and continue to live that law in the Celestial Kingdom with our Father in Heaven."[32]

The sunlight of celestiality shines through the sometimes dark path ahead with the love of God that encourages us to keep moving forward, bringing ineffable peace and joy into our spirits. Thus, in the celebratory rays of this divine sunlit vision, the Lord says to each individual who will listen, "I love you."

Scriptural images possess the power to reveal enlightening insights into principles of the gospel of Jesus Christ and affirming feelings of the heavenly ambience, feelings of love and peace. But the Lord's educational plan makes us stretch intellectually and emotionally to see as He sees and feel as He feels. "Study it out in your mind," He says (D&C 9:8); "seek learning . . . by faith" (D&C 88:118), submitting the conclusion of our study to Him in prayer, then patiently waiting upon His answer—whether it be a burning in the bosom or a stupor of thought, both are revelation (see D&C 9:8-9). Every image, being a window revealing an instant of heaven, can be a sacred vision that, we may assume, our Lord does not readily open unless we take the time to knock on the image-window with sincere study to understand it, and unless we manifest, with our faith, a desire for His guidance. And, as noted in Chapter 3, over time, the same image may reveal subtexts upon subtexts as we study the scriptures seeking to know God the Son and the patterns of eternal life (see John 5:39), as we nurture our companionship with the Holy Spirit, and as we experience the efficacy of correct gospel principles in daily living.

Notes to Chapter 5

1. *TPJS*, 352.
2. Brian Greene, *The Elegant Universe: Superstrings, Hidden Dimension, and the Quest for the Ultimate Theory* (New York: W. W. Norton, 1999), 349.
3. *DNTC*, 2:236.
4. In the King Follet discourse, the Prophet said: "You ask the learned doctors why they say the world was made out of nothing; and they will answer, 'Doesn't the Bible say He created the world?' And they infer, from the word create, that it must have been made out of nothing. Now, the word *create* came from the word Hebrew *baurau*, which does not mean to create out of nothing, rather it means to organize; the same as a man would organize materials and build a ship. Hence we infer that God had materials to organize the world out of chaos—chaotic matter, which is element, and in which dwells all the glory. Element had an existence from the time he had. The pure principles of element are principles which can never be destroyed; they may be organized and reorganized, but not destroyed. They had no beginning, and can have no end." (*TPJS*, 350-352.)

5. Truman G. Madsen, "Man Illuminated," in *Five Classics by Truman G. Madsen* (Salt Lake City: Eagle Gate, 2001), 309. From a worldly, scientific view, the physicist and host of the television series, *Cosmos*, Carl Sagan, said, "We are made of starstuff."
6. Mark A. Bragg, "Brighter and Brighter until the Perfect Day," *Ensign* (May 2017), 36.
7. *Noah Webster's First Edition of an American Dictionary of the English Language* (San Francisco, CA: Foundation for American Christian Education, 2000), s.v. "quicken."
8. *Lectures*, 1:13-16.
9. Joseph Smith taught, "God dwells in everlasting burnings" (*TPJS*, 361).
10. Gordon B. Hinckley, "We Walk by Faith," *Ensign* (May 2002), 73.
11. With few exceptions, every instance where the King James' translators used the word *candle*, the original Hebrew and Greek denotes a lamp; candlestick is lampstand.
12. See the discussion of the lamp-image in the parable of the ten virgins in William J. Bohn, *Matthew 25*.
13. Margaret Barker, British theologian and Methodist minister, has written some fascinating observations about the lamp image in the scriptures in association, particularly, with the Menorah, as the symbol of the tree of life. 'The great lamp is associated with light, life, the homage of the heavenly bodies, the eyes of the Lord, the presence of the Lord, the Tree of Life and the Davidic succession. . . .

    'Both the earliest interpretation of the Menorah in Zech[ariah] 4, and the later one in numbers Rabbah, link the lamp to the presence of God on earth. . . ; but Zechariah also linked the lamp to the role and status of the anointed rulers. Standing by the *lamp*, they are said to be standing by the 'Lord of the whole earth' (Zech. 5.14). . . .

    '1 Kings 11.36 promises a reduced but still surviving kingdom for Solomon, 'so that there may be a lamp for David my servant before me ever in Jerusalem; 2 Sam[uel] records how David's men begged him not to venture onto the field of battle 'lest you put out the lamp of Israel' (*The Older Testament: The Survival of Themes from the Ancient Royal Cult in Sectarian Judaism and Early Christianity* [Sheffield, ENG: Phoenix Press, 2005], 221, 224, 227-28).
14. *HC*, 3:30.

15. On discipleship, Elder Robert D. Hales taught: "A disciple is one who has been baptized and is willing to take upon him or her the name of the Savior and follow Him. A disciple strives to become as He is by keeping His commandments in mortality, much the same as an apprentice seeks to become like his or her master. . . .

    "[G]enuine discipleship is a state of being. This suggests more than studying and applying a list of individual attributes. Disciples live so that the characteristics of Christ are woven into the fiber of their beings, as into a spiritual tapestry" ("Becoming a Disciple of Our Lord Jesus Christ," *Ensign* (May 2017), 46.
16. Someone has said: "Sympathizers are spectators; empathizers wear game shoes."
17. From Latin *liber* "free" (*SOED*, s.v. "liberal").
18. *Stand Ye in Holy Places: Selected Sermons and Writings of President Harold B. Lee* (Salt Lake City, UT: Deseret Book, 1975), 154-55.
19. Joseph Fielding McConkie, Robert L. Millet and Brent L. Top, *Doctrinal Commentary on the Book of Mormon*, 4 vols. (Salt Lake City, UT: Bookcraft, 1988), 2:191.
20. Ibid.,
21. Zodhiates, 1462-63.
22. "During their mortal probation" includes those who did not have an opportunity to hear and accept the true gospel while on earth, but do have it presented to them in the spirit world (see D&C 130:30). The vast majority of people who have ever lived are, therefore, included in this grouping. Of these the Lord told the Prophet Joseph Smith: "All who have died without a knowledge of this gospel, who would have received it if they had been permitted to tarry, shall be heirs of the celestial kingdom of God; Also all that shall die henceforth without a knowledge of it, who would have received it with all their hearts, shall be heirs of that kingdom; For I, the Lord, will judge all men according to their works, according to the desire of their hearts.

    And I also beheld that all children who die before they arrive at the years of accountability are saved in the celestial kingdom of heaven" (D&C 137:7-9).
23. The nineteenth-century, British art historian, John Ruskin, wrote: "Great nations write their autobiographies in three manuscripts, the book of their deeds, the book of their words and the book of their art. Not one of these books can be understood unless we read the other two, but of the three, the only quite trustworthy one is the last. . . . [T]he policy of a nation may be

compelled, and, therefore, not indicative of its true character. Its words may be false, while yet the race remains unconscious of their falsehood; and no historian can assuredly detect the hypocrisy. But art is always instinctive; and the honesty of pretense of it is open to the day" ("Preface to St. Mark's Rest," *The Works of John Ruskin*, ed. E.T. Cook & Alexander Wedderburn [London: George Allen, 1906], 203).

24. C. S. Lewis, *Prince Caspian* (New York: HarperCollins Publishing, n.d.), 125.
25. Jeffrey R. Holland, "Songs Sung and Unsung," *Ensign* (May 2017), 50.
26. Stephen R. Covey, *The Divine Center* (Salt Lake City: Deseret Book, 1993), 3; also *The Seven Habits of Highly Effective People* (New York: Simon & Schuster, 1989), 38.
27. Ezra Taft Benson, "Born of God," *Ensign* (Nov. 1985), 14.
28. Music, especially song, is important in time and eternity. Anciently, Lehi heard "numberless concourses of angels in the attitude of singing and praising their God" (1 Ne. 1:8). In this dispensation the Lord has declared: "My soul delighteth in the song of the heart; yea, the song of the righteous is a prayer unto me, and it shall be answered with a blessing upon their heads" (D&C 25:12). In a note I wrote to myself a number of years ago, I compared membership in The Church of Jesus Christ of Latter-day Saints to a song composed after the manner of a Bach toccata and fugue, the most famous of which is his *Toccata and Fugue in d minor*, BWV 565, that can be heard on any number of internet sites.

    A toccata is a free style, rhapsodic composition. A fugue by contrast has a very tight, disciplined structure consisting of one theme that is expressed in all the "voices" of the fugue. Each note has to be played or sung in exact order at the right time for the composition to be harmonious. Conversion can be like a toccata prelude which is rhapsodic and free flowing, without the obvious form we hear in the fugue that follows. As we're learning so many new things, as it begins to dawn on us how intimate our relationship with God can be, the excitement of hope bubbles up in us. As the missionaries teach us the loving word of Christ, we do indeed "taste that the Lord is gracious" (1 Pet. 2:2-3). What is likely not evident when we learn the first principles of the gospel, the reality of prophets of God in this day and age, or the word of wisdom—what is not likely evident is the pattern of membership. Just as the toccata introduces the fugue, conversion introduces us to the first small bits of the fulness of the gospel in which the patterns and discipline of membership, i.e., the forms of godly discipleship, are to be found.

Our first callings begin the fugal discipline of discipleship. The part we're given to sing/play is usually not difficult, though it may seem so to us at first, but it allows us to become acclimated to the structured pattern of discipleship. As we progress and receive more challenging callings, we have to exercise greater discipline to keep all aspects of our lives in harmony. The more exactly we perform our roles, the more harmonious the song.

Indeed, the gospel is like a fugue with many voices:

Now, what do we hear in the gospel which we have received? A voice of gladness! A voice of mercy from heaven; and a voice of truth out of the earth; glad tidings for the dead; a voice of gladness for the living and the dead; glad tidings of great joy. How beautiful upon the mountains are the feet of those that bring glad tidings of good things, and that say unto Zion: Behold, thy God reigneth! As the dews of Carmel, so shall the knowledge of God descend upon them! (D&C 128:19).

In a typical Church ward, as in a Bach fugue, there are many voices in different organizations and activities, but one theme, the Lord's mission statement to bring to pass the immortality and eternal life of man" (Moses 1:39). The song cycle sung includes "the song of the Lamb" (Rev. 15:3), "the songs of everlasting joy" (see Isa. 35:10; D&C 45:71; 66:11, 101:18; 109:39; 133:33; Moses 7:53), and "the song of redeeming love" (Alma 5:26). The tempo is peaceful and measured: Jesus is the Prince of Peace who left His peace with us (see Isa. 9:6; John 14:27); His gospel is the gospel of peace (see Rom. 10:15; Eph. 6:15); and we are striving to come "unto a perfect man, unto the measure of the stature of the fulness of Christ" (Eph. 4:13). The abiding sentiment of this fugal song cycle is one of glad tiding of good and great joy (see Luke 2:10). In the final analysis, all voices sing, "Glory to God in the highest, and on earth peace, good will toward men" (Luke 2:14).

Thus, membership in the Lord's Church is much like singing in the choir performing a fugal composition. Our mission is to discipline our service to harmonize our individual talents and our individual callings to assist the Lord in His great mission-theme. (Paul challenged us to "Live in harmony with one another" (New International Version of the Bible (NIV) Rom. 12:16). We do this by publishing the good tidings of great joy that God lives, Jesus is the Christ, and They have restored Their kingdom on earth through the Prophet Joseph Smith, which Church is known as The Church of Jesus Christ of Latter-day Saints. Isaiah rhapsodized: 'How beautiful upon the mountains are the feet of him that bringeth good tidings, that publisheth peace; that bringeth good tidings of good, that publisheth salvation; that saith unto Zion, Thy God reigneth! Thy watchmen shall lift up the voice; with the voice together shall they sing: for they shall see eye to eye, when the LORD shall bring again Zion. Break forth into joy, sing together, ye waste places of Jerusalem: for the LORD hath comforted his people, he hath redeemed Jerusalem" [Isa. 52:7-9]).

The basic themes of the song cycle break down three interrelated parts, including the totality of mankind since the Fall: (1) the perfecting of the saints; (2) taking the gospel into all the world to the living who are not of our faith but who will listen to the song of the Lamb; (3) family history and temple ordinances for those who have passed into the spirit world without having heard and/or accepted the gospel.

The organization and governance of the Lord's kingdom also manifests this fugal form, a pattern Paul identified in several of his epistles. To the Corinthian saints he wrote that there is one body of Christ, i.e., one kingdom of God on the earth, but that the "body" of Christ contains many members with diverse "gifts, but the same spirit," each with an important part to play/sing for the operation of the whole body to be harmonious (see 1 Cor. 12).

What we learn as members of this great chorus of Christ, declaring the divinity of Christ and the brotherhood of man, is that we have different voices at different times, passing across the stage of mortality. At one time we may have a missionary voice, another time the voice of presidency of an auxiliary; yet another time the voice of a Primary teacher, a Boy Scout leader, a bishop, Relief Society homemaking leader, a stake president's counselor, and always a father, mother, and child.

There are, however, important constants in all the voices of the Church-choir, no matter the organizational voice we may sing: we are all children of God; we are fathers and mothers, sons and daughters; ministers to families; family history researchers, who take family names to the temple; emissaries of the gospel of Jesus Christ to the world. And it's important to remind ourselves that we're all role players in the great orchestrated plan of happiness administered through the Church. Some of the roles may seem greater than others from our ground-level view, but from the Lord's eternal perspective, I think, each role is important to the song of salvation being sung. That's why President J. Reuben Clark made the point, it's not where we serve, but how (*Improvement Era* [June 1951], 412). Moreover, it is, as Alma taught, in the small acts of life that great things are brought to pass (see Alma 37:7-8).

How do we know how well we're doing in relationship to the other voices in our families, our wards, our stakes, our Church? Several questions help in this evaluation: Is ours a harmonious or discordant voice? We're going to be off key at times, especially as we are learning a new voice and a new part, but what's the overall tenor of our performance? That's what the Lord sees and hears, I think. Are we following the director of the world-wide choir, the living Prophet, who is following the Divine director, Jesus Christ? Do we accept the counsel of our local leaders and carry out that counsel? Do we seek to ennoble others, or are we guilty of murmuring or gossiping? (Both murmuring and gossip are dissonant singing no matter how we look at it.) Are we striving to bring our ear of faith more in tune with the heavenly hallelujah? Are we feeling the song of the Holy Spirit, or are we past feeling?

How we are to internalize the correct pattern of godly discipleship (or, figuratively, sing our various parts harmoniously), how we become converted to the gospel as a whole and principles in particular, is one of the many lessons we can learn from Alma 32. Beginning in verse 27, Alma tells us to experiment upon the words of the Lord, the principles of His gospel, particularly the Atonement of Jesus Christ (see Alma 33:19-23), so that we might experience and sing the forms of godliness, feeling them deep within our souls.

29. See *DS*, 1:41.
30. M. Russell Ballard, "God Is at the Helm," *Ensign* (Nov. 2015), 25.
31. Neal A. Maxwell, "The Net Gathers of Every Kind," *Ensign* (Nov. 1980), 14.
32. "Y Students Give President Lee Manhood Award," *Deseret News* (Sept. 15, 1973), 1.

CHAPTER 6

PARABLES

Mark Turner defines parable as "the projection of story." That is, "one story is projected unto another,"[1] reminding us of the process Nephi described whereby he likened the scriptural stories unto his life and the lives of his people. In other words, he superimposed Old Testament narratives unto the life narratives of the Nephites.

Narrative is the fundamental mode in which we live; we have stories running through our minds almost all our waking hours. It is through such narratives that we establish the unity and purpose of our individual lives.[2] When we write these narratives down in a life history, for example, we try to find structure to our memories that gives meaning to our lives.

Historical Parables

The scriptures are replete with stories that illustrate gospel principles. In a *New Era* article, Elder Bruce R. McConkie told the youth of the Church,

We have in the Church an untapped, almost unknown, treasury of inspiring and faith-promoting stories. They are the best of their kind and there are thousands of them.

One reason they are the best and most inspiring faith-promoting stories is because they were selected and edited by the Lord himself. They are the ones he had, his prophets choose and place in the holy scriptures so that we would have samples before us of how to act and what to do in all the circumstances that confront us in life.

They are stories of real people who faced real problems and who solved them in a way that was pleasing to the Lord. They have been preserved for us so that we will know how to act and what to do in all the affairs of our daily lives.[3]

I call these stories of real people chronicled in the scriptures "historical parables": "historical" indicates that these are narratives from the lives of real people; "parable" because they share some qualities with poetic parables discussed in Chapter 8: *concentration* (only relevant plot elements are included); *structure* (the usual meandering of a person's life is focused into a coherent process); *image-symbols* (objects and people become representative of principles); a concrete virtual reality. Taken together, the aforementioned elements create a concentrated vision of reality for the reader. Elder Maxwell added the following to the preceding list: "Searched and likened to ourselves effectively, the scriptures can thereby '[enlarge] the memory of this people' (see Alma 37:8), emancipating us from the limitations of our own time and place. . . . If we are meek, the case studies in the scriptures help us to see our own case more clearly. In fact, it is the process of likening that results in enlarging."[4] Accordingly, the symbolism of historical, and poetic, narratives exists on several levels: one, the level of principles that may extend into several subtexts; two, the level of our personal life-narratives.[5]

The life and ministry of Jesus Christ is the most sublime of these stories, narrating as it does His supernal ministry. Indeed, the scriptures as a whole testify of His Divine Sonship and Messianic mission (see John 5:39), the narration of His Atonement, Crucifixion, and Resurrection forming the essence of the gospel (see 3 Ne. 27:13-21). The details of His life provide the perfect example for how we should comport ourselves in mortality (see 3 Ne. 18:24). Our lives, in turn, can become parables of Christ-like discipleship, mirroring His light by living a gospel-centered life—or they can languish as murky reflections of half-hearted commitment. Both aspects of discipleship and illustrated in Matthew 25.

Historical parables describe the lives of common men and women called to do uncommon works for the Lord—people such as Abraham, Moses, Lehi, Peter, Paul, Alma, Sariah, and many more. We see the human drama of mortality in their lives; we can vicariously experience how disciples through the ages have exercised the principles of righteousness, or not, in a kaleidoscope of episodes that, when studied carefully and prayerfully, parallel our own life experiences. By pondering and likening them to ourselves, historical parables can become "profitable for doctrine, for reproof, for correction, for instruction in righteousness: That the man of God may be perfect, thoroughly furnished unto all good works" (2 Tim. 3:16-17).

Sometimes historical parables conclude with a verse that explains the principle or principles informing the story. In the Bible such summary statement may be introduced by "therefore"; in the Book of Mormon the phrase "thus we see" serves the same purpose. For example, after describing one the horrific battles between Nephites and Lamanites, Alma recorded the following observation:

> While many thousands of others truly mourn for the loss of their kindred, yet they rejoice and exult in the hope, and even know, according to the promises of the Lord, that they are raised to dwell at the right hand of God, in a state of never-ending happiness.
>
> And *thus we see* how great the inequality of man is because of sin and transgression, and the power of the devil, which comes by the cunning plans which he hath devised to ensnare the hearts of men.
>
> And *thus we see* the great call of diligence of men to labor in the vineyards of the Lord; and thus we see the great reason of sorrow, and also of rejoicing—sorrow because of death and destruction among men, and joy because of the light of Christ unto life (Alma 28:12-14; emphasis added).

The word *see* invites the reader to envision the preceding story symbolically, representing something beyond the surface narrative. Each episode depicts a concrete reality that can become a virtual reality reading it intensely, i.e., reading and feeling the story until the people and their world becomes a virtual reality in the imagination.

Historical narratives can appear in several different formats. Following are brief discussions of two: 1) narratives that are dispersed throughout a chapter or book; and 2) narratives that appear in contiguous verses. The examples discussed below are, first, the life of Sariah (1 Nephi), second, the miracle of the Savior walking on water (Matt.

14:22-33; Mark 6:45-52), and, third, the confrontation between David and Goliath in Chapter 7. Even though these stories may be familiar to Latter-day Saints, rereading them with fresh eyes may reveal details that hadn't previously registered in our awareness. For example, focus on the story, not on scriptural cross-references or any other references. Just the story! Try to experience each narrative vicariously, reading intensively. It may not happen the first, or even the second, try; the scriptures do not give up their inner dynamic without diligent effort on the part of the reader. Praying to be inspired by the Holy Spirit to lead us inside each narrative is always the correct course for researching the scriptures. Keep in mind, the Lord has included every story in the scriptures for each of us to garner what we need at a particular moment in our lives.

Sariah

Sariah's narrative is interspersed throughout several chapters. As Lehi's wife and mother of Laman, Lemuel, Sam, Nephi, Jacob, and Joseph, Sariah led the life of a godly woman faced with monumental challenges. In their *Commentary on the Book of Mormon*, George Reynolds and Janne M. Sjodahl suggest that her name means "of extreme beauty and force; its roots being Sara, a princess, and *Jah* or *Iah*, or Jehovah, thus meaning a princess of Jehovah, a most fitting name for the mother of a multitude of nations"[6] While few specifics of her life were recorded, there is sufficient circumstantial evidence to build a parable of a woman who can teach us about living in our world today.

For the first part of her life, Sariah's world was Palestine c. 600 B.C. She was the wife of a successful merchant and undoubtedly enjoyed prominence in the community.[7] Nephi described her as a good mother: "I, Nephi, having been born of goodly parents. . . . (1 Ne. 1:1). This is deep praise, because often in the scriptures the word *good* can be synonymous with "godly." I imagine Sariah as the type of Jewish wife and mother whom I have known: she did not sit in the background of her husband's life; rather she asserted herself into the life of her family and would have been intensely involved with her children. Since Lehi was a merchant, we can assume that he traveled extensively,[8] in which case the early education of their children (social, some intellectual, and possibly some religious education) likely fell to Sariah to teach them "somewhat in all the learning of [their] father" (1 Ne. 1:1).

Her stable life changed abruptly when Lehi had a vision in which the Lord told him to take his family and leave their home for parts unknown to them at first. Along with her family, Sariah became a desert nomad, then a seafarer, and finally the settler of a land far away, not unlike our pioneer ancestors, many of whom sailed from Europe to the United States then walked the central plains and mountains to reach the land seen by the Prophet Joseph, the high desert of the Salt Lake Valley, many dispersing thereafter to settle the intermountain West. We may ask ourselves, what qualities sustained her through such monumental disruption of her life?

From Lehi's iron-rod vision we know Sariah was a woman of faith: he saw her accept the gospel by partaking of the fruit from the tree of life (see 1 Ne. 8:14). She had a strong testimony and was neither distracted nor dissuaded by the scorn heaped upon her by the people in the great and spacious building (see 1 Ne. 8:26-27). Like Paul centuries later, she was "not ashamed of the gospel of Christ" (Rom. 1:16).

As was the case with so many pioneer women, she possessed an inner strength so that when the Lord told her husband to leave, she supported him and they left *post haste*. Theirs was not to be a fathers' and sons' overnight, or a mothers' and daughters' sleepover, or even a three-day trek; it was serious business: the complete dislocation into the unknown. In today's parlance, they became homeless refugees, but they were led by the Lord. The conditions of the journey were difficult, and Sariah, a woman accustomed to affluence, would have been taxed physically, emotionally, and spiritually.

Despite the loss of her home and the incumbent trials of the dislocation, we do not read that she complained until she "supposed that [her sons] had perished in the wilderness." Then the mountain of concerns she had harbored inside came tumbling down on her. Can you hear her reproving her husband for sending their sons off to retrieve the brass plates from Laban? "You and your visions!" (see 1 Ne. 5:2). She was afraid for her boys, all of them, but faith won out over fear, for when Lehi assured her that the Lord had indeed spoken to him, and that their sons would be all right, she was comforted. In fact, when they returned, she gave a powerful testimony of the Lord's hand in what had transpired (see 1 Ne. 5:4-6, 8). This was a humble, faithful woman; pride did not hinder her from witnessing the truth.

Her's was not an ideal family; once they started their journey, acrimony erupted: Laman and Lemuel were fiercely hostile, primarily toward their younger brother, Nephi, but also questioning their father's inspiration. They beat and bound Nephi in the wilderness, leaving him as dinner for wild animals, even planning to kill both their father and their brother. This was the family situation Sariah faced. Imagine the gamut of emotions she must have felt! "Why do my sons act this way?" "Am I a terrible mother? (Nephi certainly did not think so.) "Have I done something to offend God?" Did she utter the same lament as the Prophet Joseph in Liberty Jail? "Oh God, where art thou" (D&C 121:1). She loved her husband, and each of her sons: Nephi recorded that upon their return from obtaining the plates from Laban, "My mother, Sariah, was exceedingly glad, for she truly had mourned because of us" (1 Ne. 5:1), the word *us* including all her sons, not just Sam and Nephi.

While Sariah experienced the challenge and joy of bearing two more sons on the journey, her life was not to be lived happily ever after. Laman's and Lemuel's jealousy and animosity toward Nephi, and their father, escalated until it finally caused both Sariah and Lehi to experience grief and sorrow unto sickness in their later years. How many mothers have had similar experiences?

While little was directly recorded about Sariah, much is said and even more implied about that marvelous woman. We have here a parable—concentrating upon the significant episodes in her life; structured by a pattern of faithfulness and strength. And what emerges is the portrait of a faithful, sagacious wife and mother meeting extraordinary challenges in her life. Those men and women today who face seemingly insurmountable challenges can draw strength from the parable of her life. Even those who seem the greatest in the kingdom face great challenges. Sariah's example encourages us to have faith in every footstep, even when it takes all the faith we can muster to put one foot in front of the other and move forward. No one sails through life on a smooth sea, yet each of us can find our way home to Heavenly Father if we persevere and let Him guide us. We just want to remember, the Savior is prepared to talk with and guide us on our stormy sea and calm the turbulent waters, if we reach out to Him with faith in prayer.

The Miracle of the Savior Walking on the Sea of Galilee

This miraculous story spans only a few verses. The drama played out on the wind-whipped Sea of Galilee. Imagine being in a boat on a large body of water with heavy waves tossing it around like a cork. Jesus had sent His Apostles ahead and it was now the fourth watch, between 3 a.m. and daybreak; visibility was very limited. On the boat, there was only a lamp giving off faint light. Because the men in the boat were experienced sailing those waters, they knew how treacherous such winds could be. Understandably, they were anxious, when suddenly they saw the form of what looked like a man walking toward the boat, *on the surface of the turbulent water!*

The unfolding drama took place on several levels: for one, centered on the Apostles' fear of the turbulent water and, for another, of seeing something for which their human experience had not prepared them—humans do not walk on water! Because their faith was young and still tenuous, they momentarily reverted to the superstitious belief in apparitions that is characteristic of folk belief around the world. "It is a spirit; and they cried out in fear" (Matt. 14:26). When the Savior called to them, "Be of good cheer; it is I," their courage was buoyed, their perspective changed, and their eyes of faith opened to the vision of a higher, albeit incomprehensible, reality.

A second level of the drama involves Peter's impetuous, yet courageous display of faith. Emboldened by recognizing his Master, Peter asked, and was invited, to come unto the Savior by doing as He was doing, namely by walking out to Him on the surface of the water. Peter had a budding faith that all things were possible in the Savior, so, for a short distance, he walked on the water toward Jesus. So long as Peter kept his eye singularly focused on his Master, all was well. But, like most of us, the instant Peter became distracted by turbulent waves in the midst of his walk of faith, out of fear he took his eye off Christ. It was not because he could not "do likewise"; rather he allowed the vision of the world to intrude into his field of vision. The "rational" worldly perspective labeled such an act as contrary to the laws of nature and, therefore, undoable by a mere mortal.

At times, in every life, storms of one fashion or another arise and we feel inundated. All too quickly we can take our eye off the Savior, look at the turmoil around us, concluding that we just cannot do what it takes to resolve the problem facing us. Our faith wavers; we do not feel we can walk on the waters of adversity. Like Peter, who went as far toward the Savior as His faith would take him before his Master reached down to lift him, when a challenge swirls around us that takes us to the edge of and beyond our faith at a moment in time, the Savior promises to reach down and lift us so that we don't drown in the murk of the world. And that is part of our schooling during mortality: each day people face such tests to one degree or another, for it is the common lot of man to experience opposites and opposition (see 2 Ne. 11-12).[9]

This miracle, read as a parable, presents a powerful question to each person: Are we "of little faith," doubting the potential of our faith? One facet of the narrative's moral is not that we will walk on water, for the Lord will not direct anyone to show off the powers of heaven. The lesson gleaned is, if we simply manifest minute faith, when He calls us to do something, anything is possible. Another facet is to not be frightened away from our faith when we encounter something for which we have no previous experience. The Lord has promised to be with the prayerful always (see D&C 75:11).

Historical parables in the scriptures can teach us much in the surface text; they teach us even more when we liken them unto ourselves. When we, with informed imagination, probe between the lines of the story and below its surface, we may well discover the light of heaven informing events.

Poietic Parables

Similar to historical parables, *poietic*[10] parables illustrate principles of the gospel with the intent that we liken the story and its underlying truths unto ourselves. In both types of parables, the impact of the likening process is fortified if, while discerning the deeper vision embedded in the story, we are able to experience it "feelingly." Like any other aspect of our gospel studies, what we gain by studying a parable can grow with time and experience: from a first reading of a story we may draw an intellectual analogy to our lives; a later reading may yield a more perceptive analogy due to things we have experienced in the interim. Scriptural parables, especially *poietic* parables, continue to reveal levels of truth whenever we engage them in serious study.

While objects and characters in a *poietic* parable may have counterparts in the "real" world, the plausibility of these parables exists within themselves, not as they relate to actual persons or events external to the narrative—thus the word *poietic* from the Greek word *poiein* (ποίειν) meaning "to make, create, compose."[11] Five seminal traits create the reality of *poietic* parables: brevity, setting, realistic imagery, symbolism, and plot. *Brevity* describes the short, highly concentrated, tightly constructed nature of *poietic* parables, resulting in the heightened role each word plays in creating the overall vision of the story. The temptation is present to simply scan such stories; however, reading them slowly and reflectively, savoring each word, will yield far greater understanding.

The word *world* refers to the organic unity of the parable,[12] i.e., to the setting an author of a parable creates in which everything placed into that world makes sense, even things that ostensibly may seem counterintuitive. A *poietic* world is, therefore, a self-contained cosmos of moral laws, often the same as the world in which the author lives.[13] Were the author of the parable to introduce a figure completely foreign to the world he created, it would disrupt the action and likely the moral of the tale. Even for a short *poietic* narrative, "world" is appropriate because the plot usually takes place in one "world." Grasping the world of the parable is essential for understanding the message intended.

Poietic parables are "the natural expression of a mind that sees truth in concrete pictures rather than conceives it in abstractions."[14] Their concreteness manifests itself in the images used that are generally taken from people, places, and objects the reader would consider to be true to the life and time of their settings. Such *images* are termed "*realistic*," meaning, according to Aristotle, they "represent things as they were or are, or as they are said or thought to be or have been, [and] as they ought to be."[15] The suggestion that such images may also represent things "as they ought to be" alludes to the symbolism created. Lehi's brother Jacob put Aristotle's thought into its proper perspective: "the Spirit speaketh the truth. . . .Wherefore, it speaketh of things as they really are, and of things as they really will be" (Jacob 4:13).

Symbols and symbolism are discussed in Chapter 3, using Elder Orson F. Whitney's stated belief, based on Moses 6:63, that the universe is built on symbols, the lesser representing the greater. The Victorian Scottish philosopher, essayist, historian and teacher, Thomas Carlyle, agreed with Elder Whitney, writing in his *Sartor Resartus*, which was highly influential on American literature, that "the Universe is one vast Symbol of God." Thus, "In the Symbol proper, . . . there is ever, more or less, distinctly and directly, some embodiment and revelation of the Infinite; the Infinite is made to blend itself with the Finite, to stand visible, and as it were, attainable there."[16] We will see the efficacy of these statements in the parable of the rural schoolroom below.

Plot, or action, is all important, revealing the true character and beliefs of the central figure, and occasionally secondary figure.

"He Took My Lickin' for Me"

To illustrate the *poietic* principle discussed above, following is a story President Hinckley told in a First Presidency Christmas broadcast. He described it as "something of a parable."

> Years ago there was a little one-room schoolhouse in the mountains of Virginia where the boys were so rough that no teacher had been able to handle them. A young, inexperienced teacher applied, and the old director scanned him and asked: 'Young fellow, do you know that you are asking for an awful beating?

Every teacher that we have had here for years has had to take one.'

'I will risk it,' he replied.

The first day of school came, and the teacher appeared for duty. One big fellow named Tom whispered: 'I won't need any help with this one. I can lick him myself.'

The teacher said, "Good morning, boys, we have come to conduct school." They yelled and made fun at the top of their voices. "Now, I want a good school, but I confess that I do not know how unless you help me. Suppose we have a few rules. You tell me, and I will write them on the blackboard."

One fellow yelled, "No stealing!" Another yelled, "On time." Finally, ten rules appeared on the blackboard.

"Now," said the teacher, "a law is not good unless there is a penalty attached. What shall we do with one who breaks the rules?"

"Beat him across the back ten times without his coat on," came the response from the class.

"That is pretty severe, boys. Are you sure that you are ready to stand by it?" Another yelled, "I second the motion," and the teacher said, "All right, we will live by them! Class, come to order!'

In a day or so, "Big Tom" found that his lunch had been stolen. The thief was located—a little hungry fellow, about ten years old. "We have found the thief and he must be punished according to your rule—ten stripes across the back. Jim, come up here!" the teacher said.

The little fellow, trembling, came up slowly with a big coat fastened up to his neck and pleaded, "Teacher, you can lick me as hard as you like, but please, don't take my coat off!"

"Take your coat off," the teacher said. "You helped make the rules!"

"Oh, teacher, don't make me!" He began to unbutton, and what did the teacher see? The boy had no shirt on, and revealed a bony little crippled body.

"How can I whip this child?" he thought. "But I must, I must do something if I am to keep this school." Everything was quiet as death.

"How come you aren't wearing a shirt, Jim?"

He replied, "My father died and my mother is very poor. I have only one shirt and she is washing it today, and I wore my brother's big coat to keep me warm."

The teacher, with rod in hand, hesitated. Just then "Big Tom" jumped to his feet and said, "Teacher, if you don't object, I will take Jim's licking for him."

"Very well, there is a certain law that one can become a substitute for another. Are you all agreed?"

Off came Tom's coat, and after five strokes the rod broke! The teacher bowed his head in his hands and thought, "How can I finish this awful task?" Then he heard the class sobbing, and what did he see? Little Jim had reached up and caught Tom with both arms around his neck. "Tom, I'm sorry that I stole your lunch, but I was awful hungry. Tom, I will love you till I die for taking my licking for me! Yes, I will love you forever!"[17]

Brief and concise, consisting of only 592 words, the concentrated story moves forward with a minimum of detail. Much is left to the reader's imagination. The images, the setting in rural Virginia classroom (It could be anywhere, couldn't it?), the rowdy students, the young teacher, all these elements depict a *plausible* setting of things as they might have been at some moment in the past. The entire narrative quickly becomes a virtual reality in the reader's or listener's imagination.

The author's intent reveals itself most clearly in the movement of the plot that creates dramatic tension and anticipation on several levels. First is the question of what is going to happen to the teacher? Will the boys run him off like all the others? Next are the rules! The reader senses something is going to happen to test the rules and the resolve of the rule makers. Third, that test comes in the drama of Tom's stolen lunch—Tom, the ringleader of the boys, the rowdiest of the rowdies, the schoolyard bully. The reader anticipates ultimate revenge: Tom will want to extract his pound of flesh from the perpetrator for this affront to his dignity and power. The punishment in the classroom will only be a prelude to the much harsher punishment outside. Unfortunately, some of this story rings true as a symbol for contemporary situations that many, all too many, children face in schoolrooms and schoolyards today.

We soon learn that the guilty party is Jim, the least of the class, physically and socially. We hear and feel his embarrassment and impoverished state. Perhaps we want to hug and protect him, but we can't. (It is only a story after all, isn't it?) He helped make the rules and he has to live by them, just like everyone else. It is a heart-wrenching scene. Even though he wishes he didn't have to, the teacher has to carry out the punishment to satisfy the demands of justice.

As the young teacher is about to exact the punishment, to our surprise, Tom intervenes. His heart is deeply stirred by Jim's plight. Tom suddenly has compassion for the skinny little boy who he intuitively understands had taken his lunch out of desperate hunger. He will take the punishment for Jim. By the time the teacher breaks his switch over Tom's back, Jim had flung his arms around the big boy's neck and told him he would love him forever for taking his licking. Sobbing now, the others in the classroom realize the significance of what they were watching. (When President Hinckley told this story, I saw many in the congregation watching the broadcast with tears streaking their cheeks.) This is the resolution of all levels of the dramatic tension and anticipation in the story. The reader knows Jim will not face retribution outside the schoolhouse; he also knows the teacher will more than survive in the schoolroom.

When you read this parable the first time, did you feel Jim's humiliation for being so poor he only had one shirt to wear? What about Tom's sudden and mighty change of heart? His willingness to take Jim's punishment for him? The emotions we feel are what such stories are designed to draw out of the reader, reaching into the heart so that we feel the narration as if we are living the plot line, to live in the world of the story for a moment of our time. Just such involvement is the intent of *poietics* which creates a virtual reality in the reader's imagination. If this were all we had of the story, it would teach a great lesson in compassion and challenge all who read it to be more merciful toward those less fortunate. But this isn't all!

After having told the story, President Hinckley drew, with Apostolic vision, from a subtext of the parable's symbolism the transcendent significance of the parable's vision, likening it to the plan of salvation. "To lift a phrase from this simple story," he said, "Jesus, my Redeemer, has taken 'my licking for me,' and yours for you. Declared the prophet Isaiah: 'Surely he hath borne our griefs, and carried our sorrows: . . . He was wounded for our transgressions, he was bruised for our iniquities: the chastisement of our peace was upon him; and with the stripes we are healed' (Isa. 53:4-5)."[18]

This is the power of *poietic* parable, on and below the surface of the story.

The Parables of Jesus Christ

For most Latter-day Saints and other Christians, the word *parable* elicits thoughts of Jesus' memorable stories that most of us learned as children. They are compact, ranging in length from one to twenty-two verses, tightly structured in parallelisms. Through the characters, plots, narrative direction, and settings of His *poietic* parables, the Savior gave concrete form to the principles of eternal life, which embody "the mysteries of the kingdom of heaven" (Matt. 13:11). ("Mysteries may be defined as a truth which cannot be known except by revelation," said Elder Harold B. Lee.[19]) Jesus' parables have been described as "earthly stories with a heavenly meaning."[20]

One of the numerous paradoxes of the gospel is that parables both reveal and conceal. Jesus gave concrete form to the mysteries in His narratives because He knew the faithful would see below the surface story and discern the truths layered in them—not all at once, but gradually. He told those accompanying Him, "For verily I say unto you, That many prophets and righteous men have desired to see those things which ye see, and have not seen them; and to hear those things which ye hear, and have not heard them" (Matt. 13:17). Those with abiding faith will, with the help of the Holy Spirit, perceive the "reality of what we do not see" (Heb. 11:1). For those with little or no faith in Christ, the stories remain mysterious: "Therefore speak I to them in parables: because they seeing see not; and hearing they hear not, neither do they understand" (Matt. 13:13).

Because of the near universal vision each parable expresses, the arc of their inspiration and influence extends from the immediacy of Palestine at the meridian of time to the twenty-first century and beyond, each century, each person finding special meaning in them that describes their immediate circumstances. Christ's Palestinian audience did not have the luxury of the printed story to study, as do we; they either grasped their immediate meaning or they did not, depending on whether they had faith in the Savior's divine mission. For the early converts, the parables were calls for immediate action to higher thoughts and conduct in their daily lives—to think and see the world through eyes from which the scales of ignorance were removed by the light of the gospel He taught. Since they had no texts to study, they relied on their memories to collect and order the gospel message, and ancient people had prodigious memories compared to people in this technological time. But we can savor and ponder His words, searching as deeply into them as we are prepared to go, never forgetting the same message the ancient saints understood.

Given the 2,000 years between when he taught in parables and our day, we might ask why someone in the twenty-first century and beyond should be able to read and relate them to contemporary life, much less have any emotional response to them? Omnisciently, the Savior's vision spanned mortal time and He saw all who would people the earth to the end. (If Moses and Abraham were given the privilege of experiencing this vision, surely the Son of Man did also.) Thus, He taught the parables not just for Palestine at the meridian of time, but for all time, including ours, and with a little effort, we can relate to such images as the prodigal, or lost son, the lost sheep, a wedding, even a mustard seed. Moreover, we know that He exemplifies the principles of righteousness in the parables, something in which every Latter-day Saint should be deeply interested. It is one thing to read a definition of a principle, but quite another to see the principle in action and to understand the internal architecture of it.

As we read the Savior's parables, perhaps we can see more deeply into the profound, eternal ideals that form the hidden underthought of each story, which seeing can lift our thoughts from the first-century setting to our contemporary lives and on upward to God and eternal life.

Of all the questions we might ask of the Savior, the one that instigated the parable of the Good Samaritan, "What shall I do to inherit eternal life," asked by a certain lawyer, is one of the most important, and understanding the Savior's answer can help define our discipleship, discussed in Chapter 8.

Notes to Chapter 6

1. Mrk Turner, *The Literary Mind* (New York: Oxford University Press, 1996), 5, 7. Dr. Turner is Institute Professor and Professor of Cognitive Science at Case Western Reserve University, Cleveland, OH.
2. See Alastair MacIntyre, *After Virtue* (Notre Dame, IN: Notre Dame University Press, 1984), 211.
3. Bruce R. McConkie, "The How and Why of Faith-promoting Stories," *New Era (July 1978)*, https:// www. lds.org/new-era/1978/07/the-how-and-why-of-faith-promoting-stories?lang=eng.
4. Neal A. Maxwell, *Lord, Increase Our Faith* (Salt Lake City: Deseret Book, 1994), 103.
5. Living in the twenty-first century, we have the same ability to capture the Lord's vision in the narratives He has chosen to include in the body of the scriptures, to superimpose the different motion pictures presented in those narratives on our own lives in order to grow into the people He envisions us to become. When our vision of reality grows closer to His, our thoughts and actions will conform to the principles of the gospel. We are fortunate to be members of the Lord's kingdom on earth, having living prophets who act as watchmen on the tower. Elder M. Russell Ballard said, "As Apostles of the Lord Jesus Christ, it is our duty to be watchmen on the tower, warning Church members to beware of false prophets and false teachers who lie in wait to ensnare and destroy faith and testimony" ("Beware of False Prophets and False Teachers," *Ensign* [Nov. 1999], 62). Most often, like Nephi, they forewarn and caution us by likening the scriptures unto our times for our profit and awareness.
6. George Reynolds and Janne M. Sjodahl, *Commentary of the Book of Mormon*, 7 vols. (Salt Lake City: Deseret Book, 1962-1976), 1:14.
7. David G. Woolley has written a series of novels about Lehi, Sariah, and their family. His writing is assiduously researched and provides the reader with a

picture of and feeling for the time and place in which Lehi and Sariah's family lived. See particularly the first novel in the series, *Pillar of Fire* (American Fork, UT: Covenant Communications, 2000).

8. See Hugh B. Nibley, *Lehi in the Desert & The World of the Jaredites* (Salt Lake City: Bookcraft, 1952), 36-37. It is also available in a joint FARMS/Deseret Book publication. Nibley, of course, wrote extensively about the period and offered great insights into it.

9. The principle of opposites and opposition is as true in the physical universe as in morality. Matter is balanced by anti-matter into the smallest particles; positive and negative charges are part of the atomic structure.

10. See Chapter 3 for a discussion of the word *poietic*.

11. See *Liddel and Scott's Intermediate Greek-English Lexicon* (Oxford: Clarendon Press, 1994), s.v. "ΠΟΙΕΩ," imper. "ποίειν," "*poiein*" (pp. 650-51).

12. "Organic unity" is briefly discussed on pp.36-37.

13. I studied with another renown Germanist named Emil Staiger who wrote an, at the time, seminal book on *poietics* entitled *Grundbegriffe der Poetik* (*Basic Concepts of Poietics*) in which he defined "world" philosophically as "the order, the cosmos, in which something may first reveal itself" ("in dem sich etwas erst als etwas zu zeigen vermag"). That is, each of us creates our own orderly reality with a network of moral, physical, social, political, etc. laws. When we encounter something new to our established reality, we try to assimilate that new into our reality, which is another way of saying, we try to envision it within our established vision. If it fits, we accept it; if it doesn't we discard it.

14. C. H. Dodd, *The Parables of the Kingdom* (London: The Religious Book Club, 1942), 15-16.

15. Aristotle, *Poetics*, trans. Ingram Bywater (New York: Modern Library, 1954), chapter 25:10-12. Even though Aristotle was referring to tragedy, I use this quote for several reasons. One, I want to show that the principle articulated in Jacob 4:13 ("things as they really are, and . . . things as they really will be") is a principle that was in the air in the region around the eastern Mediterranean at least four to five centuries before Christ, secondly, it was an integral part of literary theory in the area at the time.

16. Thomas Carlyle, *Sartor Resartus*, Book 3, Chapter 3: Symbols; http://www.gutenberg.org/files/1051/1051-h.htm#link2HCH0003.

17. Gordon B. Hinckley, "The Wondrous and True Story of Christmas," *Ensign* (Dec. 2000), 4.

18. Op. cit.
19. *Ye are the Light of the World. Selected Sermons and Writings of President Harold B. Lee* (Salt Lake City: Deseret Book, 1974), 211; *The Teachings of Harold B. Lee*, ed. Clyde J. Williams (Salt Lake City: Deseret Book, 1998), 575.
20. William Barclay, *The Parables of Jesus* (Louisville, KY: Westminster John Knox Press, 1999), 12. While it goes beyond the scope of this study to discuss the historical development of parable interpretation in depth, following is a brief overview. The question of how to understand the Savior's parables dates back to early Christian theologians who read them as allegories, i.e., the stories, the characters, and the plots related to specific events extrinsic to the stories themselves. Modern parable interpretation began with Adolf Jülicher's *Die Gleichnisse Jesu* (*The Parables of Jesus*), published in 1886 and 1889. Jülicher went away from allegorical reading and considered the Savior's parables as vivid stories that convey a singular, unique event intended to exemplify a single idea. His methodology held sway for a number of years. Charles H. Dodd (*The Parables of the Kingdom*) represented the next major step in the evolution of methodology. He described parables as "a metaphor or simile drawn from nature or common life, arresting the hearer by its vividness or strangeness, and leaving the mind in sufficient doubt about its application to tease it into active thought" (London: The Religious Book Club, 1942, pg. 16). Consequently, he proposed that one had to have an understanding of the historical setting of each parable in order to properly grasp its meaning. A more recent trend asserts that parables ought to be read in terms of their literary qualities, their aesthetics and ontology. Dan O. Via makes this case in his book, *The Parables. Their Literary and Existential Dimension*. In the last decade of the twentieth century, cognitive science entered the picture. Mark Turner, who is quoted in Chapter 6 (Historical Parables), defined parable as "the projection of story," that is, "one story is projected unto another." Indirectly this parallels the likening process described by Nephi who sought to establish "the narrative unity" between scriptural narratives and the lives of his people (see 1 Ne. 19:23; also Alastair MacIntyre, *After Virtue*, 211).

CHAPTER 7

DAVID AND GOLIATH

In Chapter 6 we briefly discuss two historical parables: with the parable of Sariah, we pulled together the fragments of her narrative and observe a woman of great faith and courage in very trying circumstances; from the miracle of the Savior walking on water, we determine that the narratives of the Savior's miracles can often be read as historical parables. In the narrative of David and Goliath we will look at a few of the subtexts that often add an important dimension of depth to historical parables, keeping in mind Elder Orson F. Whitney's observation that the universe is built on symbols, the lesser revealing the greater, therefore, some of the seemingly insignificant images in this story become symbols of things far greater.

The confrontation between David and Goliath has become a staple image and motif for the confrontation between the little guy and the big guy, the weak against the strong. But the story reveals a profound spiritual moment and monument in world history. While it is the battle between two individuals, it also represents the archetypal battle in which every individual may engage daily to one degree or another, namely the macro-battle between good and evil that began during the Great Council in heaven.

The objective here is to see and feel our way into this well-known story. It is discussed in the present tense to establish its virtual reality concretely in the imagination.

The Scene

Below is a picture of the Elah Valley today where the young shepherd, David, will confront the giant, Goliath. Try to imagine two armies aligned against one another on opposite sides of the valley, the army of Saul on one side, the Philistines on the other. The initial difference in the two forces is Goliath who stands over nine feet tall (six cubits and a span). He descends into the valley, full of pride, challenging any man in Saul's army to meet him in single combat—winner take all. Saul's soldiers only have swords and spears to fight against this huge warrior. No modern weaponry! And they are paralyzed with fear.

Elah Valley

In the midst of Saul's army, unnoticed, stands a young shepherd, too young to be a soldier. He is talking with his older brothers, to whom he has brought provisions. Their father's name is Jesse; the young man is David. As we pan the focus of our mind's eye over to David, we notice his reaction when he hears the giant once again roar his challenge at Saul's men. While others quake, David, with more than a little indignation in his voice, asks, "Who is this uncircumcised Philistine, that he should defy the armies of the living God?" (1 Sam. 17:26). With this question, David grows in spiritual stature to the height of Michelangelo's statue of him (15 feet tall). By comparison, Goliath, at nine feet, is a spiritual pygmy.

Michelangelo's David

The difference in vision between the young shepherd and Saul's soldiers lies in the words "the armies of the living God." With the appearance of of Goliath, Saul's men have forgotten that the Lord God of Israel is standing at the head of their army; they are like Elisha's servant who could at first not see the host of heaven surrounding the battlefield whereon stood the Syrian army, until the Lord opened his eyes (see 2 Kgs. 6:15-17). Saul's army has allowed its faith to flee in the face of their fear. David's eye of faith, however, is focused singularly on his God.

Concrete Virtual Reality 1: David's Battle Preparations

Few descriptive details are found in Old Testament narratives, so any included warrant further investigation. Such is the case with David's preparations for battle. He tries on the traditional armor of a soldier, but rejects it as too cumbersome. The ways of the Lord are seldom conventional from a worldly perspective. The scriptures tell us, "And he took his staff in his hand, and chose him five smooth stones out of the brook, and put them in a shepherd's bag which he had, even in a scrip; and his sling was in his hand: and he drew near to the Philistine" (1 Sam. 17:40). He is comfortable with the sling he has used to protect his flock from wild animals, like the Good Shepherd who protects His flock. In addition to the sling, three other images stand out: the staff, the five smooth stones, and the brook.

The Staff

The image of the staff and the rod often overlap in the scriptures, significantly in Psalm 23 composed by David: "Thy rod and thy staff they comfort me" (Ps. 23:4). The staff comforts because the Good Shepherd uses it to protect and correct His flock. It is "a rod of iron." representing the word of God, with which Christ will rule when He returns the second time to the earth (see 1 Ne. 11:25; Rev. 2:27; 12:5; 19:15). The iron rod of God's word encompasses the testimony of Jesus, His gospel and its truths, and the vision of eternal life (see John 5:39). (The connotation associated with the rod and staff is also found in the image of the two-edged sword, the only weapon in the whole armor of God [see Eph. 6:17; Heb. 4:12; D&C 6:2; et al].) Symbolically, then, David carries the word of God into his battle against the force of evil, the same battle fought in heaven between the spirits loyal to Heavenly Father and Jesus Christ and those who followed Satan.

The Brook

David reaches into a small brook to choose five smooth stones. Streams are flowing or living water. In Lehi's vision, the rod of iron leads "to the fountain of living waters" representing Jehovah-Jesus Christ (see Jer. 2:13; 17:13; Ether 12:28), the love of God (see 1 Ne. 11:25), and the inspiration of the Holy Ghost (see 1 Ne. 11:21-22; John 7:38-39; 14:26). As a symbol, David, carrying the staff-word of God, reaches into the source of inspiration from the Holy Spirit for the appropriate weapon to fight the gigantic obstacle confronting the army of the living God. This could be construed as the act of prayer. There is a logic to the sequence of the symbolism here: first the word of God then the inspiration of the Holy Ghost. Elder Robert D. Hales said, "When we want to speak to God, we pray. And when we want Him to speak to us, we search the scriptures; for His words are spoken through His prophets. He will then teach us as we listen to the promptings of the Holy Spirit."[1] As members of the Lord's army, Latter-day Saints are blessed with the word of God, not only in the Old Testament and New Testament, but also in the Restoration scriptures, the Book of Mormon, the Doctrine and Covenants, and the Pearl of Great Price, allowing us to hear the words of the Lord more clearly. In addition, when we receive the gift of the Holy Spirit, we enter into a companionship with the Third Member of the Godhead, a companionship of such sacred import that we want to keep our temple-bodies cleansed to be able to discern his still, small voice, trying always to understand and heed his counsel to the best of our ability, guarding vigilantly against taking his inspiration for granted. And so, as we read this historic parable of David versus Goliath, we may see ourselves in David, battling evil every day, but never needing to be alone, for the Holy Spirit, through whom Christ manifests Himself, is always with us, if we seek him out.

Five Stones

The image of the stone carries an undertone referencing the Savior Who is "the stone of Israel" (Gen. 49:24; D&C 50:44) and "the rock of heaven" (Moses 7:53). Upon Him we are to build the sure foundation of our houses of faith (see Matt. 7:24-25; 3 Ne. 14:24-35), the construction of which begins at baptism when we take His name upon us and He adopts us into His family, thereafter to become rock-solid disciples in His kingdom.

Significantly, after Simon Bar-jona testifies to Jesus, "Thou art the Christ, the Son of the Living God," Jesus gave Simon a new name, Peter, saying: "upon this rock," the rock of revelation,[2] "I will build my church," thereupon conferring "the keys of the kingdom of heaven" upon Peter, with which to administer the affairs of His earthly kingdom as directed by the Holy Spirit. Like most names in the scriptures, especially new names, symbolism lies behind it. "Peter" comes from the Greek word *petros,* meaning "small stone" (see Matt. 16:18, footnote). With his new name, Peter was imprinted with the image of Christ (see Alma 5:19), but, compared with the Savior of mankind, he was but a small Christian. In his first epistle, Peter applied this image to all of Christ's disciples: "Ye also, as *lively stones,* are built up a *spiritual house* [the house of Israel], an holy priesthood, to offer up spiritual sacrifices, acceptable to God by Jesus Christ" (1 Peter 2:5; emphasis added). To be a lively, viz. living, stone, at least five things are requisite: 1. a testimony that Jehovah-Jesus Christ is *the Son* of the living God and, therefore, have faith in Him as the Messiah; 2. repentance unto baptism; 3. commitment to follow in His footsteps; 4. receive and remain worthy of the gift of the Holy Spirit; and 5. endure faithfully to the end of our mortal sojourn. At this time in his life, David's words attest that he possesses these attributes. By employing a stone, representative of Jehovah, "the Stone of Israel," David manifests, on a symbolic plane, that he is on Jehovah's side, that he, David, is prepared to be a lively stone in the

Lord's kingdom, and that he has faith Jehovah will be on his side in the looming epic confrontation with gigantic evil challenging the armies of the Living God. Moreover, not only is he a progenitor of Jesus Christ, as a shepherd he serves as a type of the good Shepherd Who will slay death, atoning for the sins of all mankind that all may have immortality in some degree of glory.

The narrative includes the fact that the stones are smooth. "Smooth" and "polished" relate to the progressive refinement that committed disciples undergo in life. Joseph Smith wrote of himself:

> I am like a huge, rough stone rolling down from a high mountain; and the only polishing I get is when some corner gets rubbed off by coming in contact with something else, striking with accelerated force against religious bigotry, priest-craft, lawyer-craft, doctor-craft, lying editors, suborned judges and jurors, and the authority of perjured executives, backed by mobs, blasphemers, licentious and corrupt men and women—all hell knocking off a corner here and a corner there. Thus I will become a smooth and polished shaft in the quiver of the Almighty. . . .[3]

Is this not the desire of Latter-day Saints, i.e., to become "smooth and polished" as disciples of Christ so as to be instruments in His hands to wield "the sword of the Spirit" (Eph. 6:17) in defense of all that is true and right?

This refining process can, at times, be painful as edges are smoothed, described in words of beauty and depth by Elder James E. Faust speaking about the refining process:

In the pain, the agony, and the heroic endeavors of life, we pass through a refiner's fire, and the insignificant and the unimportant in our lives can melt away like dross and make our faith bright, intact, and strong. In this way the divine image can be mirrored from the soul. It is part of the purging toll exacted of some to become acquainted with God. In the agonies of life, we seem to listen better to the faint, godly whisperings of the Divine Shepherd.

Into every life there come the painful, despairing days of adversity and buffeting. There seems to be a full measure of anguish, sorrow, and often heartbreak for everyone, including those who earnestly seek to do right and be faithful. The thorns that prick, that stick in the flesh, that hurt, often change lives which seem robbed of significance and hope. This change comes about through a refining process which often seems cruel and hard. In this way the soul can become like soft clay in the hands of the Master in building lives of faint, usefulness, beauty, and strength.

In our extremities, it is possible to become born again, born anew, renewed in heart and spirit. We no longer ride with the flow of the crowd, but instead we enjoy the promise of Isaiah to be renewed in our strength and "mount up with wings as eagles" (Isa. 40:31).

Trials and adversity can be preparatory to becoming born anew.[4]

As in all things, we can choose how we will respond in these refining moments: we can rejoice in rough edges smoothed or choose to let such experiences create even sharper edges of criticism and cynicism.

Another quality of smooth stones is that they fly truer to their intended target. A rough-edged stone is more susceptible to the capriciousness of the wind, like the winds of doctrine and the slights of men that can toss us to and fro in our spiritual lives unless our houses are built upon the rock of Christ (see Matt. 7:24-25; 3 Ne. 14:24-25; Eph. 4:14). In the battle against evil, the Lord is able to effectively use smooth, lively stones, immersed in the living waters of inspiration, to carry the battle to the adversary.[5]

The number of stones is also significant. In his book, *Unlocking the Numbers*, George M. Peacock writes that the number 5 is the number of grace. Of the stones David chooses, he says: "He knew that if he were to defeat the giant, it would be by the grace of God. . . . David slew Goliath with the first stone, but he had five in his possession. The reader . . . gets the feeling for the power by which David had conquered the giant by paying attention to the number of stones from the brook."[6]

What these observations imply is that historic parables convey more than their surface texts: through their imagery and structure, they possess depths of symbolism to be explored, each stratum of meaning offering greater insight into the narrative. When likened unto ourselves, the uncovering of each stratum offers greater insight into our personal discipleship that we can use to become more effective servants in the Lord's work.

David then approaches Goliath, prepared as no other in Saul's army; he attacks Goliath in the service of Jehovah and the Israelites, not Saul. As we know, the young shepherd slays the giant, and like all things relating to things as they really are, the person and the means defy the world's image of power.

Concrete Virtual Reality 2: Our Battles against Evil

It is not difficult to liken this story unto ourselves because we all encounter Goliaths in our lives—those seemingly insurmountable obstacles that take a variety of shapes. Counseling Aaronic Priesthood bearers, but surely also all members of the Church, President Gordon B. Hinckley said:

> There are Goliaths all around you, hulking giants with evil intent to destroy you. These are not nine-foot-tall men, but they are men and institutions that control attractive but evil things that may challenge and weaken and destroy you. Included in these are beer and other liquors and tobacco. Those who market these products would like to enslave you into their use. There are drugs of various kinds which, I am told, are relatively easy to obtain in many high schools. For those who peddle them, this is a multimillion-dollar industry, a giant web of evil. There is pornography, seductive and interesting and inviting. It has become a giant industry, producing magazines, films, and other materials designed to take your money and lead you toward activities that would destroy you.[7]

The paradox is, our challenging mountain may be a molehill for someone else. Challenges seem to be individually tailored so the Lord can show us our weaknesses that we might, first, be humble, and, second, be made strong in our weaknesses (see Ether 12:27, 37).

In our effort to overcome our Goliaths, David's example can mentor us. He has the innocence of someone who does not know something cannot be done. Why? Because he has faith that he can accomplish any righteous endeavor through the Lord, and in the Elah Valley, slaying the idolatrous Philistine is a righteous cause. He knows he has killed both a bear and a lion with his sling, and to him, Goliath represents no greater a challenge than those wild beasts. So, because of his trust in Jehovah, he slings the stone. His is the extraordinary feat of someone who was ordinary in the world's view but extraordinary in the sight of God. In the eternal scheme of things, our challenges may seem insignificant when compared with David's, but ours may be every bit as important for us and our posterity. President Hinckley counseled:

> It is almost impossible to entirely avoid exposure to their products. You see these materials on all sides. But you need not fear if you have the slingshot of truth in your hands. You have been counseled and taught and advised. You have the stones of virtue and honor and integrity to use against these enemies who would like to conquer you. Insofar as you are concerned, you can hit them "between the eyes," to use a figurative expression. You can triumph over them by disciplining yourselves to avoid them. . . .
>
> You are a son of God. You have His power within you to sustain you. You have the right to ministering angels about you to protect you. Do not let Goliath frighten you. Stand your ground and hold your place, and you will be triumphant. As the years pass, you will look back with satisfaction upon the battles you have won in your individual lives. . . .

When temptation comes your way, name that boastful, deceitful giant "Goliath!" and do with him as David did to the Philistine of Gath.[8]

Concrete, Virtual Reality 3: The Cosmic War for the Souls of Men

On yet another symbolic level, the confrontation in a Palestinian Valley can also be seen as the rejoining of the cosmic battle between good and evil that began in heaven. The battle centers around two diametrically opposed plans of salvation. In the Grand Council in Heaven, our Father presented His plan, preserving, even celebrating, man's moral agency "to act for themselves and not be acted upon" to choose between good or evil, virtue or vice, liberty and eternal life or captivity and the power of the devil (see 2 Ne. 2:26-27). The Father's First-born Son, Jehovah-Jesus Christ, championed this plan and volunteered to condescend to earth as the Savior of the world, whereby man would be redeemed from his sins, thereby glorifying His Father. The other plan, proposed by Lucifer, the son of the morning, would have abrogated man's agency to choose by forcing him to take the direct path back to heaven and he, Lucifer, would retain the glory for himself, effectively supplanting Heavenly Father (see Moses 4:13).

When the Father chose His Beloved Son, Lucifer's pride could not tolerate what he chose to perceive as rejection, and he rebelled against the Father's plan, somehow convincing one-third of the host of heaven to join him, perhaps because they wanted everything done for them. (Elder Neal A. Maxwell incisively described the Lucifer's posturing: "Notice the ego dripping from only three lines: two me's and four I's. those vertical pronouns are usually accompanied by unbending knees."[9]) A great battle of words ensued, with the archangel Michael, destined to becoming the first man Adam, leading those who accepted the Father's plan against and defeating the minions of Lucifer (see Rev. 12:7-9), who became Satan, meaning adversary, a role he and his followers have played since the beginning of mortal time.

In slaying Goliath, David defeated an idolatrous people opposed to Israel and Israel's God. The Philistines were a people who transgressed and trampled on the first four laws of the Ten Commandments. Interestingly, Goliath's name means "uncovered," "removed," evoking the memory of Satan who was stripped of his glory and exiled from heaven. Like Satan, who is able to hold nations in his grip, Goliath held the army of Israel captive in their own fear until the forebear of the Good Shepherd confronted him. As Isaiah recorded of Lucifer, perhaps the soldiers of Israel looked upon Goliath in defeat and said, "Is this the man that made the earth to tremble that did shake kingdoms?" (Isa. 14:16).

The Garden of Eden

The cosmic battle ignited in heaven was rejoined in the Garden of Eden, the outcome of which initiated man into his mortal probation. What happened in the Garden also previews the outcome in the Valley of Elah.

In the Garden, we see Heavenly Father and Jesus Christ descend from the Celestial Kingdom to mentor Adam and Eve; Adam and Eve in their innocence, and Satan in his fallen state. Significantly, as noted above, Adam is Michael who led the host of heaven in defending the Father's plan against Lucifer (see D&C 27:11; 128:21). Though we know nothing of Eve before the Garden, we can reasonably assume that she was Michael-Adam's equal in defending truth and right. It would take two such courageous champions of the plan to accomplish what had to be done in the Garden in which state the Lord's plan of salvation was in a condition of inertia, as Lehi explained:

> And now, behold, if Adam had not transgressed he would not have fallen, but he would have remained in the garden of Eden. And all things which were created must have remained in the same state in which they were after they were created; and they must have remained forever, and had no end.
>
> And they would have had no children; wherefore they would have remained in a state of innocence, having no joy, for they knew no misery; doing no good, for they knew no sin (2 Ne. 2:22-23).

Some act was needed to set the Lord's plan of salvation in motion, advancing Adam and Eve from their paradisiacal existential state of innocence to the mortal sphere where "there is an opposition in all things," because "if not so . . . righteousness could not be brought to pass, neither wickedness, neither holiness nor misery, neither good nor bad. Wherefore, all things must needs be a compound in one; wherefore, if it should be one body it must needs remain as dead, having no life neither death, nor corruption nor incorruption, happiness nor misery, neither sense nor insensibility" (2 Ne. 2:11).

In His infinite wisdom, the Lord gave the Garden-of-Eden Adam and Eve two mutually exclusive commandments: one, to multiply and replenish the earth and, two, not to partake of the fruit of the tree of knowledge of good and evil (see Gen. 1:18; 3:15; Moses 4:21). With the commandment to multiply and replenish the earth, there was no alternative, therefore, to not keep the commandment was to transgress the law and sin (see 1 John 3:4), a commandment having ultimate ramifications for the fundamental sociality of the kingdom, namely the family unit. It was, and is, eternal in nature. However, from the little we know about them, it seems that, in their naïve state, Adam and Eve lacked the understanding to fulfill this commandment.

The second commandment, to not eat of the fruit of the tree of knowledge of good and evil, had an alternative: they could exercise moral agency, the essential principle of God's plan of salvation, and choose to eat the fruit, or not. There were two possible outcomes: if they did not eat the fruit, they alone would remain in the terrestrial state of the Garden, not having children (see Lehi quote above). Should they choose to eat the fruit, on the other hand, the Lord told them, "thou shalt surely die" (Gen. 2:17; Alma 12:23; Moses 3:17; Abr. 5:13). With what we have in the scriptures, it is impossible to know whether they understood what "die" meant. In any case, from an eternal perspective, the second commandment was proximate, relating to the specific and immediate state in which Adam and Eve found themselves. Despite what Nicene Christianity may say, this second commandment was a lesser commandment that contravened the first.

Once the first couple partook of the fruit, the Lord's plan moved forward and His great mission of salvation began. Adam and Eve reached into their latent godliness to exercise their agency, from what we know, for the first time, choosing to bring children, spiritual children of God, into the world and raise them in families. Once her eyes were opened, Eve recognized the ramifications of their choice and told Adam, "Were it not for our transgression we never should have had seed, and never should have known good and evil, and the joy of our redemption, and the eternal life which God giveth unto all the obedient" (Moses 5:11). The great irony with eternal ramifications is that exactly what Satan tried to block in heaven, namely moral agency, he provoked into activity by tempting Adam and Eve to partake of the fruit of the tree of knowledge. Thus, in exercising their moral agency, they chose the good of advancing to mortality rather than the evil of supporting Satan's plan to abrogate man's agency and remaining in their idyllic innocence.

After the first couple had eaten the fruit, Elohim and Jehovah returned. Knowing what had happened, the Father called Satan out of hiding. What transpired thereafter bears on the story of David and Goliath. When Satan threatened the spiritual survival of all the sons and daughters of Adam and Eve, Heavenly Father told him: "I shall put enmity between thee and the woman, between thy seed and her seed; and he shall bruise thy head, and thou shalt bruise his heel" (Moses 4:21; Gen. 3:15).

"Bruise his heel"

When walking, the heel is the first part of the foot to encounter the ground. Because, in the scriptures, a person's spirit life is often described as walking,[10] the Lord has counseled all who would be His disciples to have their "feet shod with the preparation of the gospel of peace" (Eph. 6:15; D&C 27:16). In this image taken from the armor-of-God analogy, Paul likely pictured the heavy Roman boot worn by soldiers, most people in Palestine at the time wore sandals. Slipping out of sandals happens frequently, both literally and figuratively. Since it is the spiritual slippage which interests us, let's consider the types of soil that might our heel might impact using the Savior's parable of the soils.

If we were to slip out of our gospel-of-peace sandal while on the path of righteousness, soft, fertile soil would cushion our heel—the kind of soil in which the word of God easily takes root (see Matt. 13:23). Such slips might be the small things that momentarily slow our progress, such as lack of focus on our destination and callings. If quickly corrected, we are able to slip our foot back into the sandal and continue our walk of faith.

Veering off on to any other path than the Lord's, the soil is quite different. We might find ourselves walking on soil containing the abundant thorns and thistles that choke out the word of God (see Matt. 13:22). Anyone who has ever gotten a nettle lodged in their foot, especially the heel, knows it hides just below the surface of the skin and festers. If it isn't dug out, it irritates with every step taken until it hurts enough that people limp to avoid stepping down on the spot where the nettle is located. Allowed to remain there, it may become inflamed with infection. We could liken these thistles to the noxious little irritants of worldliness that get under a person's skin and, all too often, are allowed to grow into more serious spiritual wounds. Such wounds could be mitigated if the little spur were dug out and disposed of immediately with repentance.

Another type of soil defining the paths of worldliness contains stones hidden under a very thin layer of topsoil, the type of soil in which the word of God puts down only shallow roots and dies in the heat of the summer sun (see Matt. 13:20-21). Some may be deceived into thinking this soil has exciting possibilities and they venture on to it. If anyone, however, has a heel slip out of a sandal on this type of soil, he will remember the breathtaking pain, often followed by a bruised heel. This can be compared to the painful events that can occur in a person's life if he chooses to go his own way on one of the myriad deceptively attractive but spiritually harmful paths of sins rather than remaining on the path the Savior trod for man. Such overstepping of the bounds the Lord has set often begins in the imagination, when one dwells on an inappropriate image. Allowed to inflate its seductive, pernicious program in the mind, without conscious intervention, such images can gain addictive control and foster actions that can cause excruciating pain and irreparable damage to person and family.

Satan also uses circumstances we do not choose to entice us on to the stony soil: for example, the inexplicable death of a loved one, the accident with lasting injuries, and the like. Many rise above the temptation, others blame the Lord, questioning Him and He becomes "a stone of stumbling and . . . a rock of offence" to them (Isa. 8:14; 1 Peter 2:8; 2 Ne. 18:14). Elder Maxwell wrote: "Rocks of offense or stones of stumbling keep the proud from making spiritual progress. No less destructive is what might be called the gravel of grumpiness, which keeps us off balance and annoyingly turns ankles. Even though we do not fully fall or stumble, we progress more slowly, painfully, and fitfully. The meek, however, make stepping-stones of stumbling blocks."[11] Because of the victory in the epic heavenly battle, it is our inalienable right to choose how we will respond to such events.

The healing process for a spiritually bruised heel is repentance, beginning with the sacrifice of a broken heart and contrite spirit (see 3 Ne. 9:20; D&C 20:37). Again Elder Maxwell: "The real act of personal sacrifice is not now nor ever has been placing an animal on the altar. Instead, it is a willingness to put the animal that is in us upon the altar—then willingly watch it be consumed! Such is the 'sacrifice unto [the Lord] of a broken heart and contrite spirit.'"[12] Without such repentance, we run the risk of bruising our heel so often that we become inured to the pain, exactly as Laman and Lemuel came to a spiritual moment when they "were past feeling" (1 Ne. 17:45).

Spiritually, in the Valley of Elah, David's feet were properly shod and securely fastened to his feet. His heels were not bruised. He felt the spirit; he knew the direction; he had faith in Jehovah, and, therefore, he had the courage to meet Goliath when others retired. And he crushed his head!

"Bruise his head"

Though Satan is able to bruise the heels of the sons and daughters of Adam and Eve, they possess the power to crush his head, as David did to Goliath. (The footnote to Genesis 3:15 in the LDS Bible tells us that another meaning of the Hebrew word translated as "bruise" can be to "crush, or grind.")

The mind dwells in the head; it is the source of thought that identifies who we really are (see Prov. 23:7).[13] Goliath represents the mind set of Satan and idolatry: by worshipping idols, like the other Philistines, he affronted God. (As noted above, more than once the exiled house of Israel adopted just such practices from their captors and were severely chastened by Jehovah.) The great, eternal threat Goliath represents is that he would usurp the agency of the Jews by forcing them to worship false idols, exactly Satan's plan.

When the stone David launches fells Goliath, his victory represents the victory of agency over captivity, or worshipping the living Christ, not stony idols.[14] Similar battles are waged every day in every corner of the world, and perhaps in every corner of the cosmos, "worlds without number" (Moses 1:33). Each individual is engaged in this cosmic battle of opposites on a very intimate, personal level. David's action tells us that, in many instances, we need to confront the threat to our agency head-on. By cowering, we tacitly give in to Satan's tactics. We have the promise that, while he may bruise our heels as we move forward spiritually, we have been empowered to crush evil and overcome the world. We just need to make certain that our feet are properly shod and secured with the preparation of the gospel of peace, and our eye single to the glory of God. If we are prepared, we will be able to see through the temptations he advertises to distract us from walking squarely in the Savior's footsteps.

We see, therefore, in this well-known historical parable that there are important subtexts, offering us a deeper vision into our daily struggles. Not that the intensity of our struggles diminish knowing others have experienced and are experiencing like challenges; rather we gain confidence in just how significant they are in Heavenly Father's view and why He wants to help us if we but petition Him. He knows exactly what help to offer and the precise moment to offer it. Just as He was quietly and invisibly with David, so He will be with us when we need to overcome our Goliaths.

Notes to Chapter 7

1. Robert D. Hales, "Holy Scriptures: The Power of God unto Salvation," *Ensign* (Nov. 2006), 26-27.
2. *TPJS*, 274.
3. *TPJS*, 304.
4. James E. Faust, "The Refiner's Fire," *Ensign* (May 1979), 53-54.
5. Another intriguing potential subtext for the stones is found in Isaiah 57:6 in which the Lord compares "the smooth stones of the stream" to the alien idols Israel had embraced. His people had allowed themselves to be seduced into worshipping inanimate stone figures whose small size suggested their abject vapidity, especially when compared with the mountain of the Lord where true, consequential worship occurred. Seen from this symbolic perspective, David is launching the Philistine idols against their evil embodiment, Goliath.
6. George M. Peacock, *Unlocking the Numbers – An LDS Perspective on Scriptural Use of Numbers* (Springville, UT: CFI, 2005), 84. He also points to the five virgins as an example of grace and the use of five in the account of Joseph's treatment of his brothers (Gen. 43, 45, 47).
7. Gordon B. Hinckley, "Overpowering the Goliaths in Our Lives," *Ensign* (May 1983), 46-47.
8. Ibid., 51.
9. Neal A. Maxwell, "Yet Thou Art There," *Ensign* (Nov. 1987), 32.
10. See the Topical Guide, s.v. "walk."
11. Neal A. Maxwell, *Meek and Lowly* (Salt Lake City: Deseret Book, 1988), 56-57; see also David A. Bednar, "And Nothing Shall Offend Them," *Ensign* (Nov. 2006), 89-92.
12. Ibid., 94.
13. The heart and the head often represent the mental faculty of the mind. The heart can also represent the spirit of man.

14. In a wonderful, sardonic observation on the felling of Goliath, President Boyd K. Packer said, "When David swung his sling, that was the first solid idea that had ever entered Goliath's head" ("The Play and the Plan," CES Fireside for Young Adults [May 1995], 7).

CHAPTER 8

PARABLE OF THE GOOD SAMARITAN

The parable of the Good Samaritan illustrates longer *poietic* parables. It has a long interpretative history, which BYU professor John Welch discusses in his "The Good Samaritan: A Type and Shadow of the Plan of Salvation."[1] It is so familiar to Christians that we may take it for granted, reading it rapidly, thinking we know everything there is to know about it. Yet pondering and prayer can reveal rich veins of gospel vision and understanding each time we explore it deeper.

That the scriptures inhere a significant *poietic* base is evident in the images found in them. But one of the most important elements of scriptural *poietics*, not readily evident in the traditional formatting of the scriptures and, therefore, not appreciated for its contribution to the meaning of the texts, is the extensive "parallelism of meaning"[2] in the original texts. John Breck wrote: "parallelism usually expresses some form of *thought progression*. Rather than simply repeating the sense of the first line by the use of synonymous terms, it expresses gradation: the *second line intensifies, specifies, or completes in some essential respect the thought or feeling expressed in the first line.* Long recognized but little appreciated, this characteristic is a basic feature of Hebrew poetry."[3]

POIETIC ORGANIZATION OF THE PARABLE: CHIASMUS

The Savior taught the parable of the Good Samaritan in beautiful double chiasmi. The overarching chiasmus, including the dialogue with the lawyer, is as follows:

    A Eternal life – Laws of Love (Luke 10:25-27)
        B Do and Live (v. 28)
            C Question of Neighbor (v. 29)
                D Parable of the Good Samaritan (vv. 30-35)
            C´ Question of Neighbor (v. 36)
        B´ Do (v. 37)
    A´ (Eternal life implied)

Isolating the center of the chiasmus, the parable itself (D), we find a second chiasmus:

    A Descent from Jerusalem into the valley (v. 30a)
        B Thieves rob and beat man (v. 30b)
            C Response of the priest and Levite: Avoidance (vv. 31-32)
            C´ Response of the Samaritan: Compassion (v. 33)
        B´ Healing the man: pattern of consecration (v. 34)
    A´ Ascent to the safety of the inn; delegation of healing (v. 35)

The responses of the three men who came upon the beaten man constitutes the center of the chiasmus, focusing attention on why the priest and the Levite acted as if the man were not there on the side of the road, and why the Samaritan halted his journey to care for him. Consequently, the development of the plot becomes a vital element of the virtual reality the Savior created in this narrative.

Context: The Lawyer's Question

The context of the parable is fundamental for understanding the story itself. The Seventy had just returned and reported to Jesus that, in His name, even the devils were subject unto them (see Luke 10:17). Rejoicing in spirit, the Savior thanked His Father for revealing marvelous things to the seventy disciples, but in such a way that those things unfolded to them remained obscure to "the wise and prudent" (Luke 10:21). Echoing what He had told His disciples earlier about teaching in parables, He "turned him unto his disciples, and said privately, Blessed are the eyes which see the things that ye see: For I tell you, that many prophets and kings have desired to see those things which ye see, and have not seen them; and to hear those things which ye hear, and have not heard them" (Luke 10:23-24; see Matt. 13:17). Once again He expressed a common motif of His teaching, the motif of seeing and yet not seeing, hearing, yet not hearing.

At this juncture in the narrative, Luke records that "a certain lawyer" in the larger group of listeners asked Jesus, "Master, what shall I do to inherit eternal life?" (Luke 10:25).[4] (Is there a supercilious tone in the word "Master" coming from one learned in the law—one of "the wise and prudent"—addressing someone he likely considered a country bumpkin?) While the sincerity of the lawyer is certainly dubious, his question goes to the heart of the gospel of Jesus Christ.

There is great irony in the Savior's response; the Eternal Lawgiver asked the student of His law, "What is written in the law? how readest thou?" In essence, He was asking the ostensibly learned man,

"What do you think the essence of *My* law is?" It was a question with a straightforward answer for anyone conversant with the law of Moses because the answer is found in the Shema, the prayer every adult male Jew uttered twice daily. The lawyer therefore said, "Thou shalt love the Lord thy God with all thy heart, and with all thy soul, and with all thy strength, and with all thy mind" (Deut. 6:5); and "[thou shalt love] thy neighbour as thyself" (Lev. 19:18). Jesus counseled him, "This do, and thou shalt live" (Luke 10:26, 27).

The striking simplicity of the Savior's counsel both stunned and confused the lawyer who was accustomed to having every jot and tittle spelled out so he could strictly follow the letter of the law. Seeking to catch the Savior in a conundrum and "willing to justify himself [he] said unto Jesus, And who is my neighbour?" (Luke 10:29). On the surface, this is the crux of the problem for the lawyer: in his reading of the law, the authoritative rabbis had made it clear that only those of the covenant were neighbors; Gentiles were not. But there was an even more deeply embedded conflict for the man, namely the question of neighbor and kinship, discussed below in the Second Order Virtual Reality. Consequently, the lawyer wanted to pin the Savior down and determine with just how broad a brush stroke Jesus was painting His picture of eternal life. What he was about to hear was that the attitude of the act is as important as the act itself, that the spirit of compassion precedes acts of mercy, and that the word *neighbor* includes anyone in need.

The Concrete Virtual Reality of the Parable: First Order[5]

The narrative is set in first-century A.D. Palestine, along the road between Jerusalem and Jericho, a road known as "the Path of Blood"[6] because it was fraught with the danger of robbers and murderers. Given the road's infamous reputation, the Savior created a setting whose virtual reality would have engaged the imagination of anyone listening to Him. Many of those in His presence may well have risked their lives traveling the road. Equally important to the Savior would have been the millions of listeners and readers over the subsequent centuries; He told the story in such a way that it could apply to anyone in the world at any time in history so that they could liken it unto themselves.

As the curtain goes up on the parable of the Good Samaritan, we might think of ourselves as time travelers observing what is depicted.

First, we see a man lying off on the side of the road, badly beaten; even his clothes have been ripped off. Robbers have taken everything of value and left him for dead. We note that the Savior does not identify the beaten man with any religion, culture, or country; he is simply "a certain [= some] man." He may be Jewish, but for the purposes of the parable, his religious affiliation is immaterial.

Down the road comes "a certain [meaning "some"] priest" whom we want to believe will help the man. Order will be restored in this chaotic scene of blood. The priest looks at the man, but then crosses over to the opposite side of the road, going around him and continuing his journey without stopping. Why?! Is he afraid to stop because robbers may still be lurking in the area?

Next, a Levite appears on the scene. The reader anticipates that he will certainly stop and help the man, but he does exactly the same as the priest: after looking at the man, he too crosses over to the other side of the road and continues on his way. Why is the beaten man such a pariah to these two priesthood holders? these two temple workers? In the Joseph Smith translation of this scene, we read that "they desired in their hearts that it might not be known that they had seen him [the man]" (JST Luke 10:33). Crass at best! Yes, the law forbid them to touch a dead person (see Num. 19:10), however, the Savior describes the man as "*half* dead" (Luke 10:30), in other words, he shows signs of life. The actions of the priest and Levite go to the heart of the question of neighbors: by their actions, both decide that the beaten man is not a neighbor and, therefore, they are not obliged to help him. Both understand the rabbinic interpretation of the law; both practice the letter; neither had an inclination as to the spirit of the law. And this was also the lawyer's quandary.

Then a third man appears, described as "a certain [some] Samaritan." We might well wonder what a Samaritan is doing on this road. The area is doubly hostile for him: not only does he have to watch for thieves and murderers, but the Jews despise Samaritans as no better than heathens.[7] Because of the enmity between Jews and Samaritans, it would seem unlikely that he would stop. He would not want to become involved because, if the beaten man were a Jew, he might revile the Samaritan for helping him. But, he does stop!

Feeling our way into the *poietics* of the story, we sense the astringent cleansing of the wound with wine and the soothing effect of the oil as a healing balm. But to the Samaritan, compassionate caring is not a one and done ministration; he puts the man on his donkey, takes him to an inn, and cares for him there. We do not know how long he tends the man, but when the Samaritan departs, he leaves two pence (Gk. *denarii*) with the innkeeper to continue the man's care, promising the innkeeper that, should the bill exceed the two *denarii*, he will pay the additional amount upon his return.

What the Savior depicted was righteousness in action. The story had to be a bitter pill for the lawyer to swallow—to have a Samaritan portrayed as a paragon of virtue.

Second Order Virtual Reality: Blessed are the Merciful

The story brings into sharp relief one of the imposing challenges to disciples trying to keep the second great commandment, set forth in the Savior's Sermon on the Mount and before the Nephite temple in Bountiful:

> Ye have heard that it hath been said, Thou shalt love thy neighbour, and hate thine enemy.
>
> But I say unto you, Love your enemies, bless them that curse you, do good to them that hate you, and pray for them which despitefully use you, and persecute you;
>
> That ye may be the children of your Father which is in heaven: for he maketh his sun to rise on the evil and on the good, and sendeth rain on the just and on the unjust.
>
> For if ye love them which love you, what reward have ye? do not even the publicans the same? (Matt. 5:43-46).

Love our enemies?! That can be a troubling question depending on the situation one finds oneself in. While the man lying beside the road is not identified, it is quite possible to read him as being a Jew, given the place cited. If we assume the beaten man to be Jewish, it is remarkable that the Samaritan stops to help, especially when the two priesthood bearers passed him by. Why did the Samaritan stop? The Savior said, because "he had compassion on [the beaten man]" (Luke 10:33). Was his compassion for the man because he was Jewish? Hard to say, but, given the animosity between the two tribes, it seems unlikely. Did he have compassion for the exigency of the man's situation? Quite possibly! Enemy or not, the man was in a dire circumstance.

When the Savior concluded His parable, He asked the lawyer, "Which now of these three, thinkest thou was neighbour unto him that fell among the thieves?" Though unwilling to identify the Samaritan by name, the lawyer had to concede, "He that shewed *mercy* [Heb. *hesed*, for they were likely speaking first-century Hebrew or Aramaic] on him" (Luke 10:36-37; emphasis added). Acting with mercy toward one another, then, is to love one's neighbor as oneself, perhaps because we can envision ourselves in a similar situation and, therefore, do unto the person in need, enemy or no, as we would want that person or someone like him to do unto us (see Matt. 7:12; 3 Ne. 14:12).

His undoubtedly reluctant answer, along with his second question, "who is my neighbour," reveal a defining difference between Hebrew vision of responsibility to others and Christ's heightened vision, both of which are based on two fundamental principles: the *go'el*-redeemer and its bedrock principle, *hesed*-mercy.

When the Lord proclaimed His name to Moses, He said:

> The LORD, The LORD God, merciful [Heb. *rachuwm*, "compassionate"] and gracious, longsuffering, and abundant in goodness [Heb. *hesed*] and truth, Keeping mercy [Heb. *hesed*] for thousands, forgiving iniquity and transgression and sin (Exod. 34:6-7; emphasis added).

That He cited *hesed* twice emphasized the great significance He places on mercy as a quality of godliness. Prophets have long understood this. Ammon taught that the Lord "is a merciful Being" (Alma 26:35). Exhorting the people to correctly worship the Lord, the prophet Zenos used the word *merciful* six times within eight lines (Alma 33:4-11). Elder Jeffrey R. Holland taught, "Mercy is at least a beginning synonym for the perfection God has and for which all of us must strive."[8] Surely, if, as the Prophet Joseph taught, one's faith in Jesus Christ is built on, among other things, "a *correct* idea of his character, perfections, and attributes,"[9] then understanding the principle of *hesed*-mercy is one of the most important qualities of His being that we would want to grasp.

Unfortunately, no single word adequately translates *hesed* into English, making it, therefore, difficult for English speakers to grasp the theology inherent in the term and to act accordingly. The closest English approximation conveying the inner meaning of *hesed* is the somewhat archaic term "loving-kindness."[10] For example, centuries after He personally revealed Himself to Moses, He appeared to Jeremiah, saying, "I have loved thee with an everlasting love: therefore with lovingkindness [*hesed*] have I drawn thee" (Jer. 31:3). Based on this seminal portrayal of mercy in the Good Samaritan and its association with the principle of compassion, I prefer to use the term "compassionate kindness" rather than "lovingkindness" to render *hesed*.[11]

In an *Anchor-Bible-Dictionary* article, "Love (OT)," Katherine Doob Sakenfeld cites some

> common features . . . that together describe the character of an act of *hesed*. First, the help of another is essential; the person in need cannot perform the action. Second, help itself is essential; the needy person's situation will turn drastically worse if help is not received. Third, the circumstances dictate that one person is uniquely able to provide the needed assistance. . . . Fourth, the person in need has no control over the decision of the person who is in a position to help. . . . The potential helper must make a free moral decision, based essentially on commitment to the needy person within the relationship,[12]

which closely describes the actions of the Samaritan who stops to help the man by the side of the road.

Mercy is the pivotal principle in the Savior's Beatitudes, marking the chiastic turn toward Christlike discipleship.[13] Mercy, pure in heart, and peacemaking form a compound in one, each complementing, amplifying, and extending the other. That is, mercy, meaning compassionate kindness, out of a pure heart, informs the spirit of a disciple's peacemaking efforts.

We have mercy toward others when we empathize with their circumstances and seek to minister to them as Christ would. To emphasize is to feel into, even envision, their situation so as to know how to help. It is also to pray for heavenly help. Remember, the Savior invites us to become a yokefellow with Him; it takes a great deal of faith unto vision to see ourselves in His yoke, stopping to tend to someone in need lying on or off the strait path, someone we may or may not like. But Christ loves them and our assistance at a particular moment may be just what they need to bring them back to or introduce them to the Savior.

Shakespeare penned these beautiful verses about mercy:

> The quality of mercy is not straine'd,
> It droppeth as the gentle rain from heaven
> Upon the place beneath: it is twice blest,
> It blesseth him that gives, and him that takes,
> 'Tis mightiest in the mightiest, it becomes
> The throned monarch better than his crown
>
> . . . .
>
> Mercy is above this sceptred sway,
> It is enthroned in the hearts of kings,
> It is an attribute of God himself;
> And earthly power doth then show likest God's
> When mercy seasons justice. . . .[14]

A related Old Testament principle undergirding the story is the *goʾel*, or redeemer. (The Supreme Redeemer is Jehovah-Jesus Christ; when we find the word *redeemer* in the Old Testament the Hebrew word is *goʾel*. [The Hebrew verb for "redeem" is *gaʾal*.]) The redeeming responsibilities of a *goʾel* are found, first, in Leviticus 25:47-55 in which the Israelite is told to rescue his brother if he were to become indentured:

> And if a sojourner or stranger wax rich by thee, and thy brother *that dwelleth* by him wax poor, and sell himself unto the stranger *or* sojourner by thee, or to the stock of the stranger's family:
>
> After that he is sold he may be redeemed again; one of his brethren may redeem him:
>
> Either his uncle, or his uncle's son, may redeem him, or *any* that is nigh of kin unto him of his family may redeem him; or if he be able, he may redeem himself.
>
> And he shall reckon with him that bought him from the year that he was sold to him unto the year of jubile: and the price of his sale shall be according unto the number of years, according to the time of an hired servant shall it be with him.
>
> If *there be* yet many years *behind*, according unto them he shall give again the price of his redemption out of the money that he was bought for.
>
> And if there remain but few years unto the year of jubile, then he shall count with him, *and* according

unto his years shall he give him again the price of his redemption.

And as a yearly hired servant shall he be with him: *and the other* shall not rule with rigour over him in thy sight.

And if he be not redeemed in these *years*, then he shall go out in the year of jubile, *both* he, and his children with him.

For unto me the children of Israel *are* servants; they *are* my servants whom I brought forth out of the land of Egypt: I *am* the LORD your God.

Second, he was also responsible to his brother's wife, should his brother die, leaving her a widow, called the Levirate Contract or Law[15]:

> If brethren dwell together, and one of them die, and have no child, the wife of the dead shall not marry without unto a stranger: her husband's brother shall go in unto her, and take her to him to wife, and perform the duty of an husband's brother unto her.
>
> And it shall be, *that* the firstborn which she beareth shall succeed in the name of his brother *which is* dead, that his name be not put out of Israel.
>
> And if the man like not to take his brother's wife, then let his brother's wife go up to the gate unto the elders, and say, My husband's brother refuseth to raise up unto

his brother a name in Israel, he will not perform the duty of my husband's brother.

Then the elders of his city shall call him, and speak unto him: and *if he* stand *to it,* and say, I like not to take her;

Then shall his brother's wife come unto him in the presence of the elders, and loose his shoe from off his foot, and spit in his face, and shall answer and say, So shall it be done unto that man that will not build up his brother's house.

And his name shall be called in Israel, The house of him that hath his shoe loosed (Deut. 25:5-10).

An example of a *goël* fulfilling his kinsman's obligation is Boaz in the book of Ruth. Not being the next of kin, Boaz gave the first kinsman in line the opportunity to do his duty,[16] which the man declined to do. Boaz then redeemed Naomi's land for her and redeemed Ruth's widowhood by marrying her, manifesting *hesed*-compassionate kindness toward both women, evident in what Naomi said to her daughter-in-law: "Blessed be he of the LORD, who hath not left off his kindness [Heb. *hesed*] to the living and to the dead. And Naomi said unto her, The man *is* near of kin unto us, one of our next kinsmen" [Heb. *goël*] (Ruth 2:20).[17]

This vision of neighbor, meaning the next-of-kin *goël* in the most limited sense, informed the lawyer's question, which was an undernarrative among the Pharisees, as the Savior knew from experience. To illustrate the ramifications of this worldview, the Savior used the figures of a priest and a Levite whose narrow interpretation of the law of a *goʼel* led to their shameful behavior in passing by the badly beaten man. (It's not too difficult to hear a derisive tone in the Savior's brief description of the two religious leaders, esteemed in the Jewish community, who should have been examples of how a *goʼel* was supposed to act.)

Following the wanting display of humanity exhibited by the priest and the Levite, along came the Samaritan, despised by the Jews for what they considered to be the Samaritans' aberrant religious practices,[18] a view that didn't hinder the Savior from traveling in Samaria to take the good news of His gospel to the people, evidenced in his encounter with the woman at Jacob's Well and other Samaritans who accepted Him as the Messiah (see John 4). The Samaritan in the parable, not the Jewish religious leaders, became the *goʼel* of the parable who rescued the beaten man from his life-threatening situation, manifesting *hesed*, compassionate kindness, toward his "neighbor."

We learn two important principles on this level of the story: first, "neighbor" means the brother- and sisterhood of man, especially someone in need. Second, *goʼels* do not hesitate to *act* with *hesed*-mercy toward others; they don't have to weigh whether there are theological regulations or limitations. One indication of a disciple's heightened spiritual maturity in the gospel is that he or she looks for and is sensitive to opportunities to lift others toward righteousness:

> For behold, it is not meet that I should command in all things; for he that is compelled in all things, the same is a slothful and not a wise servant; wherefore he receiveth no reward.
>
> Verily I say, men should be anxiously engaged in a good cause, and do many things of their own free will, and bring to pass much righteousness;

> For the power is in them, wherein they are agents unto themselves. And inasmuch as men do good they shall in nowise lose their reward (D&C 58:26-28),

whereby he or she manifests "the wisdom that is from above [which] is first pure, then peaceable, gentle, *and* easy to be intreated, *full of mercy and good fruits, without partiality, and without hypocrisy. And the fruit of righteousness is sown in peace of them that make peace*" (James 3:17-18; emphasis added), in other words, they are the peacemakers of the kingdom.[19] Elder James E. Faust said: "There is no higher form of worship than the unpurchased service to another soul of whatever faith, belief, or social stratum."[20]

Moreover, to act with *hesed*-mercy as a *go'el*-redeemer toward anyone in need is not only to love one's neighbor, but also to love the Lord (see Matt. 25:40; Mosiah 2:17).

The parable of the Good Samaritan, I would submit, directly relates to every Latter-day Saint: Latter-day Saints are baptized to be *go'el*-redeemers in Israel, to rescue those on this side of the veil and on the other, the living and the dead, acting with *hesed*-compassionate kindness. This dimension of our discipleship was explained by Alma at the waters of Mormon:

> Behold, here are the waters of Mormon (for thus were they called) and now, as ye are desirous to come into the fold of God, and to be called his people, and are willing to bear one another's burdens, that they may be light;
>
> Yea, and are willing to mourn with those that mourn; yea, and comfort those that stand in need of comfort, and to stand as witnesses of God at all times and in

all things, and in all places that ye may be in, even until death, that ye may be redeemed of God, and be numbered with those of the first resurrection, that ye may have eternal life—

Now I say unto you, if this be the desire of your hearts, what have you against being baptized in the name of the Lord, as a witness before him that ye have entered into a covenant with him, that ye will serve him and keep his commandments, that he may pour out his Spirit more abundantly upon you? (Mosiah 18:8-10).

Alma's words identify the actions of the Christlike discipleship of a merciful *go'el*: one who ministers righteously to those in need with long-suffering when necessary, gentleness, meekness, love unfeigned, the pure knowledge with which the Holy Spirit inspires us, "which shall greatly enlarge the soul without hypocrisy, and without guile, . . . having our bowels full of charity [the pure love of Christ], let[ting] virtue garnish [our] thoughts unceasingly" (D&C 121:41-43, 45), in other words, with compassionate kindness. This is the comportment we aspire to, not perhaps where we begin our spiritual journey at baptism. One of the beauties of the organization of the Lord's Church is that each calling He gives us therein can become a stepping stone toward realizing the full measure of our potential in our growth "unto a perfect man [or woman], unto the measure of the stature of the fulness of Christ" (Eph. 4:13). Lest we feel we are too far from the principle of perfection, President Brigham Young said:

> We all occupy diversified stations in the world, and in the kingdom of God. Those who do right, and seek the glory of the Father in heaven, whether their

knowledge be little or much, or whether they can do little or much, if they do the very best they know how, they are perfect. . . .

It is possible for a man or woman to become perfect on this earth. It is written "Be ye therefore perfect, even as your Father which is in heaven is perfect." . . .

If the first passage I have quoted is not worded to our understanding, we can alter the phraseology of the sentence, and say, "Be ye as perfect as ye can," for that is all we can do, though it is written, be ye perfect as your Father who is in heaven is perfect. To be as perfect as we possibly can, according to our knowledge, is to be just as perfect as our Father in heaven is. He cannot be any more perfect than He knows how, any more than we. When we are doing as well as we know how in the sphere and station which we occupy here, we are justified in the justice, righteousness, mercy, and judgment that go before the Lord of heaven and earth.[21]

While not speaking to becoming perfect, the words of caution from President Ezra Taft Benson certainly apply to this often-perplexing principle:

We must be careful, as we seek to become more and more godlike, that we do not become discouraged and lose hope. Becoming Christlike is a lifetime pursuit and very often involves growth and change that is slow, almost imperceptible. The scriptures record remarkable accounts of men whose lives changed dramatically, in an instant, as it were: Alma the Younger, Paul on the road to Damascus, Enos praying far into the night, King Lamoni. Such astonishing examples of the power to change even those steeped in sin give confidence that the Atonement can reach even those deepest in despair.

But we must be cautious as we discuss these remarkable examples. Though they are real and powerful, they are the exception more than the rule. For every Paul, for every Enos, and for every King Lamoni, there are hundreds and thousands of people who find the process of repentance much more subtle, much more imperceptible. Day by day they move closer to the Lord, little realizing they are building a godlike life. They live quiet lives of goodness, service, and commitment. They are like the Lamanites, who the Lord said "were baptized with fire and with the Holy Ghost, *and they knew it not.*" (3 Ne. 9:20; italics added.)

We must not lose hope. Hope is an anchor to the souls of men. Satan would have us cast away that anchor. In this way he can bring discouragement and surrender. But we must not lose hope. The Lord is pleased with every effort, even the tiny, daily ones in which we strive to be more like Him. Though we may see that we have far to go on the road to perfection, we must not give up hope.[22]

Merciful discipleship goes beyond duty: when duty becomes desire to serve, *hesed*-mercy constitutes the spirit of that desire. Most often compassionate service is rendered privately and personally, out of the gaze of public scrutiny. Merciful disciples do not look over their shoulders for pats on the back; rather they look forward for opportunities to serve with "charity out of a pure heart, and of a good conscience, and of faith unfeigned" (1 Tim. 1:15). Paradoxically, though they keep their eyes of faith "single to the glory of God" (D&C 4:5; 82:19), their walk of discipleship includes acute peripheral vision, seeing both those who have fallen along the road as well as being alert for the spiritual thieves who would assault their souls or the souls of others. And, having received comfort and compassion from the Lord, they are committed to extending that same comfort and compassion to others (see 2 Cor. 1:3-4).

Here, then, is the reality described in the parable of the Good Samaritan through the first and second orders: Love is a verb of action whereby disciples act to help the Lord in bringing to pass the immortality and eternal life of men, women, and children (see Moses 1:39). Even enemies can be ministered to with this *hesed*-mercy; we do not have to wait for the ephemeral feeling we associate with the word *love* to become involved in the work of the Lord. Active mercy manifests itself as disciples do good and help the downtrodden bear their burdens with kindness. The scriptures tell us that when someone acts with compassion by helping another bear their burdens, they are living "the law of Christ" and thereby acting with some degree of "the pure love of Christ" (Gal. 6:5; Moro. 7:47).[23]

It is in this light that we understand the Savior's call to "Be ye therefore merciful as you Father is merciful" (Luke 6:36), a variation of His call to disciples to be perfect even as His Father in heaven (see Matt. 12:48). *Hesed*-mercy-charity is "the bond of perfectness and peace" (D&C 88:125; also Col. 3:14), implying that the merciful are also the peacemakers of the Kingdom of God, i.e., those who help others attain a measure of peace in their lives (see Matt. 5:7-9; 3 Ne. 12:7-9), boosting their confidence that they can do "the work of righteousness" (Isa. 32:17) which "the Son of righteousness," "the Prince of Peace" would do (2 Ne. 26:9; 3 Ne. 25:2; Ether 9:22; Isa. 9:6; 2 Ne. 19:6). Therefore, by feeling and acting with mercy toward others, disciples manifest that, through experience, they have "knowledge of the Son of God."

The Pattern of Consecration

From three distinct yet interwoven acts by the Samaritan a pattern of consecration emerges: 1. He gave his time by stopping to help the man bear his life-threatening burden from his beating, thereby comforting him; 2. He employed his talents, cleansing and binding the man's wounds, took him to an inn where he stayed to care for him; 3. he used what means he had—the wine, the oil, and two *denarii*, the latter of which he gave to the innkeeper upon continuing his journey, promising he would reimburse him for any additional cost incurred from the man's restoration to health. Given the lawyer's first question, "what must I do to inherit eternal life?," we surmise that the merciful sharing of our time, talents, and means in ministering to others is the essence of eternal life and, as disciples of Jesus Christ recognizing these prime principles, we can aspire and strive to enact both the spirit and practice of the values of eternal life in our mortal walk, if not perfectly, then to the best of our ability.

Time

A person's willingness to share his or her time with others expresses, to a great extent, the depth, dimension, and commitment of their discipleship. Rick Warren, author of *The Purpose-driven Life*, writes: "If you want to know a person's priorities, just look at how they spend their time.... When you give someone your time, you are giving them a portion of your life that you'll never get back. Your time is your life.

That is why the greatest gift you can give someone is your time."[24] The parable of the Good Samaritan teaches us that a mere moment of time spent helping another person bear his burden is infinitely significant in the paradigm of eternal life. Freezing any particular timeframe in our lives by stopping and tending to the need of another brings into focus what is important eternally. And the Samaritan was focused. Paradoxically, in the journey of life, man progresses by stopping to help others; being oblivious to such needs and rushing on is really regression.

Talents

The talents the Samaritan displays in dressing the man's wounds do not appear extraordinary for travelers at that time; undoubtedly, the priest and Levite had the same skills and means. The difference in the men is that the Samaritan used his talents in the Lord's prescribed manner, namely "that all may be profited thereby" (D&C 46:12). There is no exclusivity in the kingdom of God, especially when there is a need that someone with the appropriate talent can address. By hiding their talents from the man desperately in need, the priest and the Levite align themselves with the "wicked and slothful servant[s]" who have to be commanded in all things before they do anything.

Means

The means available to the Samaritan are oil, wine and a few *denarii*. Wine, red in color, is the astringent the Samaritan uses to cleanse the man's wounds and start the healing process. After cleansing the wound with wine, He pours healing, soothing olive oil into. In doing so, the Samaritan represents a compassionately kind disciple of Christ, ministering to another child of God who may have succumbed to the thieves of telestiality and who may need astringent compassion at first, when the ministering disciple is moved upon by the Holy Spirit (see D&C 121:43), but follows that astringent love with the balm of comforting, burden-bearing compassionate kindness needed over the long haul of spiritual recovery.

"Means" includes money as evidenced in the parable by the two *dinarii* the Samaritan left with the innkeeper to continue the care of the man. Money and the materialism it can engender, or the lack of money, has been a source of trial and tribulation for people for centuries. Two of the Ten Commandments address issues related to things with monetary implications: "Thou shalt not steal" and "Thou shalt not covet . . . anything that is thy neighbor's" (Exod. 20:15, 17). Centuries after Moses, Paul wrote that "the love of money is the root of all evil" (1 Tim. 6:10). Not that money is evil; rather it is the utter focus on money to the exclusion of things of the spirit that is the problem. We laugh at the phrase "shop till you drop," but it has become so endemic in the United States that many families find themselves overextended in their debt load with the clock of negative interest ticking relentlessly onward.

Money, like talents, comes in various quantities, but the *quality* of one's monetary means is, however, determined by how we view them—as the result exclusively of our hard work, or as a stewardship from the Lord. It is important, therefore, to keep the vision in front of us that everything belongs to the Lord and we are the stewards of all He bestows upon us. By investing some of his means in the rehabilitation of the beaten man, the Samaritan exemplified a vision of money that sharply contrasts with a self-absorbed, self-indulgent materialism prevalent in some areas of the world today.

Though economic means may be the least effective way of helping someone, nevertheless, at times it is a necessary first step. For Latter-day Saints, the right vision of monetary means is to pay a full tithing and contribute a generous fast offering. Our individual means may be modest, but through the addition of small means, the Lord's servants, charged with administering the funds of the Church, can bring great things to pass. For example, today temples are being built around the world so that many more members can take out their endowments and be sealed, husband to wife, parents to children, for eternity, a blessing they can only receive in temples. Moreover, millions of disaster victims have been helped to recover through the Humanitarian Fund of the Church. We need only remember how tenderly the Lord spoke of the widow contributing her two mites to realize just how sacred such funds are (see Mark 12:41-44; Luke 21:1-4).

As represented with the wine and oil the Samaritan applied to the man's wounds, sometimes means are the means to help whatever they may be. One day a man lame from birth begged alms of Peter and John as the two Apostles were about to enter the temple. Though not men of means, they had something to offer which was far more meaningful than money. Reaching down to the man, Peter said, "Silver and gold have I none; but such as I have give I thee: in the name of Jesus Christ of Nazareth rise up and walk" (Acts 3:6). Notice in the next verse that Peter extended his right hand to the man, lifting him up, a gesture that reveals three nuances of the blessing: 1. Peter's abiding faith in the authority he had as a priesthood bearer and as an Apostle of Jesus Christ. 2. Peter's was a proactive faith: not only did he command the man to be healed and walk in the name of Jesus Christ, Peter became a part of the solution by literally helping to bear the man's burden and, thereby, living the law of Christ (see Gal. 6:2); 3. Peter was a witness of Jesus Christ, extending the light of his (Peter's) good work to the Lord of the universe and glorifying thereby Christ.

When we investigate and ponder the subtexts of the parable of the Good Samaritan, they can surrender "treasures of knowledge, even hidden treasures" (D&C 89:19) that enrich and deepen our vision of things as they really are. Having discovered the hidden treasures, the

Lord expects his disciples to invest these newfound mysteries into the wisdom of inclusive actions, bringing goodness into the lives of our brothers and sisters.

Third Order Virtual Reality: Symbolism

Lying below the surface narrative, in this third order of virtual reality, resides an expanded vision of eternal life that we can access through the image-symbols the Savior employed.

A Certain Man and the Thieves

The certain man descends from the high spiritual plan represented by Jerusalem, "the holy city" (Isa. 52:1), "the holy mountain" (Dan. 9:16), into the telestial valley of thieves and murderers, who are remarkably similar to the human predators we read about today in newspapers, on the internet, and see daily on television. They are the Gadianton robbers who stalk the innocent, and one another, intent on taking advantage of others, whereby they commit evil. Their objective is "to murder, and to rob, and to gain power, (and this was their secret plan, and their combination)" (Hel. 2:8). Legions of thieves and murderers worldwide rob and maim people spiritually, such as those who deal in drugs that addict people, or who enslave, or brutally slaughter.

More subtle are those described by the Savior in the Sermon on the Mount: "Ye have heard that it hath been said by them of old time, and it is also written before you, that thou shalt not kill, and whosoever shall kill shall be in danger of the judgment of God; But I say unto you, . . . whosoever shall say to his brother, Raca, shall be in danger of the council; and whosoever shall say, Thou fool, shall be in danger of hell fire" (3 Ne. 12:21-22; Matt. 5:21-22). "Raca" means worthless[25];

using the word *raca*, or any variants, to describe any person, amounts to character assassination, a phenomenon that has become widespread with social media. We live in a culture of the put-down. Think of how much dialogue on television, on radio, and in the movies is based on getting the advantage of another person through the use of words that belittle them. Think of the deluge of text messages, among adolescents in particular, that denigrate the character of classmates, causing, in some instances, irreparable psychological-spiritual harm. Is it any wonder that so many of our children, and people in general, feel worthless? Each put-down can sap a bit of life from a person's spirit. Such debasing, ridiculing language has anesthetized our collective sensibility and significantly lowered the civility among people, not to mention the negative vision so many have of life in general.

Seen symbolically from a different subtext, the unseen thieves of the parable strip the man of his "armour of God" (Eph. 6:13) and he lays there defenseless against those who spread the spirit of worldliness. Having willingly descended into the shadowy world of telestiality (see "The Starlight of Telestiality" above), he may even have given up pieces of his armor to "enjoy" the vices of the world, not realizing, like the prodigal son, that "wickedness never was happiness" (Alma 41:10). Only when it was too late might he discover that, by having ignored the warnings and chosen to travel the road to Jericho, he had acted irresponsibly and walked into a sinister predicament.

Throughout history, the watchmen who see the furthest ahead because of their direction from the Lord Himself, i.e., the prophets, seers, and revelators, often warn us of threats far in advance of their appearance, for examples, the Proclamation on the Family, issued by the First Presidency and the Quorum of the Twelve which clearly states that the Lord ordained marriage between a man and a woman. This declaration came years before the Supreme Court of the United States legalized marriage between two men or between two women, clearly contradicting the Lord's intent that started with the marriage of Adam and Eve. We can choose whether or not to heed the warnings of ordained watchmen; if we decide our vision of life is superior to their God-given vision, we begin the descent down our own Jericho road. Instead of being an undershepherd, we risk becoming one of the lost sheep who stray from the path Christ trod, turning to our own way (see Isa. 53:6; Mosiah 14:26), perhaps succumbing to the jeers of those in the great and spacious building of worldly pride and vain imaginations (see 1 Ne. 8:33; 12:18).

In sum, the man beaten and lying off the side of the road may be one who had been physically beaten or spiritually assaulted—robbed and beaten for his physical possessions or stripped of his self-worth. In either case, the Savior placed him at the nadir of this telestial world in which we live. As a sidebar, *we* need to watch carefully that we are not one of the thieves of self-worth; we are charged to lift people up.

The Priest and the Levite

The priest and the Levite represent ecclesiastical leaders, people who profess to be God's representatives, but whose prejudice and doctrinaire attitudes inhibit real godly service. In the overarching schematic of the parable, they could help heal the man, symbolically finding his way faithfully back to Christ, but they use their moral agency instead to ignore him.

Could there be a warning in these two figures for the priesthood of the Church today? Can men in the Church become so caught up in Church callings and everyday life that we pass people by who are hurting and need our help? Can we become so hurried that we do not stop for those "certain" individuals who lay along the strait path that the Savior laid out with His own life, the path we are traveling? Do we allow ourselves to become so wrapped up in our own lives that we find ourselves in a time-whirlpool from which we only extricate ourselves when we become aware of it and exercise a great deal of willpower to escape? Or, do we major in minors, letting programs get in the way of ministering to specific individuals? By and large, most priesthood bearers are actively engaged in ministering to the cares of others, but, under pressure, the potential is ever present to diffuse our focus and become stuck in the bog of busyness. Simplify is the message coming from the prophets today. With the heading "Simplify," President Dieter F. Uchtdorf asked, "First: are we making our discipleship too complicated?" giving then this counsel:

> This beautiful gospel is so simple a child can grasp it, yet so profound and complex that it will take a lifetime—even an eternity—of study and discovery to fully understand it.
>
> But sometimes we take the beautiful lily of God's truth and gild it with layer upon layer of man-made good ideas, programs, and expectations. Each one, by itself, might be helpful and appropriate for a certain time and circumstance, but when they are laid on top of each other, they can create a mountain of sediment that becomes so thick and heavy that we risk losing sight of that precious flower we once loved so dearly.[26]

The Samaritan

Noted above is that Samaritans were, from the Jewish cultural perspective, the looked-down-upon, near "infidels" from whom nothing good was expected, i.e., among the least of all people. In their attempt to denigrate Jesus, one of the worst names those who hounded him could think of was "thou art a Samaritan, and hast the devil" (John 8:48). Yet, though the Samaritan was last in their eyes, in the parable he proved to be among the first in the essential things of eternity. The priest and the Levite, who would have been considered the first religiously, showed themselves to be the last spiritually (see Matt. 19:30; 20:19; Mark 10:31). Furthermore, in the Samaritan's actions lies one of the great symbolic revelations of this parable—the pattern of consecration by which we love our neighbors, including our enemies.

Wine and olive oil have a rich symbolic heritage. Red wine suggests the blood Christ shed in atoning for the sins of man, whereby even scarlet sins can be white as snow (see Isa. 1:18; 1 Ne. 12:10) as the sinner comes faithfully unto Christ. Jesus tread the winepress of His Atonement alone to overcome the sins of and redeem man (see Isa. 63:3; Matt. 26:27-29; 3 Ne. 20:8); when He comes a second time, His robes will be wine-red, having been "dipped in blood" (Rev. 19:13; also D&C 133:48).

Olive oil evokes the presence of the Holy Spirit: when the Prophet Samuel anointed David with oil, "the Spirit of the Lord came upon David from that day forward" (1 Sam. 16:13). As we read the parable, then, and watch the Samaritan pour the oil into the man's wounds, it represents both a soothing healing agent as well as a medium through which the Holy Spirit applies his power to heal the spirit of man with the comforting love of heaven. In Isaiah we read that part of the Messiah's mission would include coming to all the disconsolate and "give unto them . . . the oil of joy for mourning" (Isa. 61:3).

Significantly, the images of wine and oil, then, represent two members of the Godhead invested in man's wellbeing—the wine the Savior, the oil the Holy Ghost—Who are ever ready and desirous to administer the powers of heaven to anyone with a broken heart and contrite spirit, who comes unto Christ, indeed, "Blessed are the poor in spirit who come unto me, for theirs is the kingdom of heaven" (3 Ne. 12:3).

Fourth Order Virtual Reality: Allegory

In an allegory, the images and the plot of a narrative represent specific historical people and events. From the first through the twelfth centuries, this was the principal method for understanding the parable of the Good Samaritan.[27] Rather than following the specifics of those early allegorical readings, the following discussion of the parable as allegory integrates the gospel as we know it in the Church, as much as possible.

The Samaritan represents Jesus Christ. Noted above is that He was once derogatorily called a Samaritan. The man lying beside the road would be Adam, whose name in Hebrew means "man" or "mankind."[28] The unseen thieves could be understood as either the devil's disciples who assault man's spirituality, or their human agents. The priest and Levite are ecclesiastical leaders. The inn is the Church. One is reminded of Elder Holland's comparison of the Church to "a hospital or an aid station, provided for those who are ill and want to get well, where one can get an infusion of spiritual nutrition and a supply of sustaining water in order to keep on climbing."[29] On one level, the innkeeper is the head of the Church in the Savior's absence, the President of The Church of Jesus Christ of Latter-day Saints; on another level, every member who, when baptized, the Lord entrusts to care for others and each disciple becomes thereby a keeper of an aid station within the great inn of the Church. Elder Maxwell offered this cautionary thought: "Each of us is an innkeeper who decides if there is room for Jesus!"[30]

Jerusalem is the Garden of Eden, the location of the mountain of the Lord, the temple mount; Jericho the world. The area where the man was beaten could be seen as "the valley of the shadow of death" (Ps. 23:4). The descent of the man from the Jerusalem evokes the Fall of Adam, and, by analogy, all mankind, from the terrestrial state of the Garden of Eden into the telestial world where assaults on the spirit of men and women occur daily. We do not see the thieves just as we do not see the devils who try to orchestrate the sins of man.[31] The man's wounds may represent the general sins of telestiality, Satan having influenced man to fall into a state of carnality, sensuality, and devilishness, i.e., the state of the natural man (see Moses 5:13; 6:49). In this sense, the clothing stripped off of him is his armor of righteousness. His implied nakedness, then, connotes his spiritual vulnerability after having been stripped of his garments.

In avoiding the beaten-man, the ecclesiastical leaders show that they deem their own status as being more important than the well-being of their congregations, and they protect their personal status to the exclusion of others, like the Pharisees and Sadducees. The appearance of the Samaritan corresponds to the Savior's mortal ministry: as established before the earth was formed, He came to this planet to redeem Adam-man from his sinful state. This moment in the plot graphically depicts the Lord's words to Isaiah, referred to in several instances above:

> The Spirit of the Lord GOD is upon me; because the LORD hath anointed me to preach good tidings unto the meek; he hath sent me to bind up the brokenhearted, to proclaim liberty to the captives, and the opening of the prison to them that are bound;
>
> To proclaim the acceptable year of the LORD, and the day of vengeance of our God; to comfort all that mourn;
>
> To appoint unto them that mourn in Zion, to give unto them beauty for ashes, the oil of joy for mourning, the garment of praise for the spirit of heaviness; that they might be called trees of righteousness, the planting of the LORD, that he might be glorified (Isaiah 61:1-3).

In a synagogue in Nazareth, Jesus affirmed that these words referred to His ministry (see Luke 4:16-21). To the end described in the Isaianic verses above, the Samaritan-Jesus Christ cleanses the man-Adam's wounds with wine and anoints him with olive oil to soothe the wounds like a balm. The allegorical and symbolic meanings of the wine and oil overlap: the Savior cleanses the sins of man in the wine-blood of His Atonement (Alma 5:21; 3 Ne. 27:19); with the olive oil He confers the companionship of the Holy Ghost upon the man to comfort him as his sins heal, often painfully, and helps him realign his inner Liahona so that he might get back on and continue walking in the path of righteousness (see 1 Sam. 10:1, 6; 16:13).

Having cleansed and anointed the man's worldly wounds, the Samaritan-Savior gathers him into His Church, the inn, where He continues to minister to him. When the Savior departs, He charges the innkeeper, the President of His Church and, by extension, all member-undershepherds, to continue nurturing the man back to spiritual wellness. The two *dinarii* He leaves with the innkeeper may be understood in several ways. One is to see them as "the earnest [i.e., downpayment] of the Spirit in our hearts" (2 Cor. 1:22), i.e., His redemption; or as "the earnest of our inheritance" (Eph. 1:14), alluding to both the immortality and eternal life of man, as well as to all that the Father hath awaiting the faithful who magnify their callings (see Rev. 21:3; D&C 84:38). This view follows from the word *redeem* that refers to the end of a financial transaction involving debt.

Another way some have interpreted the two coins is to see them representing the Old and New Testaments, though they were not yet codified, which the innkeeper would use to help the man understand the source of his spiritual poverty, encouraging man to take responsibility for his own sins, repenting as he learns the will of God by "feast[ing] upon the words of Christ; for behold, the words of Christ . . . tell [him] all things what [he] should do" (2 Ne. 32:3). From our

Latter-day Saint understanding, the two coins would denote the stick of Judah (the Bible) and the stick of Joseph (the Book of Mormon) (see Ezek. 37:19).

The promised remuneration for the additional care of the man corresponds to the grace of Christ's perfection that is sufficient after all the man could do for himself in serving the Lord (see 2 Ne. 25:23). In his book, *Believing Christ*, Stephen E. Robinson writes: "The good news is not that perfect people can be reconciled to God, but the *imperfect* people can.... The great secret is this: Jesus Christ will share *his* perfection, *his* sinlessness, *his* righteousness, *his* merits with us. In his mercy he offers us the use of his perfection, in the absence of our own, to satisfy the demands of justice."[32]

Fourth Order of the Virtual Reality: Likening unto Ourselves

Each of the Savior's parables is a call to action. Having read the parable, "see[ing] it feelingly," having considered its symbolic subtexts and allegorical implications, Jesus fully meant for each of His disciples to liken this narrative unto the narrative of their own lives and to augment what they are already doing befittingly or to make whatever course corrections needed. His words to the lawyer, "Go, and do likewise," apply equally to Latter-day Saints in our twenty-first century world.

Each of us may arrive at different visions of what this parable means for our lives because the details of our personal narratives differ as much as our biological DNA. We have to realize that our opportunities to be good Samaritans in peoples' lives are likely to be much less dramatic than what we see in the parable—less dramatic, but no less important. Moments to serve may be more like what we observe on the pioneer treks in which our young people participate.

Inevitably, one or more of them, who may not be in the first echelon of popularity, step up to help others during the most strenuous part of the trek. They are not showy; they do not look for praise; they may even hide from it. When help is needed, they simply get in, put their shoulders to the wheel, and help, without being asked. They are the kind of good Samaritans who surely came forward as our pioneer ancestors trekked westward to the Salt Lake Valley, then throughout the intermountain west. Their stories were mostly unsung in life, but "the song of redeeming love" was in every faith-filled footstep they took (Alma 5:36). Being a good Samaritan can occur in an infinite variety of circumstances, usually in the small and simple acts of life, but each such act has a common thread: it lifts another person in some way that is ultimately spiritual.

The question for each of us is: After reading the Savior's parable on several levels of meaning, can we see and feel ourselves as God's good Samaritans, having a positive impact on another person's life? I suspect that the reader of this book is already impacting others in uplifting ways, so maybe the Lord is challenging all of us to take another step upward in our discipleship to a level of compassion that we may not have thought was in us. We may need to feel more intensely after Christ (Acts 17:27; D&C 101:8). We may need to learn to feel the promptings of the Holy Spirit with greater sensitivity. He is *God* the Holy Spirit. Each such impression is, therefore, a sacred communication for us individually, meriting being written down just as much as Isaiah's or any of the other scriptures we have. What would have happened if Isaiah had not written down the impressions he received? The alternative to writing our impressions down is that we lose the meaning of these sacred communications in the vacuum of memory.

In each of us is the Light of Christ that we may "shine before men" as a lamp set high on a lampstand, making sure they see that the source of the light is the glory of God.[33] They may not perceive it the first, the second, the third time, or even in a lifetime, but when they arrive in the second part of our second estate, the spirit world, they will remember and rejoice in Christ.

Far from being just a wonderfully told story, the parable of the Good Samaritan is a powerful, multi-dimensional representation of the gospel of Jesus Christ that can continue to reveal its hidden layers of meaning over a lifetime as we search, research, and feel our way deeper into its narrative. The same applies to all the narratives the Lord has chosen to include in the scriptures.

Notes to Chapter 9

1. John W. Welch, "The Good Samaritan: A Type and Shadow of the Plan of Salvation," *BYU Studies* 38, 2 (1999), 50-115; hereafter Welch, Samaritan; also "The Good Samaritan: Forgotten Symbols," *Ensign* (Feb. 2007), 40-47.
2. Robert Alter, *The Art of Biblical Poetry* (New York, NY: Basic Books, 2011).
3. John Breck, *The Shape of Biblical Language* (Crestwood, NY: St. Vladimir's Seminary Press, 1994), 23-24; see Chapter 3 for a discussion of parallelism and its oft-used variation chiasmus.
4. By definition, eternal life is the quality of life that God lives, thus "Eternal" is one of His names (see Moses 7:35). When we accept Christ into our lives, we commit to knowing Him and His Father (see John 17:3). As used in the Old and New Testament, "to know" means to know through experience, reflected in the Savior's statement, "If any man will do his will, he shall know of the doctrine, whether it be of God, or whether I speak of myself" (John 7:17). Therefore, we gradually come to know eternal life by living the life that the Father and the Son live as best we can. Knowing also includes training our minds and spirits to think and feel as They would. Thus a disciple can live a degree of life eternal during his or her mortality.
5. The word *order* is used here in the sense of the "formal, regular, or methodological arrangement in the position of the things in any area or group" (*SOED*, s.v. "order").
6. See Richard Chenevix Trench, *The Miracles and Parables of Christ* (Chattanooga, TN: AMG Publishers, 1996), 505.

7. Evidence of this animus toward Samaritans is found in the episode at Jacob's Well when the Savior asked a Samaritan woman for a drink of water to which she replied: "How is it that thou, being a Jew, askest drink of me, which am a woman of Samaria? for the Jews have no dealings with the Samaritans" (John 4:9).
8. Jeffrey R. Holland, "He Hath Filled the Hungry with Good Things," *Ensign* (Nov. 1997), 66; hereafter Holland, "Good Things."
9. *Lectures*, 3:4.
10. *TWOT*, 1:307; also *Vine's Complete Expository Dictionary of Old and New Testament Words* (Nashville: Thomas Nelson, 1996), 142-43. In *The Interpreter's Dictionary of the Bible*, Elizabeth R. Achtemeier writes: "Generally, ... [mercy] denotes the divine love, manifested in saving acts of grace, which God holds for his covenant people. Human mercy, on the other hand, is usually a consideration, manifested in outward works, for the condition and needs of one's fellow men. . . . / God's mercy in the OT, like his faithfulness, his steadfast love, his righteousness, his judgments (cf. Hos. 2:19), represents his continual regard for the covenant which he has established with his chosen people, Israel (cf. Exod. 33:19; Isa. 63:9). . . . Further, although mercy signifies ... an affection or love within the divine person (cf. II Chr. 36:15), it is never described in the OT apart from its concrete manifestation in some outward act by Yahweh within history. It is, in general, a loving act of Yahweh by which he faithfully maintains his covenant relationship with his chosen people. . . . / In the [New Testament] gospels, those who are sick or suffering repeatedly appeal to Jesus for mercy . . . , and such appeals are naturally understood as cries for succor or healing. Thus Jesus' mercy is understood first in this sense. To have mercy—and here the verb ἐλεέω is used—means to render aid. / When describing Jesus' reaction to such need, ... the NT uses the verb σπλαγχνίζομαι, literally 'to be moved in one's bowels.' . . . [T]he Hebrews regarded [the bowels] as the center of tenderer affections, especially of kindness, benevolence, and pity" ("Mercy, Merciful; Compassion; Pity," *The Interpreter's Dictionary of the Bible*, ed. George Arthur Buttrick, 5 vols. (Nashville, TN: Abingdon Press, 1962), 5:352-353 passim.
11. See "he had *compassion* on him" (v. 33) and "he that showed *mercy* on him" (v. 37). In the Greek New Testament both words are translations of the same word: *eleéo*. In English, "compassion" is a compound of "-passion" that derives from the Greek *pathos* and the prefix "com-" from the Latin *cum* meaning "together," "with."
12. Katherine Doob Sakenfeld, "Love (OT)," *ABD*, 4: 380.

13. See Bohn, *Beatitudes*, 21.
14. William Shakespeare, *The Merchant of Venice*, act iv, sc 1, ll. 180-193.
15. See Richard Kalmin, "Levirate Law," *ABD*, 4:296-97.
16. In his article, "The 'Ceremony of the Shoe': A Ritual of God's Ancient Covenant People," Alonzo L. Gaskill takes issue with the almost universal understanding of the marriage of Ruth to Boaz as a levirate marriage. He finds that such requisite as Ruth not spitting in the face of her "next of kin," (which would have been out of character for Ruth), she didn't remove the man's shoe, the unnamed kinsman is *not* Ruth's husband's brother, etc. disqualify the marriage as levirate. I respectfully disagree with Professor Gaskill that the points he mentions disqualify the marriage as levirate since Naomi identifies Boaz as a near kin *go'el* and encourages Ruth to approach him as such. The spreading of the skirt is part of the levirate tradition. The fact that Boaz goes to the city gate to confront the next of kin with his duty, the man declines, and removes the shoe, are all indicative of the levirate tradition. The deviations may have had more to do with local flexibility and/or tradition from the law (https.//rsc.byu.edu/archived/our-rites-worship-latter-day-saint-views-ritual-history-scripture-and- practice/ceremony, 4-5.
17. For a somewhat more complete discussion of the book of Ruth, cf. Bohn, *Beatitudes*, 150-160. From the marriage of Ruth to Boaz came a son, Obed, given to Naomi, Ruth's first husband's mother—a son who became the father of Jesse, the grandfather of David, and, therefore, in the direct lineage of the Savior, lifting the story from a local occurrence into a symbol for the marriage of the Lamb to His Church and well as to individual members thereof.
18. The Jews perception of the Samaritans may parallel the underlying tone of their disdain for the Moabites in the book of Ruth and, therefore, their initial, though unexpressed, reception of Ruth, a Moabitess. But, like the Samaritan in the parable, Ruth overcomes any negative regard for her with her goodness in the way she tends to her mother in law, Naomi. In the end, Ruth acts as a *go'el* toward Naomi, something reserved for men in the society, by giving Naomi her [Ruth's] firstborn to perpetuate Naomi's husband's family line, a line that leads to the Savior.
19. For a discussion of peacemakers, see Bohn, *Beatitudes*, 98-101.
20. James E. Faust, "A Second Birth," *Ensign* (June 1998), 5.
21. JD, 2:129-30; italics added. What President Young described, Elder Russell M. Nelson termed "mortal perfection" vis à vis "immortal or eternal perfection" ("Perfection Pending," *Ensign* [Nov. 1995], 86.)

22. Ezra Taft Benson, "A Mighty Change of Heart," *Ensign* (Oct. 1989), 5.
23. The pure love of Christ is the ultimate disposition of a righteous disciple; his or her penultimate goal in the proximate reality of worldliness is to pray for and seek to act with such a degree of merciful kindness that he or she might manifest a "measure of the stature of Christ" (Eph. 4:13) in order that the Savior's "arm of mercy," extended to all who come unto Him (see 3 Ne. 9:14), might wrap them in His salvific love after all they *can* do (see 2 Ne. 25:23).
24. Rick Warren, *The Purpose-driven Life* (Grand Rapids, MI: Zondervan, 2002), 127.
25. See *TDNT*, 6:973-76: s.v. "ῥακά."
26. Dieter F. Uchtdorf, "It Works Wonderfully," *Ensign* (Nov. 2015), 21. (20-23)
27. A good example of the allegorical interpretation of the parable of the Good Samaritan is found in the "Good Samaritan" window of the famous Gothic cathedral in Chartres, France. The top of the window depicts the story of Adam and Eve that is linked to the parable of the Good Samaritan in the bottom panel. See Welch, Samaritan, esp. 51-90.
28. *TDNT*, 1:10, s.v. "adam."
29. Holland, "Good Things," 66.
30. Neal A. Maxwell, ""'Settle This in Your Hearts,'" *Ensign* (Nov. 1992), 66. (65-67)
31. C. S. Lewis wrote an imaginative, thought-provoking story about how the devils try to orchestrate the sins of man in the small book entitled *The Screwtape Letters*, a work familiar to many.
32. Stephen R. Robinson, *Believing Christ* (Salt Lake City: Deseret Book, 1992), 13, 14.
33. The significance of envisioning the light of Christ as a lamp becomes clearer in the parable of the ten virgins, each of whom has a lamp. That lamp is the outward manifestation of the inner lamp representing the light of Christ in each individual. It is to be used to light the path for the Bridegroom returning to fetch His bride at the time of the Second Coming, meaning that lamp shines to prepare for His return, something that the Apostles today are asking members to do with greater urgency. See Bohn, *Matthew 25*, 27 (parable of the ten virgins).

CHAPTER 9

THE LORD'S VISION OF BEAUTY IN THE SCRIPTURES

In chapter 3 (page 51), I cite Doctrine and Covenants 82:14 to certify that the Lord does indeed have a standard of beauty. Using that same verse as a building block, the present chapter explores the vision of beauty expounded in the scriptures.

> For Zion must increase in beauty, and in holiness; her borders must be enlarged; her stakes must be strengthened; yea, verily I say unto you, Zion must arise and put on her beautiful garments.

The Beauty of the Lord

In the wording of D&C 82:14, the word *holiness* stands in apposition to beauty, holiness, therefore, is inherently beautiful.[1] Significantly,

Heavenly Father declared that "Man of Holiness is my name" (Moses 7:35), encompassing beauty as an essential characteristic of His being. Thus, as with all other principles of the gospel, beauty is first associated with and finds its perfection in the Father and the Son. Psalm 27:4 states: "One thing have I desired of the Lord, that will I seek after; that I may dwell in the house of the Lord all the days of my life, to behold *the beauty of the Lord*, and to enquire in his temple" (emphasis added); the psalmic prayer of Moses asks: "let the *beauty of the Lord* be upon us" (Ps. 90:17; emphasis added); Isaiah 28:5 reads: In that day shall the Lord of hosts be for a crown of glory, and for *a diadem of beauty*, unto the residue of his people" (emphasis added); Zechariah 9:17: "For how great is his goodness, and how great is his beauty," drawing a parallel between goodness and beauty, tandem principles discussed below.

When Jesus said, "he that hath seen me hath seen the Father" (John 14:9), implicit in that statement were the principles of beauty, holiness, and goodness. He is the Son of Man of Holiness, possessing the divine beauty of His Father. When the Spirit of the Lord caught Nephi away into an exceeding high mountain, and allowed him to view the tree of life, as had Lehi, Nephi saw that "the beauty thereof is far beyond, yea exceeding of all beauty; and the whiteness thereof did exceed the whiteness of the driven snow" (1 Ne. 11:8). (White is the color of beauty, perhaps because it can easily be associated with light.) The angel then gave Nephi to understand that the tree represented the Lamb of God, Jesus Christ (1 Ne. 11:14-21). In his great apocalyptic vision, John saw the tree of life, a symbol of Jesus Christ and His love (see 1 Ne. 11:21-25), "in the mist of the street [proceeding from the throne of God and the Lamb], and on either side of the river, which bear twelve manner of fruits, yielded her fruit every month" (Rev. 22:2), "the fruit thereof [being] white to exceed all . . . whiteness (1 Ne. 8:11) and, therefore, representing the beauty of the tree of life (see 1 Ne. 11:8), whose subtexts include the Lord's love, faith, light, and truth, the perfection of beauty. Which brings us to perhaps the cardinal quality of divine beauty, for Nephi recognized that inner beauty of the tree of life was "the love of God, which sheddeth itself abroad in the hearts of the children of men; wherefore, it is the most desirable above all things" (1 Ne. 11:22). The love of God is, then, an aesthetic quality of paramount significance, defining the beauty of God, and the point at which a discussion of beauty as it relates to the Lord begins, followed by four qualities deeply interrelated to it: faith, light, truth, and goodness.

God is love

In his gospel, the Apostle John wrote: "For God so loved the world, that he gave his only begotten Son, that whosoever believeth in him should not perish, but have everlasting life" (John 3:16); and in his first epistle we read simply, "God is love" (1 John 4:8, 16). Among the synonyms for the love of God, including charity (Gk. *agape*), none is repeated more often in the scriptures than "mercy" and "merciful," appearing 550 times, most referring to the Lord. The Hebrew word for "mercy" in the Old Testament, and informing the New Testament Greek word translated as mercy (*eleéō* [ἐλεέω], e.g., Matt. 5:7; Luke 10:37), is *hesed*, discussed in chapter 9 in conjunction with the parable of the Good Samaritan. But, in addition to the Good Samaritan, many of the Savior's parables illustrate *hesed*, e.g., the parable of the prodigal (lost) son; each expresses a divine moral beauty that has inspired people over the centuries. Any expression of love in mortality is beautiful: a husband for his wife, a wife for her husband; parents for children, children for parents—each projecting a degree of godliness.

God is love; God is mercy; God is charity, the pure love of Christ, and it is through His all-encompassing love that He exercises the power of His faith, for "faith . . . worketh by love" (see Gal. 5:6; see also chapter 1).

God of Faith

Faith as the power by which God created and governs the universe is discussed in chapter 1 (pp. 20-21). We see the Lord's powerful faith and His beauty in the cosmos He created, in the magnificent pictures taken from space by the Hubble telescope, a black and white image of perhaps the most famous of those picture appears below. He is also discernible in the telestial world of nature (not cities). No wonder He has revealed through the theophanic experience of one of His prophet that "all things are created and made to bear record of me, both things which are temporal, and things which are spiritual; things which are in the heavens above, and things which are on the earth, and things which are in the earth, and things which are under the earth, both above and beneath: all things bear record of me" (Moses 6:63). The gist of these verses seems to be that those with faith-conditioned eyes can perceive His presence in the grand scope as well as in the details of Creation.

"Mystic Mountain": A Pillar of Gas and Dust in the Carina Nebula · HUBBLESITE.org

If faith is the power whereby God governs the universe, then it is closely related to light, the Light of Christ, "which is the law by which all things are governed, even *the power of God* who sitteth upon his throne, who is in the bosom of eternity, who is in the midst of all things" (D&C 88:13; emphasis added).

God is light

Also in his first epistle, John wrote, "God is light" (1 John 1:5), echoing the Savior's declaration, "I am the light of the world: . . . the light of life" (John 8:12; also 3 Ne. 9:18; D&C 11:28; 12:9). "The light of life" is more than merely a metaphor; it expresses the cosmic reality that the Light of Christ "giveth life to all things" (D&C 88:13), a profound integer in the heavenly calculus of existence, represented in the Lord's name, YHWH, Yahweh. The inner significance of the name Yahweh is found in the title by which the Lord told Moses to identify Him to the Israelites, "I AM THAT I AM" (Exod. 3:14). "I AM" signifies that He "is a self-existent being,"[2] whereas all other beings, man included, have life through Him. That this applies to both the Savior and His Father He made clear when He declared, "For the Father hath life in himself; so hath he given to the Son to have life in himself" (John 5:26). When, in the scriptures, Jesus is reported to have said "I am," it carries with it all the meaning contained in "I AM THAT I AM."[3]

It is the Savior's live-giving light that "proceed[s] forth from the presence of God to fill the immensity of space" (D&C 88:12), represented in "a pure river of water of life, . . . proceeding forth from the throne of God and the Lamb" (Rev. 22:1). His light also indwells "every man that cometh into the world and . . . enlighteneth every man . . . that harkeneth to the voice of the Spirit" (D&C 84:46), meaning the Holy Spirit. Elder Bruce R. McConkie explained the symbiotic relationship between the Holy Spirit and the Light of Christ: "Visions and revelations come . . . by the power of the Holy Ghost, and the Light of Christ, the all-pervading, universally present Spirit, is the vehicle used by the Holy Ghost to operate and function in all the world. That is, the Holy Ghost uses the Light of Christ to manifest his power and make available his gifts to all men everywhere at one and the same time."[4] Thus, when the Holy Spirit gently caresses our indwelling Light of Christ with the heaven-sent, love-filled warmth of inspiration, whether like a gentle breeze whispering revelation to us or, perhaps once or twice in a lifetime, like a gale-force wind that drives us to our knees, shedding tears of gratitude for "the love Jesus offers us."[5] Whatever the case may be, that inspiration enlightens our minds with understanding (see Alma 32:28), we feel the love of God encouraging us along the path toward eternal life, helping us more clearly see and follow the markers the Savior left along the way, markers set forth in the Beatitudes. Our proactive response to God's love would be to take one step of faith after the other toward the light—"the light and life of the world" (3 Ne. 9:18; 11:11; D&C 10:70; 11:28). Whenever man is privileged to partake of the divine light, it is a very sacred instant of love and beauty offered by the Third Member of the Godhead.

One of the most common metaphors in the scriptures is light of truth, united supernally in the Holy Spirit, "the Spirit of truth," who indwells every confirmed, righteous person. The love of God, then, is an essential part of both the light and truth from heaven; because He loves us, He wants to reveal as many eternal truths as we're prepared to receive, enlightening our minds to discern the beauty of the principles that, together, form the gospel of Jesus Christ. Elder Maxwell taught, "Those who have eyes to see and ears to hear, it is clear that the Father and the Son are giving away the secrets of the universe!"[6]

God of Truth

Centuries of prophetic writings have proclaimed, in one way or another, that the Lord is "the God of truth" (Isa. 65:16). In a modern revelation we read, "The glory of God . . . is light and truth" (D&C 93:36). During His earthly ministry, Jesus declared, "I am the way, the truth, and the life" (John 14:6). Wherever and whenever we find truth, God's light is in the details.

By divine definition, "truth is knowledge of things as they are, and as they were, and as they are to come" (D&C 93:24), in other words, "things as they really are" (Jacob 4:13), both physically and metaphysically. The overarching truths of eternity emanate from heaven, truths revealed in the four standard works of the Church and through continuous revelation to individuals in their spheres of responsibility. In the first instance this would be the Lord's living prophet; he is the voice of the Lord for the theology and administration for the Church as a whole (see D&C 1:38); but the will and mind of the Lord may also be declared by any of the fifteen Apostles: when moved upon by the Holy Spirit, their counseling and teaching becomes scripture, meaning "the word of the Lord, . . . the voice of the Lord, and the power of God unto salvation" (D&C 68:4). Having had the gift of the Holy Spirit bestowed upon them, continuing, personal revelation of truth from heaven is also the privilege of every baptized member of the Church in their spheres of responsibilities: father, mother, children in their families, in Church callings, etc.

God is Goodness

Alma made clear that "whatsoever is good cometh from God" (Alma 5:40); likewise Mormon: "All things which are good cometh of Christ" (Moro. 7:24).

While beauty is seldom mentioned in the King James New Testament, beauty is revealed in a less obvious way, namely in the Greek word *kalos*, appearing over ninety times in the New Testament, usually translated as "good." Christ, for instance, is "the good [*kalos*] shepherd" (John 10:11, 14). *Kalos* has a strong undertone of beauty resulting from its usage among the ancient Greeks for whom it expressed moral beauty in action. William Barclay, twentieth-century Scottish theologian, has written:

> Wherever this word [*kalos*] is found there is the idea of loveliness, of attractiveness, of graciousness, of that which delights the heart and gives pleasure to the eye. . . .
>
> [*K*]*alos* is that which is not only practically and morally good, but that which is also aesthetically good. . . .
>
> *Kalos* is the word of the goodness which is a lovely thing, the goodness which not only satisfies the conscience, but which also delights the heart, and gives pleasure to the eye. . . .
>
> One of the most interesting and significant uses of *kalos* is that it is repeatedly and consistently used to describe the *good deeds* which should characterize the life of the Christian. . . .
>
> In all his efforts to be good, in all his striving toward moral holiness, the Christian must never forget the *beauty of holiness*. . . .

> The basic idea in the word *kalos* is the idea of winsome beauty; and we are bound to see that nothing can be *kalos unless* it be the product of love. Deeds which are *kalos* are the outcome of a heart in which love reigns supreme. The outward beauty of the deed springs from the inward magnitude of the love within the heart. . . .
>
> That which tugs at men's hearts and pulls them to Christ is the winsome attractiveness in Jesus Christ himself, the attractiveness which ought to reside in those who claim to be his.[7]

As the ancient Greeks thought, truth is good and beautiful; goodness is true and beautiful; beauty is true and good.

In Sum

The five qualities of godly nature discussed above—love, light, faith, truth, and goodness—constitute a compound in one whose central, unifying principles is God's all-encompassing merciful love for His children, i.e., the compassionate kindness that informs His creative, quickening faith and the light of His truth that fills the immensity of space, qualities associated with our Savior, Jesus Christ, the Jehovah of the Old Testament as well. His is "the pure love . . . [that] endureth forever" (Moro. 7:47). These qualities and more[8] combine to make the Father and the Son the perfection of beauty. Consequently, all things associated with the Father and the Son mirror Their beauty, attested to by the Prophet Joseph, recorded in his theophanic vision of the celestial kingdom:

> The heavens were opened upon us, and I beheld the celestial kingdom of God, and the glory thereof, whether in the body or out I cannot tell.
>
> I saw the transcendent beauty of the gate through which the heirs of that kingdom will enter, which was like unto circling flames of fire;
>
> Also the blazing throne of God, whereon was seated the Father and the Son.
>
> I saw the beautiful streets of that kingdom, which had the appearance of being paved with gold (D&C 137:1-4)[9]

The "circling flames of fire" appear in most descriptions of the celestial kingdom found in the scriptures[10]; they are metaphoric representations to give man a proximate description of the otherwise indescribable beauty of the glory of God.

Zion – The City of Enoch

In Psalm 50 we read: "Out of Zion, the perfection of beauty, God hath shined" (Ps. 50:2). While the root of the word *Zion* has been the source of scholarly research, centered on Jerusalem,[11] ancient scripture translated by, and a modern revelation revealed through, Joseph Smith have provided two references that clarify the essence of Zion, contributing to our understanding of the divine vision of beauty.

The prime example of the Lord's beauty indwelling and thereby inspiring His people to act in a godly manner is the City of Enoch, "the City of Holiness" (Moses 7:19), therefore, the City of Beauty.[12] Three qualities defined their holiness and, therefore, the beauty of their community: "the Lord called his people ZION, because they were of *one heart and one mind*, and *dwelt in righteousness*; and there was *no poor among them*" (Moses 7:18; capitalization in text; emphasis added).

Oneness

The oneness of purpose that exists among the members of the Godhead is a high priority They have for the disciples of Christ: "That they all may be one; as thou, Father, art in me, and I in thee, that they also may be one in us: that the world may believe that thou hast sent me" (John 17:21). Paul fleshed out the qualities that form the kind of unity the people of the City of Enoch embodied, writing:

> There is one body, and one Spirit, even as ye are called in one hope of your calling;
> One Lord, one faith, one baptism,
> One God and Father of all, who *is* above all, and through all, and in you all (Eph. 4:4-6).

One body that "hath need of every member, that all may be edified together, that the system may be kept perfect" (D&C 84:110; see also 1 Cor. 12). "One Spirit": the Holy Spirit, the Third Member of the Godhead, who unites disciples with Christ and, thereby, with one another. "One Lord," Jesus Christ, and, therefore, "one faith" in Jesus Christ as the Son of the Living God, the Savior of the world by virtue of His Atonement for the sins of man and His Resurrection whereby He has overcome death and secured immortality for all and eternal life for those who choose to come unto Him, who enter into covenants with Him through the prescribed ordinances of the priesthood, and obey His commandments. "One baptism" in two stages: by immersion in water followed by the sanctifying fire and commission of the Holy Spirit. With this twofold ordinance, the person to be baptized takes the Savior's name and pledges fidelity to Him by words and actions. This baptism, furthermore, unites them with the Savior's Atonement and Resurrection:

> That by reason of transgression cometh the fall, which fall bringeth death, and inasmuch as ye were born into the world by water, and blood, and the spirit, which I have made, and so became of dust a living soul, even so ye must be born again into the kingdom of heaven, of water, and of the Spirit, and be cleansed by blood, even the blood of mine Only Begotten; that ye might be sanctified from all sin, and enjoy the words of eternal life in this world, and eternal life in the world to come, even immortal glory;
>
> For by the water ye keep the commandment; by the Spirit ye are justified, and by the blood ye are sanctified (Moses 6:59-60).

The promise is magnificent:

> Therefore it is given to abide in you; the record of heaven; the Comforter; the peaceable things of immortal glory; the truth of all things; that which quickeneth all things, which maketh alive all things; that which knoweth all things, and hath all power according to wisdom, mercy, truth, justice, and judgment (Moses 6:61).

When stated in such concentrated, telegrammed style, the promise is both thought provoking and stunning in its expansiveness from the macrocosm of eternity to the microcosm of mortal man who is a god in embryo. The record in heaven may well be in us as the Light or Spirit of Christ (see D&C 84:45-46). I imagine our inborn, indwelling Light of Christ to be like a lockbox: we have one key to unlock it, that being the prayer of a sincere heart wanting to know truth, with faith in Jesus Christ as the Son of the Living God and our Savior, having done our due diligence by searching and pondering the scriptures (see John 5:39; Moro. 10:4). The other key is held by the Holy Spirit who knows when to open the box to reveal and release line upon line of eternal truth as we are prepared to receive and act upon it. The Spirit brings "the wisdom that is from above is first pure, then peaceable, gentle, and easy to be intreated, full of mercy and good fruits, without partiality, and without hypocrisy" (James 3:17). Out of this promise can come the oneness among disciples, mirroring the oneness among the Godhead, for which the Savior so fervently prayed (see John 17:11, 21).

Oneness among the Saints is a serious matter: in this last dispensation, God has warned Latter-day Saints, "if ye are not one ye are not mine" (D&C 38:27). The key to becoming one is the shared feelings of revealed truth from the Holy Spirit. Said the Prophet Joseph, "by union of feeling we obtain power with God."[13] The power of oneness in and among Latter-day Saints is becoming increasingly important as the work hastens in our time against an ominous backdrop of evil and amorality. Maturing into the beauty of holiness by keeping our hearts tuned to the Spirit and our eyes single to the glory of God, searching the scriptures, heeding the words of the living prophet, keeping the commandments of God, being proactively engaged in the ministering mission of the Savior is vital in growing our testimonies of Jesus Christ, His gospel, and His Church to help others find their way to all three.

Reyna I. Aburto, second counselor in the Relief Society General Presidency, gave a profound, insightful address on the importance of unity among Latter-day Saints, using a colony of Monarch butterflies as her metaphor.

> A group of butterflies is called a kaleidoscope. . . . Each butterfly in a kaleidoscope is unique and different, yet these seemingly fragile creatures have been designed by a loving Creator with the ability to survive, travel, multiply, and disseminate life as they go from one flower to the next, spreading pollen. And although each butterfly is different, they work together to make the world a more beautiful and fruitful place.
>
> Like the monarch butterflies, we are on a journey back to our heavenly home, where we will reunite with our Heavenly Parents. Like the butterflies, we have been given divine attributes that allow us to navigate through life, in order to "[fill] the measure of [our] creation" (Doctrine and Covenants 88:19; see also Doctrine and Covenants 88:25). Like them, if we knit our hearts together (see Mosiah 18:21), the Lord will protect us "as a hen [gathers] her chickens under her wings" (3 Nephi 10:4) and will make us into a beautiful kaleidoscope. . . .
>
> Jesus Christ is the ultimate example of unity with His Father. They are one in purpose, in love, and in works, with "the will of the Son being swallowed up in the will of the Father" (Mosiah 15:7). . . .

Every one of our paths is different, yet we walk them together. Our path is not about what we have done or where we have been; it is about where we are going and what we are becoming, in unity. When we counsel together guided by the Holy Ghost, we can see where we are and where we need to be. The Holy Ghost gives us a vision that our natural eyes cannot see, because "revelation is scattered among us," and when we put that revelation together, we can see more.

As we work in unity, our purpose should be to look for and do the Lord's will; our incentive should be the love we feel for God and for our neighbor (see Matthew 22:37-40); and our greatest desire should be to "labor diligently" (Jacob 5:61), so we can prepare the way for the glorious return of our Savior. The only way we will be able to do so is "with one accord."

Like the monarch butterflies, let us continue on our journey together in purpose, each of us with our own attributes and contributions, working to make this a more beautiful and fruitful world—one small step at a time and in harmony with God's commandments.

Our Lord Jesus Christ has promised us that when we are gathered together in His name, He is in the midst of us.[14]

Dwell in Righteousness

To dwell in righteousness means to live and act according to the principles of righteousness:

> by persuasion, by long-suffering, by gentleness and meekness, and by love unfeigned;
>
> By kindness, and pure knowledge, which shall greatly enlarge the soul without hypocrisy, and without guile—
>
> Reproving betimes with sharpness, when moved upon by the Holy Ghost; and then showing forth afterwards an increase of love toward him whom thou hast reproved, lest he esteem thee to be his enemy;
>
> That he may know that thy faithfulness is stronger than the cords of death.
>
> Let thy bowels also be full of charity towards all men, and to the household of faith, and let virtue garnish thy thoughts unceasingly . . . . (D&C 121:41-45).

The promise is, again, resplendent:

> . . . then shall thy confidence wax strong in the presence of God; and the doctrine of the priesthood shall distil upon thy soul as the dews from heaven. The Holy Ghost shall be thy constant companion, and thy scepter an unchanging scepter of righteousness and truth; and thy dominion shall be an everlasting dominion, and without compulsory means it shall flow unto thee forever and ever (D&C 121:46).

This assurance amplifies the promise in Moses 6:61 above. In short, to dwell in righteousness is to live in the image of Christ, for one of His titles is "THE LORD OUR RIGHTEOUSNESS" (Jer. 23:6; also 33:16; capitalization in text).

No Poor Among Them

That the City of Holiness had no poor among them reminds us of the Lord's oft-repeated call to care for the poor—those needing the necessities of life, as well as the poor in spirit. Caring for the poor is what the righteous sheep in the Last Judgment did (see Matt. 25:40). Regarding the word *beauty* in "beauty of holiness," William A. Dyrness has written that "of all the [Hebrew] words of beauty, this one seems best suited to God himself and seems appropriate in people only when they reflect something of his character,"[15] which apparently the people of Enoch's city did to have the Lord, the Man of Holiness, attribute holiness to them. To so care for others is of major import in "worship[ping] the Lord in the beauty of holiness" (1 Chron. 16:29; Ps. 29:2; 96:9). As President James E. Faust said, "There is no higher worship than the unpurchased service to another soul of whatever faith, belief, or social stratum."[16] Such good works are beautiful in the eternal sense because they are rendered in the name of the Lord for the sake of those being helped. In this way, the disciple comes to know, i.e., experience, God the Father and Jesus Christ which is, by definition, is eternal life (see John 17:3). And there is a difference between good works in the name of the Lord and those without any reference to the Lord: the former glorify God and invite others to come unto Christ and know Him.

Years ago the young women of the Church released balloons with their own personal messages for whomever might find their balloon. It was reported that a young Korean sister's note read: "May those who know you, but don't know Him, want to know Him because they know you."

Zion – The Pure in Heart

The second reference to the Zion discipleship is found in Doctrine and Covenants 97:21: "Zion—the pure in heart" (small caps in verse). The word *pure* refers to the process of purification or sanctification that is fundamental to the progression of a disciple toward a degree of perfection during mortality and after, a process Moroni explained:

> Yea, come unto Christ, and be perfected in him, and deny yourselves of all ungodliness; and if ye shall deny yourselves of all ungodliness, and love God with all your might, mind and strength, then is his grace sufficient for you, that by his grace ye may be perfect in Christ; and if by the grace of God ye are perfect in Christ, ye can in nowise deny the power of God.
>
> And again, if ye by the grace of God are perfect in Christ, and deny not his power, then are ye *sanctified in Christ by the grace of God, through the shedding of the blood of Christ*, which is in the covenant of the Father unto the remission of your sins, that ye become holy, without spot (Moro. 10:32-33; emphasis added).

Commenting on Doctrine and Covenants 133:62 ("And unto him that repenteth and sanctifieth himself before the Lord shall be given eternal life."), Stephen E. Robinson and H. Dean Garrett have written:

> To be sanctified is the process of overcoming sin and becoming subject to the laws of God. It involves not only the atoning power of Christ but also the individual doing his or her part through repentance and obedience

to the gospel of Jesus Christ. Therefore, the command is to "sanctify yourselves; yea, purify your hearts, and cleanse your hands and your feet before me, that I may make you clean" (D&C 88:63, 74). These verses teach that as we remove ourselves from sin through repentance and focus on the mind and will of God, the cleansing and healing power of the Atonement will then prepare our souls for exaltation and eternal life.[17]

In the Beatitudes, Jesus framed purity of heart between acting mercifully and being a peacemaker, the three, in effect, form another "compound in one" (2 Ne. 2:11) of mature, discipleship, i.e., finished spiritually.[18] Since mercy, or compassionate kindness, is a prime quality of God's nature,[19] to act with any degree of mercy toward another of His children is to act with godliness, manifesting the spirit of the second great commandment to love one's neighbor.[20] It's hard to imagine any degree of mercy without a corresponding degree of purity of heart, for the merciful act on the principle that "charity," viz. mercy, "out of a pure heart is the end of the commandment" (1 Tim. 1:5).[21] Because their hearts are purified of prejudice, the pure in heart see the divine image in others, recognizing that all people are the spiritual offspring of Heavenly Father and not "mere mortals."[22] The renowned nineteenth-century British critic, John Ruskin, wrote: "All great men [and women] . . . have a curious . . . feeling that the greatness is not in them, but through them. . . . And they see something Divine and God-made in every other man they meet, and are endlessly, foolishly, incredibly merciful."[23]

Based on the parable of the Good Samaritan (Chapter 9), the merciful-pure-in-heart are also peacemakers who seek to emulate "The Prince of Peace" (Isa. 9:6; 2 Ne. 19:6) by helping others bear their burdens, mourning with those that mourn, comforting those needing comfort with the same comfort they receive from God (see 2 Cor. 1:3-4; Mosiah 18:8-9). The peace these peacemakers help others find is more than the resolution of a problem or a conflict; rather it is the peace the Savior promised (see John 14:27), expressed in the Hebrew *shalom*: a deep, inner harmony of spirit at one with self and, ideally, at one with the Christ Who wants to lift all who come unto Him, especially the brokenhearted.

The blessing accorded the peacemakers is to be "the children of God" (Matt. 5:9; 3 Ne. 12:9). The New Testament Greek word translated as "children" is *huíos* (υἱός), which specifically denotes a "son," therefore, the blessing is "they shall be the sons of God," which is tantamount to a declaration of exaltation. Daniel C. Peterson, professor of Islamic Studies and Arabic at Brigham Young University, has persuasively written that that the sobriquet "son of God" refers to one who has been endowed with godhood in the council of gods under the direction of Jesus Christ.[24] We are reminded of the Lord's description of those "who shall come forth in the resurrection of the just":

> They are they who received the testimony of Jesus, and believed on his name and were baptized after the manner of his burial, being buried in the water in his name, and this according to the commandment which he has given—
>
> That by keeping the commandments they might be washed and cleansed from all their sins, and receive the Holy Spirit by the laying on of the hands of him who is ordained and sealed unto this power;
>
> And who overcome by faith, and are sealed by the Holy Spirit of promise, which the Father sheds forth upon all those who are just and true.

They are they who are the church of the Firstborn.

They are they into whose hands the Father has given all things—

They are they who are priests and kings, who have received of his fulness, and of his glory;

And are priests of the Most High, after the order of Melchizedek, which was after the order of Enoch, which was after the order of the Only Begotten Son.

Wherefore, as it is written, *they are gods, even the sons of God*—(D&C 76:50-58; emphasis added).

Those described in these verses are the meek whom the Lord taught His ways (see Ps. 25;29), and they obeyed. Indeed, "the Lord will *beautify* the meek with salvation" (Ps. 149:4).

Beauty of Discipleship

The Savior instructed His disciples to "let your light so shine before men, that they may see your good [kalos] works, and glorify your Father in heaven" (Matt. 5:16). To this end, He imbued them with "the good [kalos] word of God, and the powers of the world to come" (Heb. 6:5). He taught them that "every good [kalos] tree brings forth good [kalos] fruit" (Matt. 7:17).

During the late eighteenth and early nineteenth centuries in Germany and England there was considerable discussion of a concept called the beautiful soul that traces back to Plato's *The Republic*: "And when a beautiful soul [*psychē kalē* (ψυχή χαλή)] harmonizes with a beautiful form, and the two are cast in one mold, that will be the fairest of sights to him who has an eye to see it?"[25] In a study of this concept, the German dramatist and essayist Friedrich Schiller wrote that "a beautiful soul is one in which duty and desire are in harmony, and grace [or graciousness] is its expression.[26]

The principle of duty transforming into desire is implicit in the gospel. Duty is the first step: "Wherefore, now let every man learn his duty, and to act in the office in which he is appointed, in all diligence" (D&C 107:99). But just doing one's duty is not the ideal toward which God would lead us; it is rather transforming the duty of discipleship into the desire to serve whereby disciples enter a higher niveau in which they enthusiastically engage in *good* causes, "and do many things of their own free will, and bring to pass much righteousness" (D&C 58:27). Such are the good undershepherds in the Lord's kingdom whose actions are beautiful in their graciousness. When Isaiah sang, "How beautiful upon the mountains are the feet of him that bringeth good tidings, that publisheth peace; that bringeth good tidings of good, that publisheth salvation; that saith unto Zion, Thy God reigneth" (Isa. 52:7), he sang in the first instance of the Messiah, but secondly of all those who come unto Him and take up His causes, emulating His good viz. beautiful work (see Rom. 10:15; 1 Ne. 13:37; Mosiah 15:16-18; 3 Ne. 20:40).

Few examples of such good and beautiful discipleship surpass the brief episode between Peter and a beggar, significantly, at the *Beautiful Gate* of the temple complex.

> Now Peter and John went up together into the temple at the hour of prayer, *being* the ninth *hour.*
>
> And a certain man lame from his mother's womb was carried, whom they laid daily at the gate of the temple

which is called Beautiful, to ask alms of them that entered into the temple;

Who seeing Peter and John about to go into the temple asked an alms.

And Peter, fastening his eyes upon him with John, said, Look on us.

And he gave heed unto them, expecting to receive something of them.

Then Peter said, Silver and gold have I none; but such as I have give I thee: In the name of Jesus Christ of Nazareth rise up and walk.

And he took him by the right hand, and lifted *him* up: and immediately his feet and ankle bones received strength.

And he leaping up stood, and walked, and entered with them into the temple, walking, and leaping, and praising God.

And all the people saw him walking and praising God:

And they knew that it was he which sat for alms at the Beautiful gate of the temple: and they were filled with wonder and amazement at that which had happened unto him (Acts 3:1-10).

We notice that the beggar, who could then walk, praised God, not Peter, as it should be.

In a Brigham Young University devotional, Elder Ulisses Soares said that, "Figuratively, we all have the potential to become beautiful works of art [beautiful souls?] in the Lord's hands. In this sense, He is the sculptor and He uses a hammer and chisel to mold us through our experiences day by day. If we allow the Lord to shape us, the result will be wonderful."[27]

Kalos works are godly deeds of goodness, because "whatsoever is good comes from God" (Alma 5:40); and if godly in nature, such acts express mercy in the broad sense of the word. And through their godly works disciples worship the Lord in the beauty of holiness (e.g., Matt. 25:40; Mosiah 2:17).

Beautiful Garments

The beautiful garments the Lord commanded Zion to put on in this dispensation evoke the wedding motif in the scriptures that pictures the Lord betrothing Himself to His people, as individuals and together in which the beautiful garments play an important role.[28]

When we think of weddings, we may well see in our mind's eye the bride in a white gown of elegant material. For the righteous invited to the great wedding feast after the Last Judgment, both the Bridegroom and brides will be resplendently beautiful: the bride "clothed . . . with garments of salvation, . . . covered with the robe of righteousness"; the "bridegroom deck[ed] . . . with ornaments" (Isa. 61:10). (A footnote in the LDS scriptures tells us that "ornaments" is more properly translated as "a crown of beauty.") In his great Ilse-of-Patmos vision, John saw the meaning of the robe the brides will wear for the feast and its meaning:

> Let us be glad and rejoice, and give honour to him: for the marriage of the Lamb is come, and his wife hath made herself ready.
>
> And to her was granted that she should be *arrayed in fine linen, clean* [sanctified] *and white: for the fine linen is the righteousness of saints.*
>
> And he saith unto me, Write, Blessed *are* they which are called unto the marriage supper of the Lamb. And he saith unto me, These are the true sayings of God (Rev. 19:7-9; emphasis added).

As mentioned above, white is the color associated with beauty in the scriptures, from which we understand that from the heavenly perspective, righteousness is beautiful, and beauty is a spiritual and not a physical quality. We further understand that **THE ROBE OF RIGHTEOUSNESS IS THE BEAUTIFUL GARMENT** that Zion saints must wear to reside in the celestial temple in the presence of Heavenly Father and Jesus Christ.

As any Latter-day Saint knows, preparing to be ultimately worthy for the Lord to clothe one in a robe of righteousness is anything but easy in this life, surrounded as we are by the distractions, temptations, and full-out evil that are part of the mortal experience. Consequently, we may spend most of life in an armor of righteousness as Victor L. Ludlow, emeritus professor of religion at Brigham Young University, has written:

> The imagery of special clothing conveys lasting impressions to the reader. For example, Isaiah's earlier use of "armor" (59:17) brings to mind the "armor of

righteousness," which all saints should wear. (2 Ne. 1:23; Eph. 6:11-12.) Armor is uncomfortable, heavy, and awkward, just as maintaining righteousness in a world of wickedness can make one feel separated from the world while living in the world. Some may feel that the armor or righteousness is too confining and shed it, thus falling to the dangers of the world. Soon they find that they have exchanged the slightly awkward armor for the absolutely confining "chains of hell." (Alma 5:7, 9-10.) On the other hand, those who faithfully wear the armor are promised a time when they will be clothed with the more comfortable "robes of righteousness." (2 Ne. 9:14.) Isaiah's repeated use of "garments," "robes," and other fine items of attire presents a picture of comfort and pleasantness (compare 59:17 with 60:3, 10).[29]

Notice in Isaiah 61:10, cited above, that the bridegroom clothes the bride. The Bridegroom is Jehovah-Jesus Christ, the merciful Judge of Judges at the Last Judgment. When He clothes His bride(s) in robes of righteousness, one hears the distant echo of an ancient temple ceremony now lost to us,[30] for there is a sense of endowment in the verb "clothe." The Greek Septuagint, the earliest translation of the Old Testament, working perhaps from more ancient documents than available to later translators, used a form of the Greek verb *enduō*, Eng. "endow," to render "clothed" in Isaiah 61:10. In the *Ensign* article, "New Testament Word Studies," distinguished BYU scholar, John W. Welch, wrote: "*The Compact Edition of the Oxford English Dictionary* notes that *endue* means 'to put on as a garment; to clothe or cover.'"[31] For instance, when we are baptized into the Church, we "put on [*enduō*]Christ" (Gal. 3:27) in the sense that we "clothe" ourselves in His name; we identify ourselves as His disciples. We "put on [*enduō*] the new man, which after God is created in righteousness and true holiness" (Eph. 4:24). We "put on" [enduō] the whole armor of God, that [we] may be able to stand against the wiles of the devil" (Eph. 6:11). As we put on the armor by "hungering and thirsting after [His] righteousness, aspiring to keep His commandments to emulate His example, we "put on" one of His righteous qualities here, another there, no matter how seemingly small each may seem. This implies that we take personal ownership of each as we take each step of faith through our second estate. Those whom the King calls His righteous sheep at the Last Judgment, i.e., those who have made a good faith effort to walk in His footsteps, those who have done what they could do in life in tending to the needs of their neighbors with their endowed talents and with compassionate kindness (see Matt. 25:35-36), to them He will extend His grace, bridging the cleft between His perfection and the brides' imperfection (see 2 Ne. 25:23), a cleft only He can bridge. He will clothe them "in white raiment," their robes of righteousness, and confess the name of each "before [His] Father, and before his angels" (Rev. 3:5), saying: "Come, ye blessed of my Father, inherit the kingdom prepared for you from the foundation of the world" (Matt. 25:34), explaining to "the righteous" (Matt. 25:37) that their actions in compassionately ministering to their neighbors with their endowed and acquired talents, they also served Him (see Matt. 25:35-36, 40). By asking their Master, what they had done that was so special, they indicate that their duty as His disciples had become the desire to serve; they had taken ownership of the principles the Savior taught. That is, the principles of righteousness became so much a part of their nature that they grew "unto the measure of the stature of Christ" (Eph. 4:13), fit to be lifted into an apotheosis of beauty, clothed in a robe of righteousness in the celestial Church of the Firstborn, the heavenly temple. From our veiled, mortal perspective this would seem to be the ultimate endowment, though there may be others at successively higher degrees of "eternal lives" (D&C 132:24, 35).

The fine linen of the robe of righteousness has several symbolic properties:
- It evokes the linen shroud in which the Savior was buried; when found lying empty in the tomb, it became the symbol of His overcoming death. Analogously, those privileged to receive a linen robe of righteousness partake of His Atonement through the baptism and temple covenants, always remembering that He gave His body and blood for the immortality and eternal life of man. Following the Savior's counsel and example, the righteous take up their crosses daily, investing their time, talents, and means in the least of their brethren and sisters.
- Woven from flax fibers, linen has been thought to have curative properties, e.g., for hygiene, to reduce fatigue, and to treat allergic disorders. Christ is the Great Healer, the Great Physician, Who came to earth to heal all wounds; by extension, disciples are the Physician's assistants through whom the Savior works to address specific needs people have.
- Because linen's tensile strength is twice that of cotton and three times wool, it is known for its durability and long life, suggesting the disciple whose strength and stability of testimony helps him endure faithfully to the end.
- Yet, with all these potent qualities, linen feels soft, suggesting the truly meek disciple whose unshakeable conviction of the truth results in spiritual strength, but who is gentle in demeanor and softly responsive to others. We think here foremost of the Savior: He had divine spiritual strength, yet manifest great gentleness and softness as He interfaced with others, especially those in need.
- Lastly, linen "is a commodity of beauty,"[32] such as a table set with linen for dining.

The properties of linen, then, circumscribe qualities of righteous discipleship: healing, strength, durability, softness, all evoking Jesus Christ. Possessing these properties and others, righteous disciples become beautiful souls in the heavenly temple, prepared to worship the Lord in the beauty of holiness.

Robes of linen also refer to temple clothing, both ancient and modern.[33] We note Joseph Smith's language when dedicating the Kirtland Temple,

> That thy church may come forth out of the wilderness of darkness, and shine forth fair as the moon, clear as the sun, and terrible as an army with banners;
>
> And be *adorned as a bride* for that day when thou shalt unveil the heavens, and cause the mountains to flow down at thy presence, and the valleys to be exalted, the rough places made smooth; that thy glory may fill the earth;
>
> That when the trump shall sound for the dead, we shall be caught up in the cloud to meet thee, that we may ever be with the Lord;
>
> That our *garments* may be *pure*, that *we may be clothed upon with robes of righteousness*, with palms in our hands, and *crowns of glory upon our heads*, and *reap eternal joy* for all our sufferings (D&C 109:73-76; emphasis added).

In the words of this prayer, he expressed the legacy of and promise to all righteous Latter-day Saints who aspire to the perfection of the

Savior. When we enter one of the Lord's temples and don the white temple clothing, we are, in fact, preparing for that grand moment in the timeless future when marriage to the Bridegroom is solemnized in celestial beauty.

Temples and Beauty

Temples of the Lord, or palaces, a meaning the ancient Hebrew word also projects,[34] are synonymous with beauty. Perhaps the first thing that comes to mind when we think of the word *temple* is the beautiful facade of each sacred edifice, and it has ever been so. From Solomon's temple to the LDS temples dotting the world in this last dispensation, their beauty has stood, and stands today, as beacons of the Lord to the world.[35]

But what transpires inside one of the Lord's temples makes each truly beautiful. David sang: "One thing have I desired of the Lord, that will I seek after; that I may dwell in the house of the Lord all the days of my life, to behold the beauty of the Lord, and to enquire in his temple" (Ps. 27:4).[36] Over the entrance to each temple of the Church is the inscription "Holiness to the Lord," representing both that the temple has been dedicated to the Lord and, more subtly, the beauty of the Lord, "the Man of Holiness" (Moses 7:35), found without and within. Anciently, the phrase "Holiness to the Lord" appeared on a gold plate fastened to the front of the mitre (headdress) worn by high priests officiating, first, in the tabernacle and, later in the temple (see Exod. 28:30). The holy garments Aaron was to wear when so officiating was "for the *glory and for beauty*" (Exod. 28:2; emphasis added). Today, The Church of Jesus Christ of Latter-day Saints builds temples "for the glory and beauty" of the Lord in which worthy members may "worship the Lord in the beauty of holiness" (1 Chron. 16:29; Ps. 29:2; 96:9).[37]

To "worship the Lord in the beauty of holiness" (1 Chron. 16:29; Ps. 29:2; 96:9) begins with "hav[ing] clean hands, and a pure heart" (Ps. 24:4). One has clean hands, wrote Elder Dallin H. Oaks, when "we do righteous acts and refrain from evil acts. . . . We have a pure heart if we act for the right motives and if we refrain from forbidden desires and attitudes."[38] When we're baptized into the Church with the heavenly fire of the Holy Spirit, we are at that moment sanctified and justified; we have cleansed hearts. But, we become susceptible to sins in one form or another very soon after baptism, so, over the centuries, the Lord has commanded His people to "sanctify yourselves that your minds become single to God . . . yea, purify your hearts, and cleanse your hands and your feet before me, *that I may make you clean*" (D&C 88:68, 74; emphasis added). In the ancient church of Yahweh, such cleansing involved a ritual washing ceremony. Since at least when the Savior appeared to the Nephites and declared the new sacrifice of a broken heart and contrite spirit (see 3 Ne. 9:20), personal inner sanctification though heart-felt repentance has required the kind of self-willed self-discipline unnatural to the natural man.

Yet, *perfect* personal sanctification is not a prerequisite for entering a temple of the Lord; rather a good faith effort. Being far less than perfect, we can, nevertheless, "worship the Lord in the beauty of holiness (1 Chron. 16:29; Ps. 29:2; 96:9) which can open one's spiritual eyes to "behold the beauty of the Lord" [and His "great plan of happiness" (Alma 42:8)] and enquire in his temple" (Ps. 27:4). "Enquire" in this context indicates an active attempt to learn of and ponder upon the plan of salvation and to gain further light and knowledge of a correct comprehension of God's character, such as His lovingkindness viz. mercy, His creative and governing faith, and the light of His glory suffusing the cosmos with divine truths, revealing things as they really are, eternally. Such knowledge is gained in the unadulterated symbolism in the temple in order that each member may have revealed to him or her that degree of understanding of the character of the Godhead and the universal truths of eternity for which they have prepared themselves by searching in and pondering upon the words of God, obeying the principles of the gospel, and, especially, through the inspiration of the Holy Spirit.

Supplementing and enhancing our understanding of the experience in the physical temple are two figurative, yet immensely important, temples, which parallel the two spiritual Zions discussed above: 1. the body and 2. a community of Zion saints, both temples of the Spirit. The Savior established the metaphor of the body as a temple when, after having driven the merchants from His Father's temple and challenged on His right to do so, He said unto the Jews who asked for a sign of His authority to perform miraculous healings,

> Destroy this temple, and in three days I will raise it up.
>
> Then said the Jews, Forty and six years was this temple in building, and wilt thou rear it up in three days?
>
> But *he spake of the temple of his body.*
>
> When therefore he was risen from the dead, his disciples remembered that he had said this unto them; and they believed the scripture, and the word which Jesus had said (John 2:18-22; emphasis added).

Later in the first century, after the Atonement and Resurrection of Jesus Christ, Paul, with apostolic insight, expanded the Savior's sacred metaphor to include all people, affirming thereby our spiritual kinship with the Son of God: "Know ye not that your body is the temple of the Holy Ghost which is in you, which ye have of God, and ye are not your own?" (1 Cor. 6:19). Christ did not mention the Spirit in conjunction with His body because He was the incarnate God; man, on the other hand, being an embryonic god, needs to be nurtured into a godly state by a personal mentor, and that mentor is the Holy Spirit, acting as the Savior's intermediary. President Joseph Fielding Smith captured the enormous ramifications of man's relationship with the Holy Spirit, when he wrote: "The man [or woman] who is confirmed receives . . . the companionship of the third member of the Godhead. Therefore, he is back again in the presence of God through the gift of the Holy Ghost."[39] Extending President Smith's vision, each confirmed member of the Church, who, by virtue of having received the companionship of the Holy Spirit, can be a prophet or prophetess in their sphere of responsibility and authority[40] and all such Latter-day Saints can experience moments like unto a personal theophany[41] when inspired by the Holy Spirit. Twentieth-century French philosopher, Henry Corbin, commented: "The Temple-archetype [in our discussion, the man's body as temple] is itself a Threshold, the communication between the celestial Temple and the Temple of the soul."[42]

The analogy of the body as temple evokes the principle of Zion as the pure in heart who will see God (see Matt. 5:8; 3 Ne. 12:8; D&C 97:21): like the pure in heart, the disciple whose temple is sanctified to the level of his or her knowledge at any given moment is a beautiful soul, mirroring the beauty of God in proportion to their own beauty.

In accord with the vision of the body as temple, when Christ appeared to the Nephites, He replaced the vicarious, symbolic sacrifice of an animal for the sins of man with the personal, inner sacrifice of a broken heart and a contrite spirit (see 3 Ne. 9:19-20), a sacrifice integral to establishing His new covenant.

Paul also saw the potential of the household of God to be a sacred edifice in which the Spirit may dwell, built upon the foundation of the apostles and prophets, Jesus Christ himself being the chief corner stone;

In whom all the building fitly framed together *groweth unto an holy temple in the Lord*:

In whom ye also are builded together for *an habitation of God through the Spirit* (Eph. 2:20-22; emphasis added).

In these verses Paul sounded an ennobling goal for Latter-day Saints today, to become united through the Spirit so that they "come in the unity of the faith, . . . speaking the truth in love, may grow up into him in all things, which is the head, even Christ: From whom the whole body fitly joined together and compacted by that which every joint supplieth, according to the effectual working in the measure of every part, maketh increase of the body unto the edifying of itself in love" (Eph. 4:13, 15-16). One can imagine that the sentiments expressed by Paul underscored the beauty of "the City of Holiness, even ZION" (Moses 7:19; capitalization in verse). Paul set the goal for any assemblage of saints, from the most basic unit in the Lord's kingdom, the family, to a ward or branch, a stake or district, and the Church as a whole, to become a Zion community of saints, manifesting the Lord's vision of beauty in holiness.[43]

Metaphorically, Isaiah compares such groupings of saints to a grove of "trees of righteousness, the planting of the Lord, that he might be glorified" (Isa. 61:3)[44] whereby they become trees of life, the fruit of whose good [viz. beautiful] works wisely "winneth souls" (Prov. 11:30; see Matt. 7:16-20; 3 Ne. 14:16-20). Daniel wrote: "And they that be *wise* shall shine as the brightness of the firmament; and they that turn many to righteousness as the stars for ever and ever" (Dan. 12:3; emphasis added). Rhapsodizing about the fast, Isaiah used elegant images in verses already cited above but worth repeating in this context that paint a picture of the spirit of beauty in individuals and community:

> Is not this the fast that I have chosen?
> to loose the bands of wickedness,
> to undo the heavy burdens,
> and to let the oppressed go free,
> and that ye break every yoke?
> Is it not to deal thy bread to the hungry,
> and that thou bring the poor that are cast out to thy house?
> when thou seest the naked thyself from thy own flesh?
> and that thou hide not thyself from thy own flesh?
> Then shall *thy light break forth as the morning,*
> and thine health spring forth speedily:
> and thy righteousness shall go before thee,
> *the glory of the Lord* [Yahweh] *shall be thy rearward.*
> Then shall thou call, and the LORD shall answer;
> thou shall cry, and he shall say, "Here I am."
> If thou take away from the midst of thee the yoke,
> the putting forth of the finger, and speaking vanity:
> and if thou draw out thy soul to the hungry,
> and satisfy the afflicted soul:
> then shall *thy light rise* in obscurity [darkness],
> and thy darkness be *as the noonday.*
> And the Lord [Yahweh] shall guide thee continually,
> and satisfy thy soul in drought, and make fat thy bones:
> and thou shalt be *like a watered garden,*
> and *like a spring of water, whose waters fail not.*

And they that shall be of thee shall build the old waste places:
thou shalt raise up the foundations of many generations;
and thou shalt be called, the repairer of the breach,
the restorer of paths to dwell in Isaiah 58:6-12; emphasis added).[45]

We note in Isaiah's picture several images relating to beauty and, therefore, holiness:
- "thy light shall break forth as the morning" is paralleled by "thy light rise in obscurity [darkness]." Around the world sunrise, such as the one pictured on the cover of this book, is regarded as beautiful and in some cultures as a spiritual moment for worship. The image of light has been discussed several times in the preceding chapters (see Index), here "thy light" can refer to the house of Israel or, if viewed as referring to an individual, to the indwelling light of Christ. Lest we forget, Isaiah reminds us that our light is not self-luminous; rather it is a reflection of the glory of the Lord that acts as the rear guard (rereward) for the righteous. We might think here of Jesus' counsel at the Sermon on the Mount and before the Nephite Temple to "let your light so shine before men, that they may see your good works [your righteousness], and glorify your Father which is in heaven" (Matt. 5:16; 3 Ne. 12:16).
- "thine health [restoration to wholeness] shall spring forth [bud or sprout like a plant] speedily." In the spring of the year, the sprouting and budding of plants is a welcomed and beautiful sight in its delicacy, perhaps not unlike a baby or the young of most mammals. So also is the restoration of the soul to whole health—physical and spiritual—often observable in photographs taken before and after a person's restoration, the latter

showing a happy, delightsome person. Such restorations often follow the Beatitudinal path from recognizing and mourning one's spiritual impoverishment with a broken heart and contrite spirit to becoming meek and teachable, hungering and thirsting after the righteousness of Christ whereby one is blessed with the powers of heaven through the Third Member of the Godhead, the Holy Spirit. A disciple's spiritual beauty shines forth as he or she grows into being a merciful-pure-in-heart peacemaker in the image of, and crediting all he or she is to, Jesus Christ Whose glorious light they reflect.

- "draw out [NKJV "extend"] thy soul to the hungry." I love the beauty of the King James' translation "draw out." In my imagination I see a disciples expanding his other circles of concern to encompass and embrace someone; willing to help bear their burden, mourning with those that mourn, perhaps those who've recognized that they are poor in spirit because of the gap between who they've become and who the Lord would have them be. A disciple draws out his soul to the hungry with the comfort from God (see 2 Cor. 1:3-4), Whose witness he is forever (see Mosiah 18:8-10).
- The metaphor, "satisfy thy soul in drought," reminds me of the exquisite image Jeremiah drew: "Blessed *is* the man that trusteth in the Lord [Yahweh], and whose hope the Lord [Yahweh] is. For he shall be as a tree planted by the waters, and *that* spreadeth out her roots by the river, and shall not see when heat cometh, but her leaf shall be green; and *shall not be careful [anxious] in the year of drought*, neither shall cease from yielding fruit" (Jer. 17:7-8; emphasis added). The waters by which the tree is planted flow from "the fountain of living waters," namely the Lord, Yahweh (Jer. 2:13; 17:13), Who shares His beauty with the righteous.

- The simile, "like a watered garden," hearkens back, perhaps, to the Garden of Eden through which a river flowed, watering the garden (see Gen. 2:10). The terrestrial state of Eden has been thought of as the epitome of earthly, though not celestial, beauty; anciently it was considered to be the prototypical temple wherein Adam-man was mentored by Elohim- Yahweh (see Gen. 2:4) in the beauty of holiness, face to face. Thus, when the Lord instructed Moses to build a tabernacle according to the pattern Yahweh gave Him and in which He could reside in the midst of the house of Israel (see Gen. 25:8-9; 26:30), the second area of the temple, the Holy Place, represented the Garden of Eden, with a Menorah, a lampstand, being a stylized tree of life.[46] The Garden of Eden also modeled the celestial garden in the temple of heaven, which John saw at the end of his apocalyptic vision: "And he shewed me a pure river of water of life, clear as crystal, proceeding out of the throne of God and of the Lamb. In the midst of the street of it, and on either side of the river, was there the tree of life, which bare twelve manner of fruits, and yielded her fruit every month: and the leaves of the tree were for the healing of the nations" (Rev. 22:1-2). Significantly, in the midst of "the holy city, New Jerusalem" that will accompany the Savior at His Second Coming is "the Tabernacle of God," perhaps the Shekinah as several scholars have suggested,[47] from which a voice from heaven declares: God himself shall be with them, and be their God (Rev. 21:3), as was the case with the ancient tabernacle. And God, meaning Jesus Christ-Yahweh, said, "I will give unto him that is athirst of the fountain of the water of life freely" (Rev. 21:6). Righteous disciples are bathed in the beauty of Eden and the Lord's heavenly residence become "like a watered garden." That water, streaming from the throne of God and the Lamb, flows into the disciple, in the spirit of Proverbs 11:25: "he that watereth shall be watered also himself." The living water is the love of God "which is shed forth in our hearts by the Holy Ghost" (Rom. 5:5) who inspires us with eternal truths. And through the Holy Spirit saints can experience a personal theophany, being back in the presence of God as they begin to assume the Lord's beauty. No more breathtaking experience can be imagined, if we treat each moment of personal revelation as the sacred moment that it is.

- "like a spring of water, whose waters fail not." From a spring comes living or potable water. In a desert, a spring is a source of joy for a thirsty traveler. Metaphorically, the thirsty traveler is someone seeking to know the truth of things as they really are in the eternities. The spring represents the disciple of the Lord Jesus Christ who receives divine guidance continually (v. 11) from Christ's fountain of living waters. (The fountain of living waters is conveyed to the disciple by the Holy Spirit [see John 7:37, 39], through whom Jesus manifests Himself [see 1 Ne. 10:11].) As he shares his testimony and knowledge of the Savior, of His Atonement, and of His gospel, his living water of revelation is continually replenished from heaven (see Prov. 11:25). Such disciples are symbolically pictured in Matthew 25 as the wise virgins, the good and faithful servants, and the sheep on the right hand of Christ at the Last Judgment.[49] They replicate as best they can their eternal source of living water, "the fountain of all righteousness," Yahweh-Jesus Christ (Ether 12:28).

These images and others like them offer us insights into the spirit of beauty in ways that abstract words cannot—insights that can unite a community of Zion saints, seeking to minister to, not only their own, but also others outside the faith in need, working together like a disciplined, practiced team, each member united in purpose and doing what each needs to do in the team.

Images are *poietic*-aesthetic words that appeal to our emotions, encouraging and exalting saints to rise to their godly potential. Twice these Isaianic verses draw attention to the light reflected from the righteous, revealing them to be guided by the glory of the Lord. Such a community of Zion saints approaches the perfection of beauty out of which God shines (see Ps. 50:2). From these verses we understand that **RIGHTEOUSNESS IS THE SPIRIT OF BEAUTY, AND WISDOM IS BEAUTY IN ACTION** (see D&C 121:41-45).

In the eternal sense, wisdom is so much more than the accumulation of knowledge, as important as that may be; it is knowing what to do, feeling when to do it, and then just doing what needs to be done. Wise disciples, acting in the spirit of heavenly mercy, seize opportunities to minister with goodness, whereby they sow the fruit of righteousness to help find Christlike peace in their lives (see James 3:17, 18; Mosiah 18:8, 9; D&C 58:27-28). Wise disciples are the righteous, peacemaking, beautiful souls of the Lord's kingdom, a sentiment James, the brother of Jesus, understood:

> Who is a wise man and endued with knowledge among you? let him shew out of a good conversation [Gk. anastrophē (ἀναστροφή), "behavior"] his works with meekness of wisdom. . . .
>
> But the *wisdom* that is *from above* is first pure, then *peaceable*, gentle, and easy to be intreated, *full of mercy* [*hesed*] *and good* [*kalos*] *fruits*, without partiality, and without hypocrisy.

And *the fruit of righteousness is sown in peace of them that make peace* (James 3:13, 17-18; emphasis added).

Isaiah wrote that "the work of righteousness shall be peace; and the effect of righteousness quietness and assurance for ever" (Isa. 32:17). Such peace is sown in the heart, like the seed of the Atonement in Alma's analogy (Alma 33:22-23), and when nourished with faith, grows into a tree springing up unto everlasting life with fruit the color of the fruit of the tree of life in Lehi's dream: "sweet above all that is sweet, and . . . white above all that is white [the color of beauty], yea, and pure above all that is pure" (Alma 32:42). Thus, in the temple on earth and in heaven people wear white robes, signifying the beauty of holiness.

The harmony of beautiful souls can significantly strengthen wards and stakes as they greet strangers to the kingdom by helping them become "fellowcitizens with the saints in the household of God" (Eph. 2:19). Each new member, or returning member, brings with him or her a unique blend of talents that adds to local units and, therefore, the Church as a whole. While it may not be immediately evident, what we do locally does impact the Church globally.

Notes to Chapter 10

1. "Stands in apposition" means two nouns or noun phrases placed side by side or in close proximity in a sentence are equivalent to one another.
2. Cf. Joseph Smith: "God himself is a self-existent being" (*TPJS*, 352).
3. In their *Charting the New Testament* (FARMS, 2002), John F. Hall and John W. Welch provide the following chart on the Savior's use of "I am":

   Jesus Affirms His Divinity with the Greek Words ἐγώ εἰμί (I AM)

   It *is I* (ἐγώ εἰμί); be not afraid (Matt. 14:27; Mk. 6:50; John 6:20)
   I am (ἐγώ εἰμί). (Mk 14:62; Mk 15:4 JST)
   Ye say that *I am*. (Lk 22:70)
   It *is I* (ἐγώ εἰμί) myself. (Lk 24:39)
   The woman saith unto him, I know that Messias cometh, which is called

Christ: Jesus saith unto her, *I* that speak unto thee *am he* (ἐγώ εἰμί). (Jn 4:25–26)
I am the bread of life. (John 6:35)
I am the light of the world. (John 8:12)
I am one that bear witness of myself. (John 8:18)
If ye believe not that *I am* he, ye shall die in your sins. (John 8:24)

When ye have lifted up the Son of man, then shall ye know that *I am* he. (John 8:28)
Before Abraham was born, *I am*. (John 8:58)
I am the door of the sheep. (John 10:7)
I am the good shepherd. (John 10:11).
I am the resurrection and the life. (John 11:25)
I am the way, the truth, and the life.
I am the true vine.
I am the vine.
I am he.
And the Lord said, *I am* (ἐγώ εἰμί) Jesus.
And he said unto me, *I am* Jesus of Nazareth.
And I said, Who art thou, Lord? And he said, *I am* Jesus.

Explanation

An important feature of the Greek Gospels is the use of the Greek words ἐγώ εἰμί, *ego eimi*, "I am." These words are used predominantly in John, but they also occur at significant moments in Matthew, Mark, and Luke as well. When Moses asked God on Mount Sinai, "When they shall say to me, What is his name? What shall I say unto them?" the answer was "I am that I am" (Ex 3:13–14). The Greek version of the Old Testament, widely used in Jesus' day, rendered this text "ἐγώ εἰμί ὁ ‰Ωv." A similar divine usage is found several places in the Hebrew Bible and in Jewish messianic literature. Thus, when Jesus repeatedly identified himself with these words, his audiences could well have understood that he was affirming his divine identity as the Lord God of Israel. This chart lists the passages in the Greek that contain the words ἐγώ εἰμί, most of which are in the Gospel of John. Interestingly, Matthew, Mark, and John record this phrase in connection with Jesus' miraculous walking on the water and stilling the storm. Mark emphasizes these words in the pointed answer of Jesus to his accusers who had asked, "Are you the Messiah" (Mk 14:61), just as John preserves them in the open declaration of Jesus to the Samaritan woman at the well. Luke reserves it exclusively for Jesus' final announcement when he appeared to his apostles after his resurrection and Paul consistently testifies that Jesus identified himself this way on the road to Damascus.

Reference: Raymond E. Brown, trans., *The Gospel According to John* (Garden City, N.Y.: Doubleday, 1966), 1:533–38; source unknown.

4. *DNTC*, 2:36.
5. Hymn 193, *Hymns of The Church of Jesus Christ of Latter-day Saints* (Salt Lake City, UT: The Church of Jesus Christ of Latter-day Saints, 1985. President Boyd K. Packer described "the burning in the bosom . . . more like a warm light shining within our being. . . .The Holy Ghost speaks with a voice we *feel* more than *hear*" ("Personal Revelation: The Gift, the Test, and the Promise," *Ensign* (November 1994), 60.
6. Neal A. Maxwell, "Meek and Lowly," BYU Devotional (Oct. 21, 1986), 9; speeches byu.edu.
7. William Barclay, *New Testament Words* (Philadelphia: Westminster Press, 1974), 241. Neal A. Maxwell wrote that "Meekness of mind recognizes God's perfect love of us and His omniscience. By acknowledging these reassuring realities and accepting that God desires our full development and true happiness, we are readied even as the learning experiences come" ("Willing to Submit," *Ensign* [May 1995], 71.
8. The discussion above cites five salient qualities of the Lord's nature informing His beauty. We must also acknowledge, however, manifold qualities, such as His Fatherhood of man, His holiness, etc. (see Bruce R. McConkie, *Mormon Doctrine*, 317) comprise His essence, many of which, if not most, we know nothing about from our veiled mortal state. Nor could we even comprehend those qualities if exposed to them now, for our spiritual and mental capacities are necessarily limited so that we learn to walk by and develop active faith (see *Lectures* 1:12). Nor would we have the vocabulary to identify such God-defining qualities—one of the reasons the Lord populated the scriptures with images to help us surmise things eternal beyond our ken.
9. Oliver Cowdery wrote something similar in describing the appearance of John the Baptist to confer the Aaronic Priesthood upon the Prophet Joseph and himself: "I shall not attempt to paint to you the feelings of this heart, nor *the majestic beauty and glory* which surrounded us on this occasion; but you will believe me when I say, that earth, nor men, with the eloquence of time, cannot begin to clothe language in as interesting and sublime a manner as this holy personage. [N]or has this earth power to give the joy, to bestow the peace, or comprehend the wisdom which was contained in each sentence as

they were delivered by the power of the Holy Spirit! . . . The assurance that we were in the presence of an angel, the certainty that we heard the voice of Jesus, and the truth unsullied as it flowed from a pure personage, dictated by the will of God, is to me past description, and I shall ever look upon this expression of the Savior's goodness with wonder and thanksgiving. . ." (*Messenger and Advocate*, vol. 1 [October 1834], pp. 15-16; emphasis added). Beauty is glorious; glory is beautiful.

10. See Rev. 1:13-15; *TPJS*, 361.
11. See *Encyclopaedia Judaica* (New York: MacMillan, 1971), 16:1030; David L. Eiler, "The Origin and History of Zion as a Theological Symbol in Ancient Israel," diss. Princeton Theological Seminary, 1968, 86-87; Jorg Jeremias, "Lade und Zion. Zur Entstehung der Ziontradition," *Probleme biblischer Theologie. Gerhard von Rad zum 70. Geburtstag*, ed. Walter Wolff (Munich: Chr. Kaiser, 1971), 188-90; Jon Levenson, *Sinai and Zion: An Entry into the Jewish Bible* (Minneapolis, Chicago, New York: Winston Press, 1985), 92. In a footnote in Eiler's dissertation, he notes that S. Krause proposed the etymology of Zion to be "place of beauty." Likewise, Hugh Nibley pointed out that beauty is one of the terms most often used to describe Zion (*Approaching Zion* [Salt Lake City: Deseret Book, 1989], 7.)
12. See Bruce R. McConkie, "The Holy Zion of God," in *The Millennial Messiah* (Salt Lake City: Deseret Book, 1982), 282-96. Elder Neal A. Maxwell wrote an imaginative epistolary story about the city of Enoch that offers consequential insight into the spirit of those wonderful saints (*The Glory of the City of Enoch: Of One Heart and One Mind* [Salt Lake City: Deseret Book, 1975]). It is also available in his collected works.
13. *HC*, 5:23.
14. Reyna I. Aburto, "With One Accord," *Ensign* (May 2018), 78-80 passim.
15. William A. Dyrness, "Aesthetics in the Old Testament: Beauty in Context," *Journal of the Evangelical Theological Society* 28, 4 (1985), 421-22.
16. James E. Faust, "A Second Birth," *Ensign* (June 1998), 5.
17. Stephen E. Robinson & H. Dean Garrett, *A Commentary on the Doctrine and Covenants* (Salt Lake City, UT: Deseret Book, 2005), 4:273.
18. See Joseph B. Wirthlin, "The Time to Prepare," *Ensign* (May 1998), 14.
19. See Bohn, *Beatitudes*, 70-71.
20. See Luke 10:25-37 (parable of the Good Samaritan); Matt. 22:39.

21. The New Testament Greek word translated as "charity" is *agápē* (ἀγάπη), the highest form of love, i.e., godly love (see Rom. 5:5). We express godly love, or charity, with acts of kindness toward our fellowmen in need, which the Savior depicted as being merciful (see Luke 10:37).
22. C. S. Lewis, *From the Weight of Glory*, in *The Essential C. S. Lewis*, ed. Lyle W. Dorsett (New York: Simon and Schuster, 1988), 369.
23. John Ruskin, *Modern Painters*, vol. 3 (Orpington, Kent: George Allen, 1888), p. 266; italics in original; in Vaughn J. Featherstone, "A Man After God's Own Heart," speeches.byu.edu/index. php?act= viewitem &id = 769.
24. Daniel C. Peterson, "Ye Are Gods: Psalm 82 and John 10 as Witnesses of the Divine Nature of Humankind," in *The Disciple as Scholar* (https://publications.mi.byu.edu/fullscreen/?pub= 1091 &index=17), 10, 11, 19, 22, 23, 28, 32, 35-40.
25. Plato, *The Republic* III, 402, trans. Benjamin Jowett, *The Great Book of the Western World*, 52 vols., ed. Mortimer Adler (Chicago: Encyclopædia Britannica, 1952), 7:333. Mystics, such as Jakob Böhme, associated the concept with the idea of the spiritual bridegroom of Christ and the betrothal of the spirit. It then entered European discussion in the eighteenth century in the Pietistic movement. In Germany, for example, Nicolaus Zinzendorff spoke of the husband of the soul and used the term "schöne Seele." In England, Shaftesbury often used the word *beauty* for spiritual perfection. In the sentimental novel *Clarissa*, Samuel Richardson used terms such as "the beauties of the mind" and "moral beauty." Richardson's novel had great influence on German writers and the concept of the beautiful soul became a popular subject during the eighteenth and early nineteenth centuries.
26. Friedrich Schiller, *Über Anmut und Würde* [*On Grace and Dignity*] (Munich: Deutscher Taschenbuch Verlag, 1966), 36. German original: "In einer schönen Seele ist es also, wo . . . Pflicht und Neigung harmonieren, und Grazie ist ihr Ausdruck in der Erscheinung."
27. Ulisses Soares, "Becoming a Work of Art," Brigham Young University devotional (Nov. 5, 2013); speeches.byu.edu.
28. See the Appendix for a discussion of the ancient Hebrew wedding process.
29. Victor L. Ludlow, *Isaiah: Prophet, Seer, and Poet* (Salt Lake City, UT: Deseret Book, 1982), 507.
30. See Matthew B. Brown, *The Gate of Heaven: Insights on the Doctrines and Symbols of the Temple* (American Fork, UT: Covenant Communications, 1999), 111-63, esp. 131-39. It might interest the reader that Methodist lay preacher

and English scholar of the Old Testament by the name of Margaret Barker is conducting research into temple theology in the New Testament. Her interest is in the evidences of the First Temple, i.e., Solomon's temple, in the teachings of Jesus and His followers. While her research remains a work in progress, it sheds a new light on many doctrines that Latter-day Saint theology takes for granted. See Margaret Barker, *Temple Theology: An Introduction* (London: Society for Promoting Christian Knowledge, 2004); see also Richard Neitzel Holzapfel & David Rolph Seely, *My Father's House: Temple Worship and Symbolism in the New Testament* (Salt Lake City, UT: Bookcraft, 1994.

31. John W. Welch, "New Testament Word Studies," *Ensign* (Apr. 1993), 29. Dr. Welch is the Robert K. Thomas Professor of Law at Brigham Young University's J. Reuben Clark Law School, editor in chief of BYU Studies, and director of publications for the university's Joseph Fielding Smith Institute for LDS History. He is the founder of the Foundation for Ancient Research and Mormon Studies. He serves on the executive committee of the Biblical Law Section of the Society of Biblical Literature.

32. Information on linen found at www.linenline.biz.

33. *Dictionary of Biblical Imagery*, eds. Leland Ryken, James C. Wilhoit, and Tremper Longman III (Downers Grove, IL: InterVarsity Press, 1998), s.v. "linen"; see also Joseph Fielding McConkie & Donald W. Parry, *A Guide to Scriptural Symbols* (Salt Lake City, UT: Bookcraft, 1990), 79.

34. See The New Strong's Exhaustive Concordance of the Bible (Nashville, TN: Thomas Nelson Publishers, 1990), H1965; *TWOT*, 1:214-15; *Vine's Complete Expository Dictionary of Old and New Testaments Words* (Nashville, TN, 1996), 258-59.

35. The focus on ancient and temples of The Church of Jesus Christ of Latter-day Saints is not to discount some of the beautiful temples other cultures have erected to worship their gods.

36. The translators of the King James Bible rendered several Hebrew words as beauty. In this verse "beauty" translates *nāam* which can also mean "kindness" and "favor," as in the grace of the Lord (Marvin R. Wilson, "[*nō'am*], *pleasantness, beauty, kindness, favor*," in *TWOT*, 2:585, s.v. 1384a). Another Hebrew word translated as "beauty" is *hădhārāh*; though denoting "decoration," it is not difficult to understand why the translators chose to use the English "beauty." In Psalm 50:2, "beauty" translates the Hebrew *yŏphî*. One other word to draw into this potpourri of Hebrew words translated as "beauty" is *tip☒ ārâ* (from the verb *pā' ra*) that can be translated as both beauty and glory.

37. From the moment Adam and Eve were expelled from the Garden of Eden, worshipping the Lord in set apart sacred spaces has been fundamental to the spiritual life of His people. One example of this was the altar Adam built to pray to Jehovah; it defined a sacred, temple-like space, a meeting place of heaven and earth for the instruction of man. Another example was Jacob's ladder-reaching-heaven vision in which he saw the Lord Who conferred the blessings of the Abrahamic covenant on him. Upon waking, Jacob understood the sanctity of the place and said, "this is none other but the house of the Lord, and this is the gate of heaven" (Gen. 28:17), whereupon he "took the stone that he had put for his pillows, and set it up for a pillar, and poured oil upon the top of it. And he called the name of that place Beth-el," or "House of God" (Gen. 28:18). Like so many things associated with the temple, the stone-pillar represented a mountain (see Isa. 2:3; 30:29; Micah 4:2; 2 Ne. 12:3) behind which lay the ultimate, eternal reality of heaven and the eternal covenant of Abraham (see also Gen. 31:45-54). A further example stems from Moses' experience going up Mt. Horeb where "an angel of the LORD appeared unto him" in a burning bush that was not consumed, reminding us of the everlasting burning of heaven, analogous to the light it produces and the glory of God. The Lord called to Moses out of the bush, saying: "put off thy shoes from off thy feet, for the place whereon thou standest is holy ground" (Exod. 3:2, 5). That sacred place on the mountain, where heaven met earth, eventually transformed into the holy of holies in, first, the tabernacle, then in the temple. Each sacred space manifests the beauty of the Lord in His desire to help and encourage His children become as righteous as they can so that they might return to their heavenly home and dwell with Him and the Son.

    See Hugh W. Nibley, "The Meaning of the Temple," in *Temple and Cosmos: Beyond the Ignorant Present*, ed. Don E. Norton (Salt Lake City: Deseret Book; Provo, UT: Foundation for Ancient Research and Mormon Studies, 1992), 1-41; *Temples in the Ancient World: Ritual and Symbolism*, ed. Donald W. Parry (Salt Lake City: Deseret Book/Provo, UT: Foundation for Ancient Research and Mormon Studies, 1994), especially Jay A. Parry and Donald W. Perry, "The Temple in Heaven: Its Description and Significance," 515-32; Hugh W. Nibley, "On the Sacred and the Symbolic," 535-621. Other articles in this volume offer additional insights.

38. Dallin H. Oaks, *Pure in Heart* (Salt Lake City, UT: Bookcraft, 1988), 1.

39. *DS*, 1:41.

40. Said President Harold B. Lee: "[A]nyone who enjoys the gift by which he may have God revealed has the spirit of prophecy, the power of revelation, and, in

a sense, is a prophet within the sphere of responsibility and authority given to him" ("The Place of the Living Prophet, Seer, and Revelator," in *Stand Ye in Holy Places: Selected Sermons and Writings of President Harold B. Lee* [Salt Lake City, UT: Deseret Book, 1975], 155).

41. The *SOED* defines "theophany" as follows: "The visible manifestation of God ... to humankind." My use of the word *theophany* does not suggest a visible encounter with Deity such as Isaiah and Lehi experienced, rather it is more like, what Blake T. Ostler terms, the narrative type involving dialogue with Yahweh (see Blake T. Osler, "The Throne-Theophany and Prophetic Commission in 2 Nephi: A Form-Critical Analysis," *BYU Studies* 26/4 [1986], 68). It is my belief that man can be part of a personal theophany-like experiences when moved upon by the Holy Spirit, the third member of the Godhead, based on President Joseph Fielding Smith's statement that through such experiences, man is in the presence of God (*DS*, 1:43).

42. Cited by Brian M. Hauglid, "Sacred Time and the Temple," in *Temples in the Ancient World: Ritual and Symbolism*, ed. Donald W. Parry (Salt Lake City: Deseret Book/Provo, UT: Foundation for Ancient Research and Mormon Studies, 1994), 636. According to the Wikipedia entry, "Henry Corbin (1903–1978) was a philosopher, theologian, Iranologist and professor of Islamic Studies at the École pratique des hautes études in Paris, France. There are several main themes which, together, form the core of the spirituality that Corbin defends. "The Imagination is the primary means to engage Creation. Prayer is the 'supreme act of the creative imagination'.... The grand sweep of his theology of the Holy Spirit embraces Judaism, Christianity and Islam. He defended the central role assigned in theology for the individual as the finite image of the Unique Divine. His mysticism is no world-denying asceticism but regards all of Creation as a theophany of the divine. This vision has much in common with what has become known as Creation Spirituality...." His regard for "all of creation as a theophany of the divine" is reflected in the Lord's revelation to Moses that "all things are created and made to bear record of me" (Moses 6:62).

43. I can think of several aesthetic performances in which the beauty of a unified effort has been manifest. One example for me is the Brigham Young University Ballroom dancers who have won a number of ballroom dancing competitions worldwide. The beauty of their movements is in the harmony between the individual couples and among all the couples together. Synchronized swimming also manifests such harmonious beauty. Torvill and Dean, ice dancing to Ravel's *Bolero* during the 1984 Winter Olympics, were beauty in

motion. In each of these examples, beauty resulted from the disciplined practice to achieve a common goal. Relating this to the Church at every level, the goal is to prepare the way for the Savior's Second Coming, precisely set forth by President James E. Faust: "The fundamental absolutes of our faith are that Jesus is the Christ, the Son of God, the Redeemer & God the Father and Jesus the Son actually appeared to the Prophet Joseph Smith, restoring the fulness of the gospel and the true Church." This dictates "the purposes of the Church, which are First, prepare its members for the perfect life (he cites 3 Ne. 12:48); second, foster and encourage its members to become a body of Saints united in faith and works; third, proclaim the message of restored truth to the world; fourth, save our dead" (CES Fireside (9/1/2002). Each of the goals President Faust cited is built on the fundamental principle of ministering. To achieve beauty of harmonious oneness, a body of Christ has need of every member. Having addressed the various gifts of the Spirit, Paul wrote:

> But all these worketh that one and the selfsame Spirit, dividing to every man severally as he will.
> For as the body is one, and hath many members, and all the members of that one body, being many, are one body: so also *is* Christ.
> For by one Spirit are we all baptized into one body, whether *we be* Jews or Gentiles, whether *we be* bond or free; and have been all made to drink into one Spirit.
> For the body is not one member, but many....
> [N]ow hath God set the members every one of them in the body, as it hath pleased him.
> And if they were all one member, where *were* the body?
> But now *are they* many members, yet but one body.
> Now ye are the body of Christ, and members in particular.
> And God hath set some in the church, first apostles, secondarily prophets, thirdly teachers, after that miracles, then gifts of healings, helps, governments, diversities of tongues (1 Cor. 12:12-14, 18-20, 27-28).

44. Comparing the righteous saints brings to mind Jacob's allegory of the tame and wild olive trees. His allegory fills in the backstory of how the Lord works with His children, cultivating and pruning them until the trees of righteousness grow together.

45. *The New Cambridge Parallel Bible with the Apocrypha: King James Version.* Following is the New English Translation (NET) version of these verses in less poetic language than the KJV, but perhaps clearer in content:

   > This is the kind of fast I want.
   > I want you to remove the sinful chains,
   > to tear away the ropes of the burdensome yoke,
   > to set free the oppressed,
   > and to break every burdensome yoke.
   > I want you to share your food with the hungry
   > and to provide shelter for homeless, oppressed people.
   > When you see someone naked, clothe him!
   > Don't turn your back on your own flesh and blood.
   > Then *your light will shine like the sunrise*;
   > your restoration will quickly arrive;
   > your godly behavior will go before you,
   > and the Lord's splendor will be your rear guard.
   > Then will you call out, and the Lord will respond;
   > you will cry out, and he will reply, 'Here am I.'
   > You must remove the burdensome yoke from among you
   > and stop pointing fingers and speaking sinfully.
   > You must actively help the hungry
   > and feed the oppressed.
   > then *your light will dispel the darkness,*
   > and *your darkness will be transformed into noonday.*
   > The Lord will continually lead you;
   > he will feed you even in parched regions.
   > He will give you renewed strength,
   > and you will be *like a well-watered garden,*
   > *like a spring that continually produces water.*
   > Your perpetual ruins will be rebuilt;
   > you will reestablish the ancient foundations.
   > You will be called 'The one who repairs the ancient walls,
   > the one who makes the streets inhabitable again
   > (NET, Isa. 58:6-10; emphasis added).

46. See Donald W. Parry, "Garden of Eden: Prototype Sanctuary," in *Temples of the Ancient World*, ed. Donald W. Parry (Salt Lake City, UT: Deseret Book; Provo, UT: Foundation for Ancient Research and Mormon Studies, 1994), 126-51; Matthew B. Brown, *The Gate of Heaven: Insights on the Doctrines*

and Symbols of the Temple (American Fork, UT: Covenant Communications, Inc., 1999), 27-29; Alex Douglas, "The Garden of Eden, the Ancient Temple, and Receiving a New Name," in *Ascending the Mountain of the Lord: Temple, Praise, and Worship in the Old Testament*, ed. David R. Seeley, Jeffrey R. Chadwick, and Matthew J. Gray (Provo, UT: Religious Studies Center; Salt Lake City, UT: Deseret Book, 2013), 39-41; Jeffrey M. Bradshaw, "The Tree of Knowledge as the Veil of the Sanctuary," ibid., 49-65; "The Temple Symbolism of the Tree of Life and the Tree of Knowledge," *Meridian Magazine* (October 24, 2019), latterdaysaintmag.com/article-1-1733/

47. See G. B. Caird, *The Revelation of Saint John* (Peabody, MA: Hendrickson Publishers, 1999), 264; David A. Aune, *Revelation 17-22*, vol. 3 The Word Biblical Commentary (Nashville, TN: Thomas Nelson Publishers, 1998), 1122-23.

48. See William J. Bohn, *Matthew 25: Symbolic Vision—Parabolic Living*.

APPENDIX

THE ANCIENT HEBREW MARRIAGE

In order to establish a better understanding of the wedding motif in the scriptures and, therefore, the beautiful garments, we will briefly survey the pattern of betrothal and marriage among the ancient Hebrews, specifically five of the steps in the process, though there are more[1]: 1. the marriage proposal; 2. the negotiation; 3. betrothal; 4. wedding procession; 5. wedding.

A Near East Betrothal and Marriage

1. As in many cultures of the Near East, rather than a young man and woman falling in love and desiring to be married, marriages were arranged. A prospective bridegroom and his father initiated the process by searching for a suitable bride, "suitable" could include similar social status and/or advantageous marriage.
2. Having chosen a young woman, the father and son approached her father with their marriage proposal, upon which a negotiation ensued, in the presence of both the young woman and the son. The

first thing to be agreed upon was a price for the bride, indicating how much the bridegroom valued her. (It is important to note that, besides being present at these negotiations, the young woman had the right, by law, to accept or reject the marriage proposal, though to reject it could damage her family's reputation in the community. Thus, there were few rejections.) Upon successfully settling on a price, there followed a Katuba, or contract to be married which formalized the engagement. Among other things, in the Katuba the bridegroom promised to cherish his bride and declared that she became a peculiar, i.e., chosen, treasure to him. At that moment, they were considered to be married, though they did not live together for a time. Before leaving, the groom presented her with a gift or gifts to express his esteem for her and for her to remember him.

3. After leaving his bride, the bridegroom spent much of his time preparing a "little" mansion for himself and his bride in his father's household, his father overseeing the construction, and only when *the father* was satisfied that all was in order would he release his son to fetch his bride. During the bridegroom's absence, which could last up to a year, a friend of the bridegroom served as an intermediary between the groom and the bride. The intermediary was also responsible for ensuring her virginity when the groom came to fetch her.

The bride, who did not know when the bridegroom would return to fetch her, spent her time honing her homemaking skills and collecting the things she would take with her. In addition, she sought to make herself beautiful and holy in various ways, including a ritual bath and wearing the gift(s) the bridegroom had given her so as to appear more beautiful in his eyes.

4. When the bridegroom's father was satisfied that all things were in order, he released his son to bring his bride back to their new home, an event depicted in the parable of the ten virgins. The bride

was alerted to the imminent arrival of the wedding party by the friend of the bridegroom. For the occasion, both bridegroom and bride were clothed in white, the symbol of purity and beauty.

5. At the new home, the father of the bridegroom gave each wedding guest gifts and a proper wedding garment. (In the parable of the marriage of the king's son [Matt. 22:2-14], one of the guests does not don the proper garment, an expression of his pride and an insult to the king, leading to his banishment.) A great wedding feast followed after the wedding ceremony.

Much has been omitted in this presentation of an Old-Testament Hebrew marriage, but the details given will suffice to discuss how the pattern appears in the Lord's relationship with His people.

The great wedding motif in the scriptures

1. The Father is Elohim, the Bridegroom is Jehovah-Jesus Christ (see Matt. 9:15; Mark 2:19; Luke 5:34-35; John 3:29). Under the direction of His Father, Jehovah created this earth, among numberless others, as a temporary residence, a mere nanosecond in eternity, for the spirits the Father created and sent to this telestial orb. In the Father's grand design, it was to be a laboratory in which men and women can exercise and school their moral agency "to act for themselves and not be acted upon," "to choose liberty and eternal life, through the great Mediator of all men, or to choose captivity and death, according to the captivity and power of the devil" (2 Ne. 2:26, 27), in other words, to choose the goodness of God, the evil of the devil, or points in between, though anything less than *choosing* the goodness of God may delimit one's eternal progression. The commencement of the Father's plan came with the Fall of Adam and Eve. After being sent from the terrestrial state of the Garden into the telestial state of mortality, and after

having obediently offered sacrifices as they had been directed, an angel of the Lord appeared to them, explaining to them that each sacrifice was "a similitude of the Only Begotten of the Father," the foreordained Messiah (see Moses 4:2), "which is full of grace and truth" (Moses 5:7).

Thereafter a vital event occurred for Adam, Eve, and all mankind: "the Holy Ghost fell upon Adam, . . . bear[ing] record of the Father and the Son, saying: I am the Only Begotten of the Father from the beginning, henceforth and forever, that as thou hast fallen thou mayest be redeemed, and all mankind, even as many as will" (Moses 5:9). Layered in these words of the Son, spoken by the Holy Spirit according to the principle of divine investiture,[2] is the first scriptural intimation of the Bridegroom-bride relationship, named in the price the Son would pay to redeem all mankind (see 1 Cor. 6:30; 7:23). (The price for the bride is discussed above.) As a result of hearing the Son's declaration, Adam and Even understood the supernal blessing they had received:

> And in that day Adam blessed God and was filled, and began to prophesy concerning all the families of the earth, saying: Blessed be the name of God, for because of my transgression my eyes are opened, and in this life I shall have joy, and again in the flesh I shall see God.
>
> And Eve, his wife, heard all these things and was glad, saying: Were it not for our transgression we never should have had seed, and never should have known good and evil, and the joy of our redemption, and the eternal life which God giveth unto all the obedient (Moses 5:10-11).

The Bridegroom-bride relationship became clearer with Abram, who, because of his great faith in Jehovah, was willing to sacrifice his only son, Isaac, an act that went completely contrary to what he had rejected in his homeland, namely human sacrifice (see Abr. 1:7). While, so far as we know, no other has had the Father and the Son ask of them what They asked of Abram, His willingness represents the reciprocal sacrifices the Lord asks each of His disciples to make in preparing to receive the great blessings of eternal life.

Though the Lord stopped Abram in the final moment of his son's sacrifice, because of his willingness to obey the Lord, the Father and the Son selected Abram and his posterity to be Son's bride, giving Abram the new name, Abraham, a temple-like act, recognizing the covenant endowment between them and solemnizing the marriage proposal (a divine Katuba) with the Abrahamic covenant whereby Abraham's posterity would become the chosen people of the Lord see (see D&C 132:29-50; Abr. 2:6-11).

2. The second phase of the marriage was not actually a negotiation. The bridal price was the Redemption of Jesus Christ: "ye are bought with a price: therefore glorify God in your body, and in your spirit, which are God's" (1 Cor. 6:20). This price, the infinite atonement, was established before the world was. The Bible Dictionary states:

> Jesus Christ, as the Only Begotten Son of God and the only sinless person to live on this earth, was the only one capable of making an atonement for mankind. By His selection and foreordination in the Grand Council before the world was formed, His divine Sonship, His sinless life, the shedding of His blood in the garden of Gethsemane, His death on the cross and subsequent bodily resurrection from the grave, He made a perfect atonement for all mankind.

Hosea 2:19-20 expresses the divine covenant-contract: "And I will betroth thee unto me for ever; yea, I will betroth thee unto me in righteousness, and in judgment, and in lovingkindness, and in mercies. I will even betroth thee unto me in faithfulness: and thou shalt know the Lord." The covenant was to be formalized at Sinai; the Lord wanted to seal the contract with a higher, spiritual law, but the children of Israel became idolatrous in Moses' absence:

> And the Lord said unto Moses, Hew thee two other tables of stone, like unto the first, and I will write upon them also, the words of *the law, according as they were written at the first on the tables which thou brakest*; but it shall not be according to the first, for I will take away the priesthood out of their midst; therefore my holy order, and the ordinances thereof, shall not go before them; for my presence shall not go up in their midst, lest I destroy them.
>
> But I will give unto them the law as at the first, but it shall be after *the law of a carnal commandment*; for I have sworn in my wrath, that they shall not enter into my presence, into my rest, in the days of their pilgrimage. Therefore do as I have commanded thee, and be ready in the morning, and come up in the morning unto mount Sinai, and present thyself there to me, in the top of the mount (JST Exod. 34:1-2; emphasis added).

The resulting covenant we know as the Ten Commandments, the first five of which explain how the children of Israel, the bride(s), were to honor their bridegroom:

And God spake all these words, saying,

I am the Lord thy God, which have brought thee out of the land of Egypt, out of the house of bondage.

Thou shalt have no other gods before me.

Thou shalt not make unto thee any graven image, or any likeness of any thing that is in heaven above, or that is in the earth beneath, or that is in the water under the earth:

Thou shalt not bow down thyself to them, nor serve them: for I the Lord thy God am a jealous God, visiting the iniquity of the fathers upon the children unto the third and fourth generation of them that hate me;

And shewing mercy unto thousands of them that love me, and keep my commandments.

Thou shalt not take the name of the Lord thy God in vain; for the Lord will not hold him guiltless that taketh his name in vain.

Remember the sabbath day, to keep it holy.

Six days shalt thou labour, and do all thy work:

But the seventh day is the sabbath of the Lord thy God: in it thou shalt not do any work, thou, nor thy son, nor thy daughter, thy manservant, nor thy maidservant, nor thy cattle, nor thy stranger that is within thy gates:

For in six days the LORD made heaven and earth, the sea, and all that in them is, and rested the seventh day: wherefore the LORD blessed the sabbath day, and hallowed it (Exod. 20:1-11).

Throughout history, beginning with Adam (see Moses 5:9, 14), the friend of the Bridegroom has been, first and foremost, the Holy Spirit, of whom the Savior said:

If a man love me, he will keep my words: and my Father will love him, and we will come unto him, and make our abode with him.

He that loveth me not keepeth not my sayings: and the word which ye hear is not mine, but the Father's which sent me.

These things have I spoken unto you, being yet present with you. (John 14:23-25).

Reminding His disciple-brides of what He has said to them is one of the duties of the Bridegroom's friend. But in addition to the Holy Spirit, the Bridegroom has called prophets, often when moved upon by the Holy Spirit, sometimes with theophonic experiences direct with the Lord,[3] to lead His people, to make sure they correctly understand the Lord's plan of salvation. Amos wrote: "Surely the Lord GOD will do nothing, but he revealeth his secret unto his servants the prophets" (Amos 3:7).

3. Over the centuries, the Bridegroom has prepared for the moment when He would fetch His bride by seeking to build a "house of prayer, a house of fasting, a house of faith, a house of learning, a house of glory, a house of order" (D&C 88:113; 109:8, 16), fit to be a "habitation of God through the Spirit" (Eph. 2:22), in other words, to build Zion. The first bride He and His Father chose was the Israelites whom He rescued from the Egyptian bondage and idolatry. From the beginning it was a troubled marriage because the people often fell into idolatry, an adulterous violation of the marriage covenant with the Lord, Who had clearly commanded that they should have no other gods before Him (Exod. 20:3; Mosiah 12:35). Finally, after centuries of falling into idolatry-adultery and being forgiven by its Bridegroom, He finally divorced Himself from the house of Israel, dissolving the divine Katuba by declaring, "she is not my wife, neither am I her husband" (Hosea 2:2), though He held out the promise of a later redemption. Nevertheless, this was a tragedy for Israel with continuing consequences.[4]

At the meridian of time, Jehovah condescended to earth, being born of the virgin Mary, and became known as Jesus of Nazareth (Hebrew *Yeshua*, English Joshua, meaning "Yahweh saved"). Though now without a bride, His mission was to pay the price for His bride, that is, to redeem the sins of all mankind, making immortality available to all and eternal life to those who choose to come unto Him, "come unto [Him] (3 Ne. 12:3), "take up [their] cross [of sacrifice] daily" (Luke 9:23), and diligently seek to keep His commandments, faithfully serving Him and God's children to the end (see D&C 63:20). Recognizing the inestimable price the Savior paid, Peter wrote of those who come unto Him: "ye are a chosen generation, a royal priesthood, an holy nation, a peculiar [Greek, *peripoiesis* (περιποίησις), "purchased"] people; that ye should shew forth the praises of him who hath called you out of darkness into his marvellous light" (1 Peter 2:9). Thus, the Atonement of Jesus Christ is the central doctrine of His gospel (see 3 Ne. 27:13-21). Nothing is greater in the lives of men.

His Redemption altered the law of sacrifice: no longer would a high priest annually offer the an unblemished lamb, symbol of the Messiah to come, and exile a scapegoat for the sins of the Israelites on the Day of Atonement (*Yom Kippur*, "*kippur* is from the Hebrew word . . . meaning to cover. . . . Yom Kippur [was] an atonement [covering] . . . made for the previous year's sins."[5]). The freely offered sacrifice of the Lamb of God, the Great High Priest (see Heb. 4:15), the Messiah, ended the Law-of-Moses sacrifices "once for all" (Heb. 10:10), instituting the law of repentance whereby His Atonement becomes active in people's lives,[6] offering their personal sacrifice of "a broken heart and a contrite spirit" (3 Ne. 9:20). Thus, the inner sacrifice of a broken heart supplanted the Old-Testament "outward performances" of animal sacrifice (Alma 24:15). The fire that cleansed the animal became the sanctifying, heavenly fire within.

As seminally important as a broken heart and contrite spirit are for the progression and refinement of man, the Lord has a vastly greater vision of our potential, a potential for godliness, that He elucidated in His seminal discourse, the Sermon on the Mount in Palestine and the Sermon before the temple in Bountiful in the Western Hemisphere. Prefacing this discourse are the Beatitudes that outline the path from a broken heart ("poor in spirit") to a pure heart[7] to become sons of God, meaning to be exalted into the state of godhood.[8] (In most ways, the remainder of the sermon, and all His other teaching, explains the undergirding principles of the prefacing Beatitudes.) The emphasis of the Beatitudes is, therefore, on the quality of the heart. While not compromising the "shalt nots" of the Ten Commandments, the Beatitudes define the "thou shalts" that will help followers make a mighty change of heart and grow into the beauty of goodness (*kalos*) and Good-Samaritan mercy, whereby a dedicated disciple of Christ may increasingly mirror "the Father of mercies" (2 Cor. 1:3) from Whom all goodness descends (see Alma 5:40), and Whose being is the perfection of beauty.[9]

As the groom leaving his bride went to build a house for her, so also did the Savior for His chosen bride.

> Let not your heart be troubled: ye believe in God, believe also in me.
>
> In my Father's house are many mansions: if it were not so, I would have told you. I go to prepare a place for you.
>
> And if I go and prepare a place for you, I will come again, and receive you unto myself; that where I am, there ye may be also (John 14:1-3).

Having divorced His first bride, through the succeeding centuries (another nanosecond of eternity), the Savior and His Father prepared the religious, intellectual, and sociopolitical climate in which to choose a new bride and restore Their original covenants and ordinances, along with Their tutoring gospel. That time arrived early in the nineteenth century of the newly created, expanding United States, whose Constitution guaranteed religious freedom. The specific location was in upstate New York, in the so-called burned-over region, so named due to the religious fervor preachers of all persuasions created. The person foreordained and selected to establish the new bride and restore the gospel was a young, inquisitive, spiritually-prepared farm youth named Joseph Smith. Because the marriage proposal was to be made by the Father and the Son, both appeared to Joseph, the Father deferring to the Bridegroom-Son, saying: *"This is My Beloved Son. Hear Him!"* (Joseph Smith—History 1:17). That was the beginning; the general name for the new bride is The Church of Jesus Christ of Latter-day Saints. The bride is the accretion of individual brides from around the world[10] who at baptism make the following "marriage" covenant with the Lord:

> All those who humble themselves before God, and desire to be baptized, and come forth with broken hearts and contrite spirits, and witness before the church that they have truly repented of all their sins, and are willing to take upon them the name of Jesus Christ, having a determination to serve him to the end, and truly manifest by their works that they have received of the Spirit of Christ unto the remission of their sins, shall be received by baptism into his church (D&C 20:37).

His inestimable gift to each newly betrothed is the gift of the Holy Spirit who will be their constant (constancy or steadfastness being a hallmark of divinity and faithful discipleship) companion so long as they remain worthy. A second level of covenants is made in the temple with the Endowment. In a Brigham Young Devotional address, Bruce C. Hafen made the following insightful comment on the baptismal and temple covenants:

> Baptism represents the first sacrifice [a newly converted bride makes]. The temple endowment represents the second sacrifice. The first sacrifice was about breaking out of Satan's orbit. The second one is about breaking

fully into Christ's orbit, pulled by His gravitational power. The first sacrifice was mostly about giving up temporal things. The second one is about consecrating ourselves spiritually, holding back nothing.[13]

Yet a third level of covenant occurs when a man and a woman are sealed for time and all eternity.

To give as many of God's children the opportunity to betroth themselves to the Bridegroom, the Lord has commanded the Church to take the gospel into all the world to find those who will believe in Christ and commit to following His gospel thereby becoming one of His individual brides. Consequently, "thy gates [the gates of thy house] shall be open continually; they shall not be shut day nor night; that men may bring unto thee the forces of the Gentiles, and that their kings may be brought" (Isaiah 60:11).

4. Only the Father knows when the Savior will return to claim His bride. After describing the events of the tribulation prior to His Second Coming, the Lord said:

> the sun shall be darkened, and the moon shall not give her light, and the stars shall fall from heaven, and the powers of the heavens shall be shaken:
>
> And then shall appear the sign of the Son of man in heaven: and then shall all the tribes of the earth mourn, and they shall see the Son of man coming in the clouds of heaven with power and great glory.
>
> And he shall send his angels with a great sound of a trumpet, and they shall gather together his elect from the four winds, from one end of heaven to the other.

Now learn a parable of the fig tree; When his branch is yet tender, and putteth forth leaves, ye know that summer is nigh:

So likewise ye, when ye shall see all these things, know that it is near, even at the doors. . . .

Heaven and earth shall pass away, but my words shall not pass away.

But of that day and hour knoweth no man, no, not the angels of heaven, but my Father only (JST Matt. 24:35-40).

But, in his apocalyptic vision, John was allowed to partially view the moment:

And I saw a new heaven and a new earth: for the first heaven and the first earth were passed away; and there was no more sea.

And I John saw the holy city, new Jerusalem, coming down from God out of heaven, *prepared as a bride adorned for her husband.*

And I heard a great voice out of heaven saying, Behold, the tabernacle of God is with men, and he will dwell with them, and they shall be his people, and God himself shall be with them, and be their God.

And God shall wipe away all tears from their eyes; and there shall be no more death, neither sorrow, nor crying, neither shall there be any more pain: for the former things are passed away.

And he that sat upon the throne said, Behold, I make all things new. And he said unto me, Write: for these words are true and faithful (Rev. 21:1-5; emphasis added).

5. As described in Matthew 25, the great wedding and feast begins as the Last Judgment proceeds. The third narrative of Matthew 25 depicts the Son of Man of Holiness (see Moses 7:35, 47)—the divine Bridegroom, Yahweh-Jesus Christ, "KING OF KINGS AND LORD OF LORDS" (Rev. 19:16), Father of all disciples (see Mosiah 5:7)—sitting "upon the throne of his glory," all nations gathered before Him (Matt. 25:31-33). Representing the worthy brides of the marriage, the righteous sheep are placed on His right hand, the right hand symbolizing righteousness, acceptance, power, and authority; the slothful goats appear on His left hand, the symbol of unrighteousness and inadmissible for eternal life.

Gifts for each wedding guest, meaning each disciple-bride who has overcome the world, are also part of the ultimate wedding, identified in the first few chapters of Revelation:

1. "to eat of the tree of life, which is in the midst of the paradise of God" (Rev. 2:7);
2. "to eat of the hidden manna" and receive "a white stone," a personal "Urim and Thummim pertaining to a higher order of kingdoms," in which "a new name is written, which no man knoweth save he that receiveth it" (Rev. 2:17; D&C 130:10);
3. receive "power over many kingdoms" (JST Rev. 2:26);

4. "clothed in white raiment," a robe of righteousness (Rev. 3:5);
5. "name not blotted out of the book of life" (Rev. 3:5);
6. "name confessed [acknowledged] before my Father, and before his angels" (Rev. 3:5);
7. "make a pillar in the temple of my Father" (Rev. 3:12);
8. "write upon him the name of my God, and the name of the city of my God, which is new Jerusalem" (Rev. 3:12);
9. "write upon him my new name" (Rev. 3:12);
10. "grant[ed] to sit with [the Savior] in [His] throne, even as I also overcame, and am set down with my Father in his throne" (Rev. 3:21)
11. to be "before the throne of God, and serve him day and night in his temple: and he that sitteth on the throne shall dwell among them. They shall hunger no more, neither thirst any more; neither shall the sun light on them, nor any heat. For the Lamb which is in the midst of the throne shall feed them, and shall lead them unto living fountains of waters: and God shall wipe away all tears from their eyes" (Rev. 7:15-17).

The throne of God resides in the Father's house where the Savior went to prepare mansions for His disciple-brides, an abode of unparalleled magnificence:

And he shewed me a pure river of water of life, clear as crystal, proceeding out of the throne of God and of the Lamb.

> In the midst of the street of it, and on either side of the river, was there the tree of life, which bare twelve manner of fruits, and yielded her fruit every month: and the leaves of the tree were for the healing of the nations.
>
> And there shall be no more curse: but the throne of God and of the Lamb shall be in it; and his servants shall serve him:
>
> And they shall see his face; and his name shall be in their foreheads.
>
> And there shall be no night there; and they need no candle, neither light of the sun; for the Lord God giveth them light: and they shall reign for ever and ever (Rev. 22:1-5).

This is the heavenly temple (see Rev. 21:22-23) where the church of the Firstborn will abide in the presence of the Father and the Son, forming the pillars of that sacred edifice (see D&C 76:51-70). When Nephi saw the tree of life in its celestial setting, he could only say that "the beauty thereof was far beyond, yea, exceeding of all beauty" (1 Ne. 11:8), the quality of all things associated with the Lord.

There is one final, inclusive gift that defies human comprehension and imagination: "He that overcometh shall inherit all things; and I will be his God, and he shall be my son" (Rev. 21:7),[12] echoed in Doctrine and Covenants 84: "For he that receiveth my servants receiveth me; And he that receiveth me receiveth my Father; And he that receiveth my Father's kingdom; therefore all that my Father hath shall be given unto him" (D&C 84:36-38). The Father and the Son will share the mysteries of the universe with each pair of marriage partners as they are prepared to receive them. Here is the culminating realization of the Lord's marriage to His people that the wedding motif anticipated through the centuries, a wedding of beautiful souls to their Master and His Father, the sources of all beauty. And to be clothed in a robe of righteousness is "to be clothed upon even as I am, to be with me, that we may be one" (D&C 29:13).

Notes to Appendix

1. I am indebted to Donna B. Nielsen's book *Beloved Bridegroom: Finding Christ in Ancient Jewish Marriage and Family Customs* (Salt Lake City: Onyx Press, 2013) that sets out the pattern of Hebrew marriage customs in detail.
2. Divine investiture was explained by the First Presidency of President Joseph F. Smith: "[T]he Father placed His name upon the Son; and Jesus Christ spoke and ministered in and through the Father's name; and so far as power, authority and Godship are concerned His words and acts were and are those of the Father" (*Messages of the First Presidency of the Church of Jesus Christ of Latter-day Saints*, ed. James R. Clark, 6 vol.s [Salt Lake City, UT: Bookcraft, 1971], 5:32). While President Smith and his counselors addressed the specific relationship between Heavenly Father and His Son, Jesus Christ, the Holy Spirit speaks by that same principle of divine investiture, as many scriptures testify. The Apostle John recorded the Savior saying: "I will pray the Father, and he shall give you another Comforter, that he may abide with you for ever; *Even* the Spirit of truth; whom the world cannot receive, because it seeth him not, neither knoweth him: but ye know him; for he dwelleth with you, and shall be in you. . . . These things have I spoken unto you, being *yet* present with you. But the Comforter, *which is* the Holy Ghost, whom the Father will send in my name, he shall teach you all things, and bring all things to your remembrance, whatsoever I have said unto you" (John 14:16-17, 25-26). In the sixteenth chapter of John we hear these words of the Savior: "[W]hen the Comforter is come, whom I will send unto you from the Father, even the Spirit of truth, which proceedeth from the Father, he shall testify of me" (John 15:26). Before the advent of Christ, Nephi wrote that "after [the Messiah] had been slain he should rise from the dead, and should make himself manifest, by the Holy Ghost, unto the Gentiles" (1 Ne. 10:11).

3. In the April 2018 General Conference, Elder Quentin L. Cook said: "[S]enior Church leaders who preside over the divinely appointed purposes of the Church receive divine assistance. This guidance comes from the Spirit and sometimes directly from the Savior. Both kinds of spiritual guidance are given. I am grateful to have received such assistance" ("Prepare to Meet God," *Ensign* [May 2018], 117).

4. For an enlightening discussion of this divorce, see Kent P. Jackson, "The Marriage of Hosea and Jehovah's Covenant with Israel," in *Isaiah and the Prophets: Inspired Voices from the Old Testament*, ed. Monet S. Nyman and Charles D. Tate Jr. (Provo, UT: Religious Studies Center, Brigham Young University, 1984), 57-74.

5. Kevin Howard and Marvin Rosenthal, *The Feasts of the Lord: God's Prophetic Calendar from Calvary to the Kingdom* (Orlando, FL: Zion's Hope, 1997), 118. Listen to Elder Jeffrey R. Holland's stirring address "Behold the Lamb of God," at lds.org.

6. See Joseph B. Wirthlin: "It is through repentance that the Atonement becomes operative in your life" (*Ensign*, Nov. 1999), 40.

7. See Bohn, *Beatitudes*.

8. See Daniel C. Peterson reference in Chapter 10, note 24 above; also David E. Bokovoy, "'Ye Really *Are* Gods': A Response to Michael Heiser concerning the LDS Use of Psalm 82 and the Gospel of John," *FARMS Review* 19/1 (2007), 267-313.

9. There is always this caveat: the *perfection* of the many qualities enunciated in the Beatitudes and elsewhere will happen only through the grace and perfection of Jesus Christ, after all we can do (see 2 Ne. 25:23). As Latter-day Saints, trying to do our best to live up to the principles of the gospel, we sometimes obsess about our imperfections, and, if not despair, we lament the disparity between who we are and the perfection the Savior has set for us. We need to take to heart the profound counsel then Elder Russell M. Nelson gave about perfection in general, but surely including all the qualities that go into it:

> If I were to ask which of the Lord's commandments is most difficult to keep, many of us might cite Matt. 5:48: "Be ye therefore perfect, even as your Father which is in heaven is perfect." . . .
>
> When comparing one's personal performance with the supreme standard of the Lord's expectation, the reality of imperfection can at times be depressing. My heart goes out to conscientious

Saints who, because of their shortcomings, allow feelings of depression to rob them of happiness in life.

We all need to remember: men are that they might have joy—not guilt trips![2] We also need to remember that the Lord gives no commandments that are impossible to obey. But sometimes we fail to comprehend them fully.

Our understanding of perfection might be aided if we classify it into two categories. The first could pertain uniquely to this life—*mortal* perfection. The second category could pertain uniquely to the next life—*immortal* or *eternal* perfection. . . .

Mortal perfection can be achieved as we try to perform every duty, keep every law, and strive to be as perfect in our sphere as our Heavenly Father is in his. *If we do the best we can*, the Lord will bless us according to our deeds and the desires of our hearts. . . .

The *perfect* man described in Paul's quotation is the completed person—*teleios*—the glorified soul!

Moroni taught how to gain this glorious objective. His instruction stands in any age as an antidote for depression and a prescription for joy. I echo his plea: "Come unto Christ, and be perfected in him, and deny yourselves of all ungodliness; ... love God with all your might, mind and strength ... [Then] ye may be perfect in Christ, . . . holy, [and] without spot" (Moro. 10:32–33).

Meanwhile . . . let us do the best we can and try to improve each day. When our imperfections appear, we can keep trying to correct them. We can be more forgiving of flaws in ourselves and among those we love. We can be comforted and forbearing. The Lord taught, "Ye are not able to abide the presence of God now . . . ; wherefore, continue in patience until ye are perfected" (D&C 67:13)

We need not be dismayed if our earnest efforts toward perfection now seem so arduous and endless. Perfection is pending. It can come in full only after the Resurrection and only through the Lord. It awaits all who love him and keep his commandments. It includes thrones, kingdoms, principalities, powers, and dominions (See D&C 132:19) It is the end for which we are to endure. It is the eternal perfection that God has in store for each of us (Russell M. Nelson, "Perfection Pending," *Ensign* [Nov. 1995], 86, 88).

10. I'm fully aware that Catholic nuns consider themselves to be brides of Christ, which may be true due to the compassionate help they give to the poor and needy, like Sister Teresa and those associated with her. But, without the ordaining power of the Melchizedek priesthood, in which godliness is manifest (see D&C 84:20), the ultimate marriage to the Bridegroom is not completed, meaning exaltation into the celestial kingdom and the presence of Heavenly Father.

11. Bruce C. Hafen, "A Disciple's Journey," https://speeches.byu.edu/talks/bruce-c-hafen_ disciples-journey/

12. Rather than referring strictly to males, "son" here denotes those who have the qualities of Christ. The same attribution appears in reference to peacemakers who "shall be called the sons [Greek *huios* (υἱός)] of God" (Matt. 5:9). The King James' translators used the word "children" to include men and women, whereas "sons" might appear to exclude women, which is obviously contrary to the Lord's gospel.

Bibliography

Abrams, M. H. *The Norton Anthology of English Literature*. New York: Norton & Co., 1968.

Aburto, Reyna I. "With One Accord." *Ensign* (May 2018): 78-80.

Anderson, Wilford W. "The Music of the Gospel." *Ensign*. November 2015: 54-????

Alter, Robert. *The Art of Biblical Poetry*. New York: Basic Books, 2011.

_____ and Frank Kermode, eds. *The Literary Guide to the Bible*. Cambridge, MA: Harvard University Press, 1990.

American Heritage Dictionary. 4th ed. Boston, MA: Houghton Mifflin, 2000.

Aquinas, Thomas *Summa Theologica*. Translated by Fathers of the English Dominican Province. In *Great Books of the Western World*. 52 vols. Edited by Robert Maynard Hutchins and Mortimer Adler. Chicago, IL: Encyclopædia Britannica, 1952. Volumes 19 & 20.

Aristotle. *Poetics*. Translated by Ingram Bywater. New York, NY: Modern Library, 1954.

_____. *Poetics*. Translated by Stephen Halliwell. Loeb Classical Library. Cambridge, MA: Harvard University Press, 2005.

Auerbach, Erich. *Mimesis: The Representation of Reality in Western Literature*. Translated by Willard R. Trask. Princeton, NJ: Princeton University Press, 2003.

Augustine. *Confessions*. Translated by Edward Bouverie Pusey. In *Great Books of the Western World*. 52 vols. Edited by Robert Maynard Hutchins and Mortimer Adler. Chicago, IL: Encyclopædia Britannica, 1952. Volume 18.

_____. *Questionum in Heptateuchum* [Questions on the Heptateuch].

Aune, David A. *Revelation 17-22*. Nashville, TN: Thomas Nelson Publishers, 1998.

Ballard, M. Russell. "God Is at the Helm." *Ensign* (November 2015): 25???.

Barclay, William. *New Testament Words*, Philadelphia: Westminster Press, 1974.

_____. *The Parables of Jesus*. Louisville, KY: Westminster John Knox Press, 1999.

Barfield, Owen. *Poetic Diction: A Study in Meaning*. Hanover, NH: Wesleyan University Press, 1984.

Barker, Margaret. *Temple Theology: An Introduction*. London: Society for Promoting Christian Knowledge, 2004.

_____. "The Lord is One." *Brigham Young University Studies* 56, no. 1 (2017): 75-97.

_____. *The Older Testament: The Survival of Themes from the Ancient Royal Cult in Sectarian Judaism and Early Christianity*. Sheffield, ENG: Phoenix Press, 2005.

Barnstone, Willis, ed. *The Other Bible*. San Francisco, CA: Harper & Row, n.d.

Beardsley, Monroe. *Aesthetics: Problems in the Philosophy of Criticism*. Indianapolis, IN: Hacket Publishing, 1981.

Bednar, David A. "A Reservoir of Living Water," Church Education System Fireside for Young Adults, Feb. 4, 2007 (https://speeches.byu.edu/talks/david-a-bednar_reservoir-living-water/)

_____. "And Nothing Shall Offend Them." *Ensign* (November 2006), 89-92.

Benson, Ezra Taft. "A Mighty Change of Heart." *Ensign* (Oct. 1989): 2-5.

_____. "Born of God." *Ensign* (November 1985): 5-7.

_____. "Flooding the Earth with the Book of Mormon," *Ensign* (November 1988): 4-9.

_____. *Teachings of the Presidents of the Church*. Salt Lake City, UT: The Church of Jesus Christ of Latter-day Saints, 2014.

Bloom, Harold. *Shakespeare: The Invention of the Human*. New York, NY: Riverhead Books, 1999.

Bohn, William J. *The Beatitudes: From Poor in Heart to Pure in Heart*. N.p. 2015.

_____. *Matthew 25: Symbolic Vision—Parabolic Living*. N.p., 2017.

Bokovoy, David E. "'Ye Really Are Gods': A Response to Michael Heiser concerning the LDS Use of Psalm 82 and the Gospel of John." *FARMS Review* 19, no. 1 (2007): 267-313.

Boorstin, Daniel. *The Discoverers*. New York, NY: Random House, 1983.

Bradshaw, Jeffrey M. "The Tree of Knowledge as the Veil of the Sanctuary. In *Ascending the Mountain of the Lord: Temple, Praise, and Worship in the Old Testament*. Edited by David R. Seeley, Jeffrey R. Chadwick, and Matthew J.

Gray. Provo, UT: Religious Studies Center; Salt Lake City, UT: Deseret Book, 2013: 49-65.

Bradshaw, Merrill. "Toward a Mormon Aesthetic." *BYU Studies* 21, no. 1 (winter 1981): 91-99.

Bragg, Mark A. "Brighter and Brighter until the Perfect Day." *Ensign* (May 2017): 36???

Breck, John. *The Shape of Biblical Language: Chiasmus in the Scriptures and Beyond.* Crestwood, NJ: St. Vladimir's Seminary Press, 1994.

Brown, Hugh B. *Eternal Quest.* Salt Lake City, UT: Bookcraft, 1956.

Brown, Matthew B. *The Gate of Heaven: Insights on the Doctrines and Symbols of the Temple.* American Fork, UT: Covenant Communications, 1999.

Buttrick, George Arthur, ed. *The Interpreter's Dictionary of the Bible.* 5 vols. Nashville, TN: Abingdon Press, 1962.

Caird, G. B. *The Language and Imagery of the Bible.* Grand Rapids, MI: William B. Eerdmans Publishing, 1997.

———. *The Revelation of Saint John.* Peabody, MA: Hendrickson Publishers, 1999.

——— & L. D. Hurst. *New Testament Theology.* Oxford: Clarendon Press, 1995.

Calne, Donald B. *Within Reason – Rationality and Human Behavior.* New York: Vintage Books, 2000.

Cambridge History of English and American Literature, The. Edited by Ward, A. W. and A. R. Waller. 14 vol.s. Cambridge, ENG: Cambridge University Press 1907-1921).

Carlyle, Thomas. *Sartor Restarus.* https://books.google.com/books? id=C4EQ AAAA YAAJ& printsec= frontcover&source=gbs_ge_summary_r&cad=0#v= onepage&q&f=false.

Chase, Mary Ellen. *Life and Language in the Old Testament.* New York: W.W. Norton, 1955.

Coleridge, Samuel Taylor. *A Critical Edition of the Major Works.* Edited by H. J. Jackson. Oxford, ENG: Oxford University Press, 1995.

Corbett, Don Cecil. *Mary Fielding Smith—Daughter of Britain: Portrait of Courage.* Salt Lake City, UT: Deseret Book, 1974.

Covey, Stephen R. *The Divine Center.* Salt Lake City: Deseret Book, 1993.

———. *The Seven Habits of Highly Effective People.* New York, NY: Simon & Schuster, 1989.

Deaton, Dennis. *Mind Management.* Mesa, AZ: MMI Publishing, 1995.

Dodd, C. H. *The Parables of the Kingdom.* London: The Religious Book Club, 1942.

Douglas, Alex. "The Garden of Eden, the Ancient Temple, and Receiving a New Name." In *Ascending the Mountain of the Lord: Temple, Praise, and Worship in the Old Testament*. Edited by David R. Seeley, Jeffrey R. Chadwick, and Matthew J. Gray. Provo, UT: Religious Studies Center; Salt Lake City, UT: Deseret Book, 2013: 36-48.

Durant, Will. *The Renaissance: A History of Civilization in Italy from 1304-1576 A.D.* New York: Simon and Schuster, 1953.

Dyer, Wayne W. *You'll See It When You Believe It*. New York, NY: Avon Books, 1990.

Dyrness, William A. "Aesthetics in the Old Testament: Beauty in Context." *Journal of the Evangelical Theological Society* 28, no. 4 (1985): 421-32.

Eco, Umberto. *The Aesthetics of Thomas Aquinas*. Translated by Hugh Bredin. Cambridge: Harvard University Press, 1988.

Edwards, Boyd F. and W. Ferrell Edwards. "Does Chiasmus Appear in the Book of Mormon by Chance." *Brigham Young University Studies* 43, no. 2 (2004): 103-30.

Eiler, David L. "The Origin and History of Zion as a Theological Symbol in Ancient Israel." Doctoral diss. Princeton Theological Seminary, 1968.

Einstein, Albert. "What Life Means to Einstein: An Interview by George Sylvester Viereck." *The Saturday Evening Post* (October 26, 1929).

Elliott, Robert E. "Parallelism." In *Princeton Encyclopedia of Poetry and Poetics*. Edited by Alex Preminger. Princeton, NJ: Princeton University Press.

Encyclopaedia Judaica. 17 vols. New York: MacMillan, 1971.

Eyre, Richard. *Life Before Life: Origins of the soul . . . knowing where you came from and who you really are*. Salt Lake City, UT: Shadow Mountain, 2000.

Eyring, Henry B. "Serve with the Spirit." *Ensign* (November 2010): 59-62.

Faust, James E. "A Second Birth." *Ensign* (June 1998): 2-5.

_____. "It Can't Happen to Me." *Ensign* (May 2002): 46-48.

_____. "The Refiner's Fire." *Ensign* (May 1979): 53-59.

Ferrell, James L. *The Hidden Christ: Beneath the Surface of the Old Testament*. Salt Lake City: Deseret Book, 2009.

Friedman, Norman. "Imagery." In *Princeton Encyclopedia of Poetry and Poetics*. Edited by Alex Preminger. Princeton, NJ: Princeton University Press, 1990.

Frye, Northrup. *Words with Power: Being a Second Study of "The Bible and Literature."* New York, NY: Harcourt Brace, Jovanovich, 1990.

Gaskill, Alonzo. "'The 'Ceremony of the Shoe': A Ritual of God's Ancient Covenant People," https://rsc.byu.edu/archived/our-rites-worship-latter-day-saint-views-ritual-history-scripture-and-practice/ceremony.

Gong, Gerrit W. "Campfire of Faith," *Ensign* (November 2018):40-43.

Greene, Brian. *The Hidden Reality: Parallel Universes and the Deep Laws of the Cosmos*. New York, NY: Alfred A. Knopf, 2011.

Hafen, Bruce C. "A Disciple's Journey." https://speeches.byu.edu/talks/bruce-c-hafen_disciples-journey/

Hales, Robert D. "Becoming a Disciple of Our Lord Jesus Christ." *Ensign* (May 2017): 46-48.

———. "Holy Scriptures: The Power of God unto Salvation." *Ensign* (November 2006): 24-27.

Harris, R. Laird, Gleason L. Archer, Jr., Bruce K. Waltke. *Theological Wordbook of the Old Testament*. 2 vols. Chicago, IL: Moody Press, 1980.

Harris, Sydney. "Love Your Enemies." *Detroit Free Press* (June 1973).

Hart, David Bentley. *The Beauty of the Infinite: The Aesthetics of Christian Truth*. Grand Rapids, MI: Wm. B. Eerdmans Publishing, 2003.

Hauglid, Brian M. "Sacred Time and the Temple." In *Temples in the Ancient World: Ritual and Symbolism*, ed. Donald W. Parry. Salt Lake City: Deseret Book/ Provo, UT: Foundation for Ancient Research and Mormon Studies, 1994: 636-45.

Hicks, Michael. "Notes on Brigham Young's Aesthetics." *Dialogue: A Journal of Mormon Thought* 16 (1983): 127-30.

Hinckley, Gordon B. "Look to the Future." *Ensign* (November 1997): 67-69.

———. "Overpowering the Goliaths in Our Lives." *Ensign* (May 1983): 46, 51-52.

———. "The Wondrous and True Story of Christmas." *Ensign* (December 2000)" 2-5.

———. "We Walk by Faith." *Ensign* (May 2002): 72-74.

Holland, Jeffrey R. "'Abide in Me.'" *Ensign* (May 2004): 30-32.

———. "He Hath Filled the Hungry with Good Things." *Ensign* (November 1997): 64-66.

———. "Songs Sung and Unsung." *Ensign* (May 2017): 49-51.

Holzapfel, Richard Neitzel & David Rolph Seely, *My Father's House: Temple Worship and Symbolism in the New Testament*. Salt Lake City, UT: Bookcraft, 1994.

Hopkins, Richard R. *How Greek Philosophy Corrupted the Christian Concept of God*. Bountiful, UT: Horizon Publishers, 1999.

Howard, Kevin and Marvin Rosenthal. *The Feasts of the Lord: God's Prophetic Calendar from Calvary to the Kingdom*. Orlando, FL: Zion's Hope, 1997.

Hunter, Howard W. *Teachings of the Presidents of the Church*. Salt Lake City, UT: The Church of Jesus Christ of Latter-day Saints, 2015.

Hyde, Orson. "The Man Called to Lead God's People, etc." *Journal of Discourses*, 26 vols., Edited by G. D. Watt. Liverpool, ENG: F. D. & S. W. Richards, 1854: 121-30.

Interpreter's Dictionary of the Bible, The. 5 vols. Edited by George Arthus Buttrick, et al. Nashville, TN: Abingdon Press.

Jackson, Kent P. "The Marriage of Hosea and Jehovah's Covenant with Israel." In *Isaiah and the Prophets: Inspired Voices from the Old Testament*. Edited by Monet S. Nyman and Charles D. Tate Jr. Provo, UT: Religious Studies Center, Brigham Young University, 1984), 57-74.

Jauss, Hans Robert. *Aesthetic Experience and Literary Hermeneutics*. Translated by Michael Shaw. Minneapolis, MN: University of Minnesota Press, 1982.

Jeremias, Jorg. "Lade und Zion. Zur Entstehung der Ziontradition." In *Probleme biblischer Theologie. Gerhard von Rad zum 70. Geburtstag*. Edited by Walter Wolff. Munich, GER: Chr. Kaiser, 1971: 188-90.

Journal of Discourses. 26 vols. Edited by G. D. Watt. Liverpool, ENG: F. D. & S. W. Richards, 1854-86.

Jülicher. Adolf. *Die Gleichnisse Jesu*. Tübingen, Germany: J. C. B. Mohr, 1889.

Kalmin, Richard. "Levirate Law." In *The Anchor Bible Dictionary*, 6 vols. Edited by David Noel Freedman. New York: Doubleday, 1992: 4:296-97.

Langer, Susanne. *Feeling and Form*. New York, NY: Charles Scribner's Sons, 1961.

Laughlin, Clarence John. *Ghosts Along the Mississippi*. New York, NY: Bonanza, 1961.

Lawrence, Larry R. "The War Goes On." *Ensign* (April 2017): 33-39.

Lectures on Faith. Prepared by the Prophet Joseph Smith. Salt Lake City, UT: Deseret Book, 1985.

Lee, Harold B. "A Blessing for the Saints." *Ensign* (January 1973): 133-34.

———. *Stand Ye in Holy Places: Selected Sermons and Writings of President Harold B. Lee*. Salt Lake City, UT: Deseret Book, 1975.

———. *The Teachings of Harold B. Lee*. Edited by Clyde J. Williams. Salt Lake City, UT: Bookcraft, 1996.

———. "Y Students Give President Lee Manhood Award." *Deseret News* (September 15, 1973).

———. *Ye are the Light of the World. Selected Sermons and Writings of President Harold B. Lee*. Salt Lake City, UT: Deseret Book, 1974.

Levenson, Jon. *Sinai and Zion: An Entry into the Jewish Bible*. Minneapolis, MN: Winston Press, 1985.

Lewis, C. Day. *The Poetic Image*. London, ENG: Jonathan Cape, 1969.

Lewis, C. S. *Prince Caspian*. New York, NY: HarperCollins Publishing, n.d.

_____. *The Essential C. S. Lewis*. Edited by Lyle W. Dorsett. New York, NY: Simon and Schuster, 1988.

Liddel and Scott. *Intermediate Greek-English Lexicon*. Oxford: Clarendon Press, 1994.

Ludlow, Victor L. *Isaiah: Prophet, Seer, and Poet*. Salt Lake City, UT: Deseret Book, 1982.

MacIntyre, Alastair. *After Virtue*. Notre Dame, IN: Notre Dame University Press, 1984.

Madsen, Truman G. "Man Illuminated." In *Five Classics by Truman G. Madsen*. Salt Lake City, UT: Eagle Gate, 2001.

Maxwell, Neal A. "'According to the Desires of [Our] Heart.'" *Ensign* (November 1996): 21-23.

_____. "'Brightness of Hope.'" *Ensign* (November 1994): 34-36.

_____. *Lord, Increase Our Faith*. Salt Lake City, UT: Bookcraft, 1994.

_____. *Meek and Lowly*. Salt Lake City: Deseret Book, 1988.

_____. *The Glory of the City of Enoch: Of One Heart and One Mind*. Salt Lake City, UT: Deseret Book, 1975.

_____. "The Inexhaustible Gospel." *Ensign* (April 1993): 68-73.

_____. "The Net Gathers of Every Kind." *Ensign* (November 1980): 14-15.

_____. "Willing to Submit," *Ensign* (May 1995): 70-73.

_____. "Yet Thou Art There." *Ensign* (November 1987): 30-33.

McConkie, Bruce R. *A New Witness for the Articles of Faith*. Salt Lake City, UT: Deseret Book, 1987.

_____. *Doctrinal New Testament Commentary*, 3 vols. Salt Lake City, UT: Bookcraft, 1974-75.

_____. *Mormon Doctrine*. Salt Lake City, UT: Bookcraft, 1972.

_____. "The How and Why of Faith-promoting Stories," *New Era* (July 1978). https://www. lds.org/ new-era/1978/07/the-how-and-why-of-faith-promoting-stories?lang=eng.

_____. *The Millennial Messiah*. Salt Lake City: Deseret Book, 1982.

McConkie, Joseph Fielding and Donald W. Parry. *A Guide to Scriptural Symbols*. Salt Lake City, UT: Bookcraft, 1990.

_____. and Robert L. Millet, *Doctrinal Commentary on the Book of Mormon*. 4 vols. Salt Lake City, UT: Bookcraft, 1988.

McMurtry, Larry. *Lonesome Dove*. New York: Simon and Schuster, 1985.

Monson, Thomas S. "Four Guideposts." *Deseret News* (August 30, 2003).

Nelson, Russell M. "Perfection Pending." *Ensign* (November 1995): 86-88.

_____. "With God Nothing is Impossible." *Ensign* (May 1988): 33-35.

Nibley, Hugh B. *Approaching Zion*. Salt Lake City: Deseret Book, 1989.

_____. *Lehi in the Desert & The World of the Jaredites*. Salt Lake City, UT: Bookcraft, 1952.

_____. "On the Sacred and the Symbolic." In *Temples in the Ancient World: Ritual and Symbolism*. Edited by Donald W. Parry. Salt Lake City: Deseret Book/ Provo, UT: Foundation for Ancient Research and Mormon Studies, 1994: 535-621.

_____. *Temple and Cosmos: Beyond the Ignorant Present*. Edited by Don E. Norton. Salt Lake City: Deseret Book/Provo, UT: Foundation for Ancient Research and Mormon Studies, 1992.

_____. "The Meaning of the Temple." In *Temple and Cosmos: Beyond the Ignorant Present*. Edited by Don E. Norton. Salt Lake City: Deseret Book/Provo, UT: Foundation for Ancient Research and Mormon Studies, 1992: 1-41.

Nielsen, Donna B. *Beloved Bridegroom: Finding Christ in Ancient Jewish Marriage and Family Customs*. Salt Lake City: Onyx Press, 2013.

Noah Webster's First Edition of an American Dictionary of the English Language. San Francisco: Foundation for American Christian Education, 2000.

Oaks, Dallin H. "Nourishing the Spirit." *Ensign* (December 1998): 7-13.

_____."Scripture Reading and Revelation." *Ensign*(January1995). https://www.lds.org/ensign/1995 /01/ scripture-reading-and-revelation?lang=eng.

_____. *Pure in Heart*. Salt Lake City, UT: Bookcraft, 1988.

Orsini, Gian Napoleone Giodano. Organism." In *Dictionary of the History of Ideas: Discussion of Selected Pivotal Ideas*. 5 vols. Edited by Philip P. Wiener. New York, NY: Charles Scribner's Sons, 1973. 3:421-27.

Ostler, Blake T. "The Throne-Theophany and Prophetic Commission in 2 Nephi: A Form-Critical Analysis." *BYU Studies* 26/4 (1986): 67-95.

Oxford Dictionary of English Etymology, The. Edited by C. T. Onions. Oxford, ENG: Clarendon Press, 1991.

Packer, Boyd K. "Inspired Music—Worthy Thoughts." *Ensign* (January 1974): 25-28.

_____. "Personal Revelation: The Gift, the Test, and the Promise." *Ensign* (November 1994): 59-62.

———. "The Play and the Plan." CES Fireside for Young Adults (May 1995).

Parry, Donald W. *A Guide to Scriptural Symbols*. Salt Lake City, UT: Bookcraft, 1990.

———. *Poetic Parallelism in the Book of Mormon: The Complete Text Reformatted*. Provo: UT: The Neal A. Maxwell Institute for Religious Scholarship, 2007.

Parry, Jay A. and Donald W. Parry. "The Temple in Heaven: Its Description and Significance." In *Temples in the Ancient World: Ritual and Symbolism*. Edited by Donald W. Parry. Salt Lake City: Deseret Book/Provo, UT: Foundation for Ancient Research and Mormon Studies, 1994: 515-32.

Perry, L. Tom. "The Gospel of Jesus Christ." *Ensign* (May 2008): 44-46.

Peacock, George M. *Unlocking the Numbers: An LDS Perspective on Scriptural Use of Numbers*. Springville, UT: CFI, 2005.

Peterson, Daniel C. "Ye Are Gods: Psalm 82 and John 10 as Witnesses of the Divine Nature of Humankind." In *The Disciple as Scholar*. https://publications.mi.byu.edu/fullscreen/?pub= 1091 &index=17), 10, 11, 19, 22, 23, 28, 32, 35-40.

Plato. *Phædo*. Translated by Benjamin Jowett. In *Great Books of the Western World*. 52 vols. Edited by Robert Maynard Hutchins and Mortimer Adler. Chicago, IL: Encyclopædia Britannica, 1952. Volume 7.

———. *Phædrus*. Translated by Benjamin Jowett. In *Great Books of the Western World*. 52 vols. Edited by Robert Maynard Hutchins and Mortimer Adler. Chicago, IL: Encyclopædia Britannica, 1952. Volume 7.

———. *The Republic*. Translated by Benjamin Jowett. In *Great Books of the Western World*. 52 vols. Edited by Robert Maynard Hutchins and Mortimer Adler. Chicago, IL: Encyclopædia Britannica, 1952. Volume 7.

Platt, Rutherford H,ed. *The Forgotten Books of Eden: The Lost Books of the Old Testament*. New York: NY: Bell Publishing, 2015.

Polk, Timothy. "In the Image: Aesthetics and Ethics through the Glass of Scripture," *Horizons in Biblical Theology: An International Dialogue* 8, no. 1 (1986): 27-59.

Preminger, Alex. *Princeton Encyclopedia of Poetry and Poetics*. Princeton, NJ: Princeton University Press, 1990.

Rasband, Ronald A. "Standing with the Leaders of the Church." *Ensign* (May 2016): 46-49.

Rawlins, F. I. G. "Religion and Aesthetics." *The British Journal of Aesthetics* 6, no. 4 (Oct. 1966): 375-84.

Ricoeur, Paul. *Interpretation Theory: Discourse and the Surplus of Meaning*. Fort Worth, TX: Texas Christian University Press, 1976.

Reynolds, George and Janne M. Sjodahl. *Commentary of the Book of Mormon*. 7 vols. Salt Lake City, UT: Deseret Book, 1962-1976.

Ricoeur, Paul. *Interpretation Theory: Discourse and the Surplus of Meaning.* Fort Worth, TX: Texas Christian University Press, 1976.

Robinson, Stephen E. *Believing Christ.* Salt Lake City, UT: Deseret Book, 1992.

_____ and H. Dean Garrett. *A Commentary on the Doctrine and Covenants.* 4 vols. Salt Lake City, UT: Deseret Book, 2000-2005.

Romney, Marion G. "Prayer and Revelation." *Ensign* (May 1978): 48-50.

Ruskin, John. *Modern Painters.* Vol. 3. Orpington, Kent: George Allen, 1888. In Vaughn J. Featherstone. "A Man After God's Own Heart." speeches.byu.edu/index. php?act= viewitem &id = 769.

_____. *The Works of John Ruskin.* 39 vols. Edited by E.T. Cook & Alexander Wedderburn. http://www.lancaster.ac.uk/ruskin-library/the-complete-works-of-john-ruskin/.

Ryken, Leland, James C. Wilhoit, and Tremper Longman III, Editors. *Dictionary of Biblical Imagery.* Downers Grove, IL: InterVarsity Press, 1998.

Sakenfeld, Katherine Doob. "Love (OT)." Vol. 4. of *The Anchor Bible Dictionary*, 6 vols. Edited by David Noel Freedman. New York: Doubleday, 1992: 4: 375-81.

Schiller, Friedrich. *Über Anmut und Würde* [*On Grace and Dignity*]. Munich, GER: Deutscher Taschenbuch Verlag, 1966.

Shakespeare, William. *King Lear.* Edited by Kenneth Muir. London, ENG: Methuen & Co., 1966.

Shorter Oxford English Dictionary on Historical Principles, The. 2 vols. Edited by Lesley Brown. Oxford, ENG: Clarendon Press, 1993.

Shkloevsky, Viktor. "Art as Technique. https://warwick.ac.uk/fac/arts/english/currentstudents /under graduate/ modules/fullist/first/en122/lecture-list-2015-16-2/shkloevsky.pdf

Smith, Joseph. *History of The Church of Jesus Christ of Latter-day Saints*, 7 vols. Salt Lake City, UT: Deseret Book, 1980.

_____. *Lectures on Faith.* Salt Lake City, UT: Deseret Book, 1985.

_____. *Teachings of the Prophet Joseph Smith.* Compiled by Joseph Fielding Smith. Salt Lake City, UT: Deseret Book, 1965.

_____. *The Teachings of Joseph Smith.* Editors Larry E. Dahl & Donald Q. Cannon. Salt Lake City, UT: Bookcraft, 1997.

Smith. Joseph Fielding. *Doctrines of Salvation. Sermons and Writings.* Edited by Bruce R. McConkie. Salt Lake City, UT: Bookcraft, 1998.

Soares, Ulisses. "Becoming a Work of Art." Brigham Young University devotional, Nov. 5, 2013.; speeches.byu.edu.

Talmage, James E. *The Vitality of Mormonism*. Salt Lake City, UT: Deseret News Press, 1919.

Tegmark, Mark. *Our Mathematical Universe: My quest for the Ultimate Nature of Reality*. New York, NY: Alfred A. Knopf, 2014.

The New Cambridge Paragraph Bible. Edited by David Norton. Cambridge, ENG: Cambridge University Press, 2005.

Thiessen, Gesa Elsbeth, ed. *Theological Aesthetics: A Reader*. Grand Rapids, MI: William B. Eerdmans Publishing, 2005.

Thomas, M. Catherine. "King Benjamin and the Mysteries of God." FARMS Reprint.

Trench, Richard Chenevix. *The Miracles and Parables of Christ*. Chattanooga, TN: AMG Publishers, 1996.

Turner, Mark. *The Literary Mind*. New York, NY: Oxford University Press, 1996.

Uchtdorf, Dieter F. "It Works Wonderfully." *Ensign* (November 2015): 20-23.

Via, Jr. Dan O. *The Parables. Their Literary and Existential Dimension*. Philadelphia, PA: Fortress Press, 1967.

Vico, Giambattista. *New Science* [Italien: *Nuova Prima*]. Translated by David Marsh. New York, NY: Penguin Books, 2001.

Vine's Complete Expository Dictionary of Old and New Testament Words. Nashville: Thomas Nelson, 1996.

Walsh, Jerome T. "Gen 2:4b-3:24: A Synchronic Approach." *Journal of Biblica Literature* 96 (1977): 172.

_____. *Style & Structure in Biblical Hebrew Narrative*. Collegeville, MN: Liturgical Press, 2001.

Warren, Rick. *The Purpose-driven Life*. Grand Rapids, MI: Zondervan, 2002.

Webster, Noah. *First Edition of an American Dictionary of the English Language*. San Francisco, CA: Foundation for American Christian Education, 2000.

Welch, John W., Editor. *Chiasmus in Antiquity*. Provo, UT: FARMS, 1981.

_____. "Criteria for Identifying and Evaluating the Presence of Chiasmus." In *Chiasmus Bibliography*. Edited by John W. Welch and Daniel B. McKinlay. Provo, UT: Research Press, 1999: 154-74.

_____. "New Testament Word Studies." *Ensign* (Apr. 1993): 28-30.

_____. "The Good Samaritan: A Type and Shadow of the Plan of Salvation." *Brigham Young University Studies* 38, 2 (1999): 50-115.

_____. "The Good Samaritan: Forgotten Symbols." *Ensign* (February 2007): 40-47.

Westermann, Claus. "Das Schöne im Alten Testament." In *Beiträge zur alttestamentalischen Theologie. Festschrift für Walter Zimmerli zum 70. Geburtstag*.

Edited by Herbert Donner. Göttingen, GER: Vandenhoeck und Ruprecht, 1977: 479-97.

Whitney, Orson F. "Latter-day Saint Ideals and Institutions." *Improvement Era* (August 1927): 851-62.

Widtsoe, John A. *A Rational Theology*. Salt Lake City, UT: Deseret Book, 1966.

_____. *Joseph Smith: Seeker after Truth, Prophet of God*. Salt Lake City, UT: Bookcraft, 1951.

Wilcox, Michael. *Ten Great Souls I Want to Meet in Heaven*. Salt Lake City, UT: Deseret Book, 2012.

Williams, Janet. "Judging Judgment." *Theology Today* (January 2002).

Wirthlin, Joseph B. "Growing into the Priesthood." *Ensign*, (November 1999): 38-41.

_____. "The Time to Prepare." *Ensign* (May 1998): 14-17.

Woolley, David G. *Pillar of Fire*. 5 vols. American Fork, UT: Covenant Communications, 2000-11.

Young's Literal Translation. https://www.biblegateway.com/versions/Youngs-Literal-Translation-YLT-Bible.

Zodhiates, Spiros. *The Complete Word Study Dictionary: New Testament*. Chattanooga, TN: AMG Publishers, 1993.

SUBJECT INDEX

A

Abraham, 270
Abrahamic Covenant, 270
Act, action, active, 110, 112, 135, 181, 191, 201, 268
Adam and Eve, 169, 171, 206, 208, 252
  Fall of, 170, 206, 268
Aesthetics, 50-52
Agency, choose, 54, 168, 171, 175, 192, 203, 268
Anarchy, 121
Angels, 119
Apostles, apostolic, 99, 248
Appearances, 127
Art, 66, 131-32
Articles of Faith, 5
Atonement, Day of, 275

B

Baptize, baptism, 162, 193, 221, 226, 234, 263, 277
Battle, war, 158, 168
Bear burdens, 103, 192, 200, 233, 251
Beatitudes, 187, 220, 233-34, 251, 275-76
Beggar at the Beautiful Gate, 200, 236-38
Beauty, beautiful, 52, 58, 68, 75, 134, 207, 215-17, 220, 223, 225, 242, 249, 251, 253, 254, 257, 259, 260-61, 262-63, 276, 282, 283
  Apotheosis of, 241
  Beautiful souls, 243
  Kalos (good), 222-223, 235-36, 238
  Of holiness, 222, 227, 231, 238, 243, 244, 252, 255
  Of the Lord, 215-17, 244, 245, 247, 253, 261
  Theories of, 51-52
Birth, born again, 164, 226
Boaz, 190
Book of Life, 281
Book of Mormon, 6, 40-41, 78, 81

C

Celestial, celestiality, 125-29
  Celestial kingdom, 107
Challenges, 166
Character assassination, 202
Charity, 193, 217, 230, 259
Christlike, 193
Church, ancient, 126
Church of Jesus Christ of Latter-day Saints, the, 7, 85-86, 126, 193, 208, 278
  Callings in, 193
  First Presidency of, 26, 206, 208
  Membership in, 132-35, 221
  Restoration of, 276-77
Church of the Firstborn, 107, 235, 241, 282
City of Enoch, 128, 224-35
Civilization(s), 121

Comfort, 111, 134, 192, 196, 207, 208, 233-34, 251
Commandments, 120
Companion(ship), 67
Compassion, 181, 196, 199, 210, 212
  Compassionate kindness, 19, 114, 186, 193, 198-99, 223, 234, 241
Confusion, 121
Consecration, pattern of, 114, 197-201, 205, 242
Counterfeits, 34
Covenants, 212, 277
Creation, create, 129, 218, 262
Culture, 45
  of eternal life, 1, 49

D

Deuteronomists, 7-8, 124
Disciple(ship), 131, 163, 165, 166, 193, 195-97, 204, 214, 233, 243, 252, 253, 254
  Beauty of, 235-38
  Prophetic d., 116
Discipline, 114, 133, 192, 245, 263
Disorientation, spiritual, 98
Divine investiture, 269, 283
Duty-desire, 195, 236, 341

E

Earth, 72
Edify, 248
Empathy, empathize, 64-70, 86, 187
Endow, endowment, 240-41
Endure, 28, 162, 242
Eternal life, 6, 18, 22, 35, 62, 101, 107, 120, 129, 152, 180, 193, 197, 198, 211, 225, 226, 231, 268, 269, 274
Existence, 219
Experiment, 135

F

Faith in Jesus Christ, 9-10, 14, 15, 25, 32, 42, 57, 65, 114, 119, 129, 143, 144, 152, 159, 167, 186, 200, 217, 220, 225, 234, 241, 255, 275
  As action, 19-20, 109, 115
  As light, 110
  As power, 20-21, 109
  Experience-informed f., 26
  Informed f., 22-25
  Spirit-informed f., 25-26
  Unity of, 185
  Walk of, 62
Family, 127
  F. History, 134
  Proclamation on, 202-03
Feel, feeling(s), emotion, 37, 42, 50, 55, 64, 99, 100, 128, 135, 151, 187, 196, 209, 210, 211, 220, 227, 254, 257
Form(s), 23, 30
Freedom, liberty, 207, 268

G

Garden of Eden, 206, 252
Gentle, 242, 254
Glory, 257
God (cf. also Heavenly Father) 10, 68-69, 126, 147, 160, 185, 199, 211, 268, 279
  Beauty of, 215-17, 244, 245, 253, 261
  Character of, 245, 257
  Children of, 234
  City of, 224
  Faith of, 20, 215-17, 223, 245
  Faithfulness, 271
  Father of lights, 109
  Grace of, 212, 232, 241
  Glory of, 46, 175, 210, 245, 249, 250, 254
  God of truth, 221, 223
  Household of, 247-48
  Is goodness, 221-23, 268
  Is light, 219-20, 221, 282
  Knowledge of, 133
  Love of, 59, 96, 115, 128, 217, 220,

223, 253
    Loving kindness, 245, 271
    Mission statement, 114, 196
    Self-existent, 108
    Throne of, 224
Godhead, 119, 227, 228, 235
Godhood, 234, 275
Godly, godliness, 23, 60, 126, 171, 185, 224, 233, 238, 254
    Form of, 135
    Mystery of, 74-75
Gods, council of, 234
Good(ness), 113, 170, 191, 201, 213, 216, 221, 231, 236, 248, 254
    Kalos, 254, 276
Gracious(ness), 236

H

Harmony, 133, 134, 229
Heavenly Father, 168, 169, 178, 216, 283
"He Took My Lickin' for Me," 147-51
Holy, holiness, 215, 222, 225, 232, 241, 244
    Beauty of, 222, 227, 231, 238, 243, 244, 248
Holy Spirit (Ghost), the, 2, 25, 47, 59, 64, 65, 96, 108-09, 111, 116, 119, 126, 161, 162, 208, 210, 219-20, 225, 226, 227, 229, 247
    Comforter, 226, 283
    Companionship of, 126, 247, 277
    Gift of, 161, 182, 234, 247, 277
    Still, small voice, 99, 119, 161
Hope, 18-19, 195

I

Idolatry (viz. spiritual adultery), 13-14, 169, 175, 224
Illusion, 39
Imagine, imagination, 3, 16, 33, 34, 53, 54, 55, 58, 70, 90, 91, 145, 149, 151, 158, 174, 182, 262
I-Max screen, 62-63, 71-72
Inform(ed), 23-24
Innocence, 166-67, 170
Insight, 61-64
Inspiration, impressions, 59, 64, 96, 161, 210, 220, 253
Intelligence, 101
Isaiah, 11
    Isaiah 21:1, 95-99
    Isaiah 58:6-12, 249-53

J

Jacob's Allegory of the Tame & Wild Olive Trees, 263
Jesus Christ/Jehovah/Yahweh, 39-40, 46, 58, 59, 106-08, 111, 125, 126, 133, 134, 135, 151, 161-62, 169, 191, 196-97, 205, 207, 208, 209, 211-12, 216, 219, 223, 225, 228, 230, 240, 242, 246, 248, 251, 252, 263, 268, 270-71, 274, 280, 283-84
    Atonement of Jesus Christ, the, 17, 67, 113, 114, 195, 205, 233, 242, 253, 255, 270, 275, 284
    Beauty of, 251
    Come unto, 205
    I Am, 108, 219, 249, 255-57, 283
    Law of, 196, 200
    Light of, 14, 39, 62, 63, 107, 108, 110, 111, 115, 119, 210, 214, 219-20, 227, 250
    Light of the world, 256
    Love of, 214
    Marriage of the Lamb, 213
    Mercy of, 209, 212
    Only Begotten of the Father, 226
    Prince of Peace, 233
    Pure love of, 196, 214
    Righteousness of, 251
    Second Coming of, 252
Justify, justification, 226

K

Kindness, 119, 186, 190, 196, 259
  Merciful k., 214
Knowledge, 23, 25, 26, 32, 34, 65-66, 85, 123, 124, 193, 197, 200, 211, 231, 245, 257

L

Language, 44-45
  Figurative, 4-5, 93
Last Judgment, 253
Law, 180-81, 183, 271
  Celestial l., 128
  Of carnal commandments, 271
Learning, 275
  By faith, 129
Levirate Contract, 189-90, 218
Life, 108, 195, 263
Liken, 34, 64, 92, 138-38, 145, 154, 165, 182, 209-11
Love, 11, 14, 49, 196, 217, 223, 248, 259, 273
  Enemies, 184
  Neighbor, 2, 181, 183, 185, 233
  The Lord, 192, 232
Lucifer/Satan, 121, 123, 168-69

M

Man, 109, 138, 207, 227
  As beautiful work of art, 238
  Children of light, 109
  Divine potential, 125
  God in embryo, 227, 247
  Natural m. 11, 17, 207, 245
  New man, 240-41
Manifest, 36-37
Marriage, 127
  Ancient Hebrew m., 266-68
  God's marriage covenant with His people, 271
Materialism, 199
Means, 197, 198-201
  Money, 199
Meek(ness), 174, 235, 242, 251, 257
Mercy, 111, 119, 181, 184-87, 192, 195-97, 209, 212, 217, 227, 234, 238, 254, 259, 276
  Hesed-mercy, 185-86, 191
Ministering, 187, 193, 227, 241, 253-54
Mortality, 18, 62, 131, 145, 239, 268
  Probationary state, 131
Music, 2, 132-35
Mysteries, 101, 152, 282
Myth, 55

N

Nature, 121, 218
  Symbolism in, 218
New name, 121, 218
New Jerusalem, 252, 279

O

Obey, obedience, 119, 126, 269
Objectivity, 13, 123, 126
Old Testament/ New Testament, 6, 8, 59, 124
Oneness, unity, 42, 226-29, 248, 254, 262, 263
Opposition, opposites, 26-28, 54, 145, 170, 175
Ordain, ordinances, 271, 286
Order, 123, 126, 274
Organic unity, 85, 94
Orientation, spiritual, 27
Overcome, 10, 11, 92, 234, 281

P

Palace (temple), 244
Parables, 136
  Characteristics of, 137-38, 146
  Historical p., 136-40, 165
  History of interpretation, 156

Fig tree, 279
Marriage of the king's son, 268
Miracle of the Savior Walking on Water, 143, 145
    Sariah, 140-43
    Ten Virgins, 112, 217, 267
Patterns, 2, 23, 24, 30, 65, 129, 133
Paul, 5-6, 7
Peace (-able), 134, 192, 196, 226, 236, 254, 255
    Shalom, 234
Perception, percipience, 38-39, 75, 122, 125
Perfect(ion), 16-17, 133, 134, 193-94, 196, 209, 216, 259, 263, 284-85
Pioneer treks, 209-10
Philosophy, 123
Plan of Salvation, 18, 170, 245
Poietics, 49-50, 52, 73-74, 83, 146
    Allegory, 206
    Ancient biblical p., 72, 76, 78-79, 159
    Chiasmus, 80-82, 179-80
    Dramatic tension, 54
    Frost, Robert, "The Road Less Taken," 53-55
    Image(ry), see entry under Image(ry)
    Literary structure, 66
    Metaphor, metaphoric, 55-60
    Narrative mode, 55-56, 136
    Organic unity, 55-56, 58, 146
    Parallelism, 77-80, 178-79
        Thought rhyme, 77
    Poetic expression, 53
    Poetic logic, 50
    Plot, 180
    Poetic world, 180
    Poetic reality, 72-73
    Poetic vision, 73
    Summary statements, 138-39
    Symbol(ism), symbolic, 72-76, 101, 147, 245, 247

Types, 6
Verse, 77-82
Ponder, 62, 100
Poor, 231, 251
Practice, 263
Prayer, 21, 28, 70, 129, 140, 262
    Sacrament p., 48-49
Priesthood, 203-04, 230, 271, 274
    Order of Melchizedek, 235, 286
    Priests and kings, 235
Principles, 2, 23, 75, 129, 153, 220
Progression, 194-95, 198, 268
Prophecy, 261-62, 283-84
    nābí, 117
Prophets, 116-20, 135, 202, 247, 273
    Living p., 92, 221, 227
Pure in heart, 232-35, 245, 247
Pure, purification, 232-33, 255

Q

Questions, 63
Quicken, 109

R

Raca, 201-02
Reading, 91
Reality, really, 2, 11, 24, 25, 30, 32, 38, 39, 45, 50, 62, 92, 100, 101, 113, 122, 144, 146-47, 152, 155, 214, 253
    Eternal r., 73
    Plausible r., 150
    Virtual r., 90-92, 139, 150-51, 158, 180, 182
    Vision of, 101, 126, 154
Reason, 200
Remember(ance), 33, 48, 60, 283
    anamnesis, 83
Repentance, 162, 174, 194, 233, 245, 275, 277, 284
Resurrection, 225
Revelation, reveal, 41, 47, 119, 221, 253, 261

Righteous(ness), 47, 112, 114, 167, 183, 191, 192-93, 214, 229-31, 239, 241, 249, 250, 251, 254-55, 271, 280
   Fruit of, 254, 255
   Principles of, 238-39, 240, 241-43, 280, 283
   Robe of, 238-39, 241, 241-43, 280, 283
   Works of, 33, 196, 213
Ruth, book of, 190, 213

S

Sacred spaces, 261
Saint, 17
Salvation, 134, 236
Sanctify, sanctification, 163-64, 226, 232-33, 245, 275
Scott, Richard G., *Campfire at Sunset*, 12-14
Scriptures, 3, 4, 22, 51, 53, 92, 100, 140, 178, 221, 227
   Breadth, 46
   Depth, 46
   Search(ing), 38, 51, 70-72
   Topography, 100-01
Second Estate, 211
Secret combinations, 121
Septuagint, 83
Servant, good and faithful, 253
Serve, service, 134-35
Shekinah, 89
Skill, 15-16, 20
Smith, The Prophet Joseph, 39-40, 126, 163, 263
   Restoration, 276-77
Smith, Mary Fielding, 21-22
Story, stories, 77
Strangers, 255

T

Tabernacle, 252, 261, 279-80
Talents, 8, 197, 198, 241, 255
Telestial(ity), 120-22, 292

Temple, 104, 130, 200, 244-55, 261
   Clothing, 244
   Temple covenants, 277-78
   Heavenly t., 241, 281, 282
   Holy Place, the, 252
   In the New Testament, 260
Ten Commandments, 271
Terrestrial(ity), 122-25, 205, 252, 268
Testimony, 6-7, 26, 85-86, 117, 152, 227, 234, 253
Theophany, 247, 253, 262
Think, thought, 211
   Overthought, 93
   Underthought, 93
Time, 197-98, 204
Trust, 17
Truth(s), 2, 6, 39, 67, 101, 108, 113, 120, 121, 123, 126, 226, 227, 245, 248, 253
   Doing t. 126

U

Universe, cosmos, 73-74, 147

V

Virtue, 193, 230
Vision, envision, 1, 6, 20, 22, 24, 28, 30, 34, 36, 37, 39-40, 45, 50, 65, 100, 113, 126, 128, 139, 144, 175, 185, 209
   Peripheral v., 196|
   Pictures, 3, 54
   See(ing), 27, 38, 41-42, 124, 152, 180, 209
   View, 37
Vision, First, 1

W

Weakness(es), 166
Wise, wisdom, 11, 49, 115, 192, 227, 248, 254, 257
Words, xi, 23, 36, 37, 38, 45, 47, 50, 63, 64, 91, 146

Abstract w., 47-48
Etymology of, 48
Everlasting w., 113
Trigger w., 76
Word of God/Christ, 42, 109, 113, 150, 175, 208, 279
Work(s), 38, 112, 114, 131, 231, 236, 238, 250, 254, 277
  Good w, 250

IMAGE INDEX

A

Armor
   of God, 160, 202, 241
   of righteousness, 207, 239-40
Arm of mercy, 214
Ashes, 207

B

Binoculars, 35-36
Blind(ness), 39
Body, 85, 134, 263
   as temple, 246-47
Bog, 204
Bread, 112, 249
   Bread of Life, 66-67, 256
Bride, 103, 243, 269, 277, 278, 279, 280
Bridegroom, 240, 259, 280
   Marriage to, 244
Broken heart, 174, 205, 207, 251, 275, 277
Brook, 161
Bruise, 172-75
Building, great and spacious, 203
Burning, 12, 64, 111, 261
   Blazing, 224
   In bosom, 13, 64, 71

C

Candle(stick), 130
Captive, captivity, 175, 207, 268
Chains, 98, 240

Chickens-hen, 228
Clay, 164
Clean hands, 245
Cleansed, 226
Coins, 208
Color, 55
   Gold, 225
   Green, 251
   White, 82, 106, 114, 216, 239, 255, 268, 280
   Yellow, 53-55
Cross, 115, 242, 274

D

Darkness, 13, 27, 98, 118, 122, 127, 275
   Mist of, 99
   Vapor of, 120
Desert, 59, 95, 98
Dew, 230
Diamonds, 101
Doors, 279
Drought, 96, 112, 249, 251

E

Earnest (down payment), 208
Eye, 38, 39, 62, 63, 106, 144, 218
   E. single, 35, 175, 227
   Of faith, 18, 32, 62, 127, 159, 196
Ear, 38
   Of faith, 135

F

Fat . . . bones, 249
Feast(ing), 208
Feet, 134, 172, 175, 236
    Footstep, 28, 241
Filled, 76
Fire, 12, 14, 27, 106, 224, 226, 245, 275
    Flames, 12
    Pillar of, 89
Fork in the road, 54
Fruit, 24, 82, 115, 192, 215, 227, 235, 252, 254, 255, 282
    Of salvation, 238

G

Garden
    Of Eden, 169-72, 206, 252
    Watered g., 112, 249, 252
Garment, raiment, 207, 244, 280
    Beautiful g., 52, 215
Gate, 261, 278
Glass, 5, 123
Goliath, 166, 167, 169, 175, 177
Gravel, 174

H

Head, 175
Heart, pure 275
Heel, 172-74
House, 276
    Of faith, 274
Hunger and thirst, 25, 94, 112, 241, 249, 251, 281
Husband, 279

I

Inheritance, 208
Inn, 206, 208
Innkeeper, 208

J

Jericho, 206
Jerusalem, 206

L

Laboratory, 62, 268
Ladder, 14, 22, 26, 261
Lamb, the, 281
Lamp, 47, 112, 130, 210, 214
Lampstand, 112, 130, 210, 252
Landscape, 98
Leaf, 251, 252, 279
Left-hand, 280
Light, luminosity, 12-13, 26, 39, 58, 76, 106-20, 210, 219, 223, 249, 250, 257, 261, 275
    Enlighten, luminosity, 19, 39, 47, 113, 220
    Of truth, 58, 63, 220
Linen, 239, 242
Lily, 204

M

Manna, hidden, 280
Mansions, 276
Member, 5, 263
Menorah, 252
Mirror, 5, 59, 121
Moon, 120, 122-23
Morning, 112, 249
Mountain, 204, 236, 261

N

Naked, 207, 249
Number 5, 165

O

Oil, 58, 208
    Of joy, 205, 207
    Olive o., 198, 205

Olive tree, 57
Ornaments, 238

P

Path, 57, 251
Pillar, 119, 261, 281
Planting, sowing, 24, 126, 207, 248, 254
Price, 214
Prison, 207
Puzzle, 100

R

Redeem, redemption, 134, 190, 193, 208, 269, 274-75
Right hand, 280
Road, 127
Robbers, 123
Robe of righteousness, 238-39, 240, 241-43, 255, 280, 283
Rod of iron, 160
Root(ed), 57, 173, 251

S

Samaritan, 204-05, 208, 209, 210
Sand, 99
Scaffolding, 62
Scales, 153
Scepter, 230
Sculptor, 238
Sheep, 127, 231, 253, 256, 280
Shepherd, 163
   Good S., 163, 256
Shire, 117
Sing, 134
Slave(ry), enslave, 166
Slums, 125
Soils, 172-74
Snow, 106, 216
Song of redeeming love, 210
Spot, 232

Spring (of water), 112, 249, 253
Staff, 160
Stars, 120-21
Stone, 162-66, 167, 173, 176, 261
   Cornerstone, 248
   Rock, 57
   Rock of heaven, 162, 165,
   Stone of Israel, 162
   Stumbling s., 36, 174
   White s., 72, 280
Storms, 144-45
Stream, 59
Sword, two-edged, 160

T

Thieves, 201, 202, 203, 206
Thorns/thistles, 164, 173
Thorncrown Chapel, 97
Throne, 281, 282
Tree of life, 24, 115, 215, 248, 252, 255, 280, 281, 282
Tree(s), 82, 114, 235, 251
   Tree of knowledge of good and evil, 170
   Trees of righteousness, 207, 248, 263
   Tree springing up unto everlasting life, 24, 258

U

Undershepherds, 203, 208
Urim and Thummim, 47, 72, 280

V

Vine, The True, 256
Virgins, wise, 253
Voice, 133, 135

W

Walk, 28, 196, 229, 241
Washed, 234

Wasteland, 103
Watchmen, 99, 134, 154, 202, 203
Water, 59, 96, 115, 116, 161, 251, 253
   Living w., 57, 96, 115, 116, 161, 251, 253
  Sea, 28, 59, 97, 98
  Watereth, 115
Wedding, 238-39
  Great wedding feast, 238-39

Wind, 28, 57, 123, 165
Wilderness, 99
Window, 23, 129
Wine, 198, 205
Winepress, 205
Wounds 207

www.ingramcontent.com/pod-product-compliance
Lightning Source LLC
Chambersburg PA
CBHW051747040426
42446CB00007B/261